Cuisine Rapide

Cuisine Rapide

PIERRE FRANEY & BRYAN MILLER

Illustrations by Lauren Jarrett

Times BOOKS

LIBRARY OF CONGRESS CATALOGING-IN-PUBLICATION DATA
Franey, Pierre.
Cuisine rapide.
Includes index.
1. Quick and easy cookery.   I. Miller, Bryan.
II. Title.
TX833.5.F73 1989   641.5′55   88-29469
ISBN 0-8129-1746-4

Designed by Beth Tondreau Design
Manufactured in the United States of America
9 8 7 6 5 4 3 2
First Edition

To Nicolas, Noël, Larissa, Tanya, and Denise
—P.F.

To Benson and Veronique
—B.M.

Contents

Introduction ◆ xi

Appetizers & Salads ◆ 1

Soups ◆ 25

Seafood ◆ 51

Poultry & Game ◆ 109

Beef ◆ 169

Ham & Pork ◆ 195

Lamb & Veal ◆ 221

Pasta & Rice ◆ 255

Sauces, Condiments, & Bread ◆ 287

Vegetables & Eggs ◆ 297

Desserts ◆ 331

Index ◆ 355

Introduction

You don't need to speak French to translate the term *cuisine rapide*, for both words, while French in origin, are closely related to their English equivalents. In a sense, that point reflects what this book is all about. My background is French, yet after nearly fifty years in this country I consider myself half American. Many of the recipes here are based on sound French techniques, yet the ingredients, flavors, and style are often thoroughly American. Bryan Miller, my collaborator, dines out more than five hundred times a year in his role as restaurant critic for *The New York Times*. He constantly scouts out dishes that are exciting yet accessible to home cooks. We have adapted many of those recipes to fit the *cuisine rapide* format.

Cuisine rapide does not mean "fast food" as Americans think of it—instead, it conveys a style of home cooking that is efficient, accessible, and refined. You will find everything here from simple hamburgers with goat cheese to home-made ravioli, couscous, moussaka, and cassoulet (my own short-cut version). All are made with the demands and limitations of busy home cooks in mind, and virtually all ingredients are widely available in supermarkets. (That is where I shop at home on eastern Long Island for my weekly column in *The New York Times*, "The 60-Minute Gourmet.") If by chance an uncommon ingredient is called for, I try to give a suitable substitute.

It is interesting to note how cooking styles have evolved in this country over the past few decades. In looking over this book and comparing it to my earlier publications, I can see how my style has changed to meet today's demand for lighter, purer, more healthful food. For example, many sauces here call for less butter and cream and more olive oil and vegetable purées. I still believe that, in some recipes, a tablespoon of butter or a dash of cream adds a silky texture to a sauce that cannot be achieved otherwise—and if you divide the amount of butter or cream by four to six, the quantity is insignificant.

Cuisine rapide applies to all levels of cooking, from the most casual family dinner to the most lavish entertaining. This book provides you with the tools to accomplish both with élan. Happy cooking!

Appetizers
& Salads

Country Pâté with Pistachios

Essentially, a pâté is nothing more than an elaborate meat loaf. Pâté, by the way, is so named because at one time it was enclosed in a pastry casing. In the classic sense, the more appropriate name for the dish as we often see it nowadays—that is, without the pastry—is a terrine.

Enclosed or not, pâtés are simple to make, and the less elaborate ones can be prepared in about an hour. One of my favorites is a pâté made with pistachios, pork, veal, and ham. The baking time is forty-five minutes. The preparation time, if you are really clock-watching, can be squeezed into fifteen minutes (it shouldn't take much longer than that even if you are not rushing). Or you can cut and chop the meat in advance and simply refrigerate the ingredients for a few hours until you are ready to cook.

1 tablespoon butter
$\frac{1}{2}$ cup coarsely chopped shallots
$\frac{1}{2}$ pound pork or veal liver, cut into 1-inch cubes
$\frac{1}{4}$ teaspoon dry thyme
$\frac{1}{2}$ bay leaf, crumbled
$\frac{3}{4}$ pound lean veal, cut into 1-inch cubes
1 pound lean pork, cut into 1-inch cubes
$\frac{1}{2}$ pound cooked ham, cut into $\frac{1}{2}$-inch cubes
$\frac{1}{2}$ cup shelled pistachios, toasted
$\frac{1}{8}$ teaspoon ground allspice
$\frac{1}{8}$ teaspoon ground cloves
$\frac{1}{4}$ teaspoon freshly grated nutmeg
$\frac{1}{8}$ teaspoon ground cumin
   Pinch ground cinnamon
   Pinch cayenne pepper
$\frac{1}{2}$ cup dry white wine
   Salt to taste if desired
   Freshly ground pepper to taste
2 slices lean bacon

1. Preheat the oven to 425 degrees.

2. Heat the butter in a heavy skillet and add the shallots. Cook briefly, stirring. Add the liver and sprinkle with the thyme and bay leaf. Cook about 2 minutes, stirring occasionally.

3. Put the veal in a food processor or blender and blend it slightly finer than store-bought hamburger. Empty the veal into a mixing bowl.

4. Put the pork in the food processor or blender and blend it a little coarser than store-bought hamburger. Add the pork to the veal.

5. Put the liver mixture in the food processor or blender and blend it as finely as possible. Pour and scrape it into the bowl with the pork and veal. Add the ham and pistachios. Add the allspice, cloves, nutmeg, cumin, cinnamon, cayenne, wine, salt, and pepper and blend well with your fingers. To test the mixture for seasoning, shape a small portion into a patty and cook it, turning once, in a nonstick skillet until cooked through. Taste the patty and add more seasonings as desired.

6. Pack the mixture in a 5- or 6-cup loaf pan. Smooth the top, rounding it slightly. Place the bacon slices on top. Cover tightly with foil and place the pan in a heatproof baking dish. Set the dish on the stove and pour in boiling water around the loaf pan. Bring the water to a boil. Place the pan in the water bath in the oven and bake 45 minutes or to an internal temperature of 150 degrees. Remove the pan from the oven and let stand until ready to serve.

7. The pâté is excellent hot or cold. Cut it crosswise into slices and serve.

    Yield: 6 to 10 servings.

Smoked Brook Trout with Horseradish Sauce

> 2 whole smoked brook trout
> ¹/₃ cup heavy cream
> 1 tablespoon chopped fresh dill
> 1 tablespoon vodka (plain or lemon-flavored)
> 2 tablespoons or more freshly grated or prepared horseradish
>   Salt and freshly ground white pepper to taste
> 4 sprigs fresh dill for garnish
>   Tomato Roses for garnish, optional (see opposite)
>   Cucumber Salad (recipe follows)

MAKING TOMATO ROSES

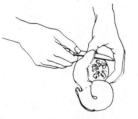

1. Hold the tomato stem-side down and make a thin incision across the top. The paring knife must be extremely sharp. Stop about ¼ inch from the other end to leave this little lid attached.

2. Place the tip of the knife on one side of the partly severed lid as shown and cut a thin strip of skin (removing just a little flesh with it) around the tomato. The strip should be about ¾ inch wide and about 4 inches long. Work all the way around the tomato using a sawing motion with the knife. Continue until you reach the other side of the lid; sever the strip from the tomato but keep the lid attached.

3. Place the lid, skin side down, on a flat surface. Curl the strip of skin around the perimeter to form a rose pattern.

4. Cut two more strips from the tomato, each slightly shorter than the previous one.

5. Roll the second strip into a tighter coil and place it inside the middle of the lid. Repeat with the third strip, rolled tighter yet. (It may take a few tries to make everything fit.)

6. You may place some parsley or other greens under the rose for extra color.

1. Carefully remove the skin from each trout, using a knife. Fillet the trout, removing all the bones. Arrange a trout fillet on each of 4 plates.

2. Whip the cream until stiff. Fold in the chopped dill, vodka, and horseradish. Add salt and pepper to taste. Serve garnished with the dill sprigs and Tomato Roses, along with Cucumber Salad.

   Yield: 4 servings.

Cucumber and Dill Salad

    4 cucumbers, about 1½ pounds
    ½ cup sour cream
    2 tablespoons heavy cream
    3 tablespoons white vinegar
    Salt to taste if desired
    Pinch cayenne pepper
    Freshly ground pepper to taste
    1 tablespoon finely chopped fresh dill

1. Trim the cucumbers and cut them in half lengthwise. Scrape away and discard the seeds. Cut each cucumber half into thin crosswise slices. There should be about 6 cups.

2. Place the slices in a mixing bowl, add the remaining ingredients, and toss well.

   Yield: 4 servings.

◆ ◆ ◆

Baked Clams with Garlic Butter

  2 cups shucked cherrystone clams
24 empty clam shells
10 tablespoons butter
    Salt to taste if desired
    Generous grinding of black pepper
  1 tablespoon finely minced garlic
  1 tablespoon finely chopped shallot
 $^1/_4$ cup finely chopped parsley
  2 tablespoons finely chopped fresh chervil
 $^1/_2$ teaspoon finely chopped fresh thyme
  3 tablespoons fine fresh bread crumbs
  3 tablespoons freshly grated Parmesan cheese

1. Preheat the broiler.

2. Cut each clam into 4 pieces.

3. Fill the clam shells with the clam pieces.

4. Blend together the butter, salt, pepper, garlic, shallot, parsley, chervil, and thyme. Spoon an equal amount of the herb butter on top of each clam shell. Smooth it slightly. Arrange the shells on a baking dish or sheet.

5. Blend the bread crumbs and cheese and sprinkle over each shell.

6. Place the shells under the broiler 5 to 6 inches from the heat and broil about 3 minutes. Set the oven at 450 degrees, transfer the clams from the broiler to the oven, and bake about 2 minutes.

    Yield: 4 luncheon or first-course servings.

◆ ◆ ◆

Cherrystone Clam and Corn Fritters

Clams are among the foods I like best, so I am fortunate that they are in season all year. One of my favorite preparations is clam fritters made with cherrystone clams, which are larger than littlenecks.

In New York the names littleneck and cherrystone indicate two different sizes of the quahog or hard-shelled clam. Littlenecks are smaller and measure about two inches in width at their widest point. Cherrystones are slightly larger and measure two or three inches across.

Other than size, there is no guide that can tell you the precise moment when a littleneck becomes a cherrystone. Chowders, the largest size, are not recommended for fritters because they tend to be tough.

These fritters are easy to prepare, and it takes about two dozen clams to produce enough meat for eighteen fritters of suitable size to serve four to six people. If you are not equipped to open your own clams, it is best to have them shucked at the seafood shop. To make the batter, combine the clam meat and juice with flour, egg yolks, baking powder, spices, and corn, and fold in a few stiffly beaten egg whites.

The fritters can be served without an accompaniment, but I prefer a delicious sauce made of roasted sweet red peppers, fresh tomatoes, mustard, vinegar, and olive oil. For spiciness, I add a small portion of finely chopped hot green pepper.

   24 **cherrystone clams**
    1 **large ear corn, about 8 ounces**
1¹/₂ **cups flour**
    3 **eggs, separated**
    1 **tablespoon finely chopped fresh tarragon or 1 teaspoon dry**
    2 **tablespoons finely chopped parsley**
    2 **teaspoons baking powder**
 ¹/₄ **cup chopped scallions**
     Salt and freshly ground pepper to taste
 ¹/₄ **teaspoon Tabasco sauce**
 ¹/₂ **teaspoon ground cumin**
 ¹/₂ **cup corn, peanut, or vegetable oil**
     Red Pepper Purée (recipe follows)

1. Open the clams, remove the meat, and save the juice. There should be about 2 cups liquid and about 1¹/₄ cups clams. Put the clams on a flat surface and chop them until they are coarse-fine.

2. Shuck the corn and cut the kernels from the cob. There should be about 1 cup.

3. Put the flour in a mixing bowl and add the chopped clams, ³/4 cup reserved clam liquid (the rest may be discarded or put to another use), corn, egg yolks, tarragon, parsley, baking powder, scallions, salt, pepper, Tabasco, and cumin. Blend well.

4. Beat the egg whites until stiff, arrange them over the batter, and fold them in.

5. Heat 2 tablespoons oil in a nonstick skillet over medium-high heat. When it is quite hot, add about ¹/4 cup of the batter at a time, keeping each fritter separated. Continue adding batter in this manner until the skillet is filled without crowding.

6. Cook about 1 minute or slightly longer on one side or until the edges of the fritters start to brown. Turn and cook 1 minute or slightly longer on the other side. As the fritters are cooked, transfer them to paper towels. Continue making fritters until all the batter is used. Use about 2 additional tablespoons oil for each batch of fritters. Serve the fritters with the sauce spooned over them.

Yield: about 18 fritters.

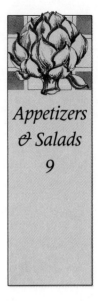
Red Pepper Purée

    1 large red sweet pepper, roasted, peeled, and seeded (see page 10)
    1 small red onion, about ¹/4 pound
    1 ripe tomato, about ¹/4 pound
    1 teaspoon finely chopped green hot pepper or ¹/4 teaspoon red
        pepper flakes
    1 tablespoon Dijon-style mustard
    3 tablespoons red-wine vinegar
  ¹/2 cup olive oil
    2 teaspoons finely minced garlic
  ¹/2 cup coarsely chopped chervil or ¹/4 cup chopped parsley

1. Cut the pepper into 1-inch pieces. There should be about ³/4 cup.

2. Cut the onion into ¹/4-inch cubes. There should be about ³/4 cup.

3. Cut the tomato into ¹/2-inch cubes. There should be about ³/4 cup.

ROASTING A PEPPER

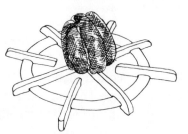

1. Place a pepper directly over a gas flame or close to the heating element of the broiler. Cook, turning often so that it blisters and blackens all over. Let stand until cool enough to handle.

3. Halve and remove seeds.

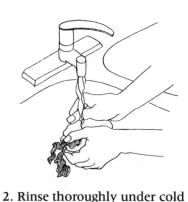

2. Rinse thoroughly under cold water, peeling off the burned outer skin.

4. Dry on paper towels.

4. Put the tomato, sweet pepper, onion, hot pepper, mustard, vinegar, oil, garlic, and chervil in a food processor. Blend thoroughly.

   Yield: about 2 cups.

◆ ◆ ◆

Clam Cocktail

This quick and tasty appetizer can be attractively presented on red leaf or bibb lettuce.

   ³/₄ cup coarsely chopped cherrystone clams
    1 cup clam juice
    2 tablespoons lime juice
    1 cup minced red sweet pepper
    1 tablespoon olive oil
   ³/₄ pound tomatoes, cored and cut into ¹/₂-inch cubes (about 2 cups)
   ¹/₈ teaspoon red pepper flakes
   ¹/₃ cup chopped fresh coriander

1. Combine all the ingredients in a mixing bowl. Blend well and refrigerate. The clam cocktail should be served very cold.

    Yield: 4 servings.

Cold Lobster with Basil Vinaigrette

    4 quarts water (see Note)
    1 tablespoon black peppercorns
     Salt to taste if desired
    4 sprigs fresh thyme or ¹/₂ teaspoon dry
    2 bay leaves
   ¹/₄ teaspoon red pepper flakes
    4 live lobsters, 1¹/₂ pounds each
     10 or 12 basil leaves
    1 teaspoon Dijon-style mustard
   ¹/₂ cup olive oil
   ¹/₄ cup finely chopped shallots
    2 tablespoons balsamic vinegar
     Three-Lettuce Chiffonade (recipe follows)

*Cuisine
Rapide
12*

1. Put the water, peppercorns, salt, thyme, bay leaves, and pepper flakes in a kettle large enough to hold the lobsters. Cover and bring to a boil.

2. Add the lobsters quickly, 1 at a time, and cover. When the water returns to a boil, cook the lobsters for 7 minutes and drain thoroughly. When the lobsters are cool enough to handle, break off the tails and remove the meat from each in one piece. Crack the large claws and remove the meat from each in one piece. Remove the meat from the remaining claw shells. Put all the meat in a bowl.

3. Stack the basil leaves and cut them into fine shreds. There should be about ¹/₂ cup. Add to the bowl.

4. Put the mustard, olive oil, shallots, vinegar, and salt in a small mixing bowl and blend well with a wire whisk.

5. To serve, cut each piece of tail meat diagonally into ¹/₂-inch medallions. Reassemble the slices from a lobster tail on each of 4 plates. Arrange 2 of the large pieces of claw meat at the top of each portion of tail meat to resemble a lobster shape. Spoon the sauce over the tail and claw meat. Scatter the small pieces of lobster meat around. Garnish each side of the tail meat with some chiffonade.

Yield: 4 servings.

NOTE: Sea water is best, and, if it is used, the peppercorns, salt, and herbs should be omitted.

Three-Lettuce Chiffonade

    1 head radicchio (about ¹/₄ pound), core removed
    2 heads bibb lettuce, about ¹/₄ pound each
  ¹/₂ head iceberg lettuce (about ¹/₄ pound), core removed
    1 red sweet pepper (about ¹/₄ pound), cored
  ¹/₄ cup olive oil
3¹/₂ tablespoons red-wine vinegar
      Salt to taste if desired
      Freshly ground pepper to taste

1. Stack the radicchio leaves and cut them into very fine shreds. There should be about 2 cups. Put the shreds in a large bowl. Repeat with the bibb lettuce and the iceberg. There should be about 2 cups of bibb shreds and 2 cups of iceberg. Add both to the bowl.

2. Cut the red pepper lengthwise into thin strips. There should be about 1 cup. Add to the bowl.

3. Add the oil, vinegar, salt, and pepper and blend well. Serve immediately.

   Yield: 4 servings.

Tomatoes Stuffed with Curried Shrimp

       32 medium shrimp, about 1 pound
        2 teaspoons finely minced garlic
        1 teaspoon curry powder
       ¼ cup olive oil
        3 tablespoons fresh lemon juice
          Salt to taste if desired
          Freshly ground pepper to taste
        4 large tomatoes
       ½ cup thinly sliced onion
        2 sprigs fresh thyme or ½ teaspoon dry
        8 thin slices mozzarella cheese
        2 tablespoons finely chopped parsley

1. Preheat the oven to 450 degrees.

2. Shell and devein the shrimp and put them in a mixing bowl. Add the garlic, curry powder, 2 tablespoons oil, lemon juice, salt, and pepper. Stir to blend.

3. Neatly core each tomato. Slice each tomato in half crosswise.

4. Select a baking dish large enough to hold the tomato halves in one layer. Brush the bottom of the baking dish with the remaining 2 tablespoons oil and scatter the onion in it. Arrange the tomato halves, cut side up, on the onion. Sprinkle with the thyme, salt, and pepper.

5. Place the dish in the oven and bake 10 minutes. Remove the dish and turn on the broiler.

6. Arrange 4 shrimp on top of each tomato half. Dribble any leftover sauce over the shrimp.

7. Place the dish on the bottom shelf of the oven and under the broiler. Cook 5 minutes. Place the dish directly under the broiler about 3 inches from the heat. Leave the oven door open and broil exactly 1 minute.

8. Cover each tomato half with a slice of mozzarrella cheese. Place under the broiler again for about 1 minute or until the cheese melts. Sprinkle with the parsley and serve immediately.

   Yield: 4 servings.

Tuna Escabeche

In recent years I have cooked fresh tuna in dozens of ways. One appetizer that is particularly popular around my house is called escabeche. *This dish of Latin American origin is prepared with sweet peppers, onions, oil, and vinegar. It is excellent when served hot, but there are those who consider it even better when refrigerated overnight and served cold. I like it both ways. Except for the chopping involved, it is a very easy dish to make and can be cooked in less than half an hour. When it is to be served hot, Rice with Mushrooms and Pistachios (see page 288) makes an excellent accompaniment.*

   ¹/₄ **cup olive oil**
    1 **tablespoon finely chopped garlic**
    2 **cups finely chopped onions**

2 cups finely diced red sweet pepper

¾ cup finely diced yellow sweet pepper

1 teaspoon finely chopped green hot pepper, preferably jalapeño

5 sprigs fresh thyme, finely chopped, or ½ teaspoon dry

1 bay leaf

Salt to taste if desired

Freshly ground pepper to taste

¼ cup red-wine vinegar

2 cups finely diced tomatoes

¼ cup drained capers

4 thin slices lemon

1¼ pounds skinless, boneless tuna, cut into 12 pieces each about 1 inch thick

¼ cup finely chopped parsley

1. Heat the oil in a heavy skillet or casserole and add the garlic and onions. Cook, stirring, about 2 minutes. Add all the peppers. Cook, stirring, about 2 minutes.

2. Add the thyme, bay leaf, salt, pepper, and vinegar and cook, stirring, about 1 minute.

3. Add the tomatoes and capers. Bring to a boil and cover. Cook 10 minutes and stir in the lemon slices.

4. Sprinkle the tuna pieces with salt and pepper and add them. Stir to coat. Cover closely and cook 5 minutes. Sprinkle with the parsley and stir gently. Remove the bay leaf and serve hot or cold.

   Yield: 4 servings.

◆ ◆ ◆

Warm Tuna and Scallop Salad with Orange-Coriander Vinaigrette

2 teaspoons Dijon-style mustard
2 tablespoons fresh lemon juice
1/3 cup olive oil
1 tablespoon red-wine vinegar
1/8 teaspoon red pepper flakes
   Salt and freshly ground white pepper to taste
1 tablespoon minced fresh coriander
2 tablespoons julienne orange zest
1 head each radicchio, bibb lettuce, and arugula
2 heads Belgian endive
2 oranges, sectioned and trimmed of the tough membranes
1 tablespoon vegetable oil
3/4 pound bay scallops or quartered sea scallops
3/4 pound skinless tuna fillets, cut into 1/2-inch cubes
2 tablespoons minced shallots

1. To make the vinaigrette, combine the mustard and 1 tablespoon lemon juice in a small bowl. Beat briskly until the mixture begins to thicken. Gradually add the olive oil, remaining 1 tablespoon lemon juice, and vinegar while continuing to beat. Add the pepper flakes, salt, white pepper, coriander, and orange zest and mix well.

2. To make the salad, tear the lettuces and endive into bite-size pieces and mix them with the orange sections in a large bowl. Pour 2/3 of the dressing over the salad and toss well. Divide the salad among 4 serving plates.

3. Coat the bottom of a nonstick pan with the vegetable oil. Sauté the scallops in the oil over high heat for 1 minute while shaking the pan. Add the tuna and shallots. Salt and pepper well. Toss briskly and cover. Cook for 1 minute, shaking the pan occasionally. Remove the pan from the heat and cool, uncovered, for 2 to 3 minutes. Drizzle the remaining vinaigrette over the tuna and scallops and distribute among the 4 plates.

Yield: 4 servings.

◆ ◆ ◆

Smoked Salmon Mousse

Many home cooks still think of mousses as tricky and time-consuming. The truth is, the mousses that I prepare—one with smoked salmon (below), the other with chicken livers (on the next page)—are easy to make; either can be ready within twenty minutes. The salmon mousse, in fact, can be prepared in five.

Making first courses like these does not demand a rapidly made main course. Consider a roast chicken as a main course: you could begin preparation of the chicken, put it in the oven, and have it ready to serve in about forty-five minutes.

After the chicken has begun to cook, there would be ample time to make the appetizer. The salmon mousse, as a matter of fact, is ready to serve the moment it is removed from the food processor. You will find, however, that the mousse improves when chilled overnight and served cool (but not cold).

The chicken liver mousse is best if it is served at slightly cooler than room temperature.

1/2 pound smoked salmon
1/2 pound cream cheese
1/3 cup chopped scallions
1/4 cup finely chopped fresh dill
    Juice of 1/2 lemon
    Freshly ground pepper to taste
1/2 teaspoon ground cumin
    Tabasco sauce to taste
2 tablespoons vodka (plain or lemon-flavored)

1. Combine all the ingredients in a food processor or blender. Blend to a fine purée. Spoon and scrape the mixture into a serving dish. Smooth the top. Chill.

2. Serve (cool, not cold) with buttered toast, chopped onion, and drained capers on the side.

    Yield: about 4 cups.

◆ ◆ ◆

Chicken Liver Mousse

3/4 pound chicken livers
Salt and freshly ground pepper to taste
1/4 bay leaf, broken into small pieces
1 sprig fresh thyme or 1/8 teaspoon dry
1/8 teaspoon ground allspice
1/2 teaspoon ground cumin
1/8 teaspoon ground cinnamon
Pinch cayenne pepper
1/4 pound butter or melted chicken fat
1/2 cup thinly sliced shallots
1/4 pound mushrooms, thinly sliced (about 2 cups)
1 tablespoon cognac

1. Pick over the livers to remove and discard any tough connecting tissues or blemished portions. Put them in a bowl and add the salt, pepper, bay leaf, thyme, allspice, cumin, cinnamon, and cayenne.

2. Heat the butter in a heavy skillet over medium-high heat and add the shallots and mushrooms. Cook, stirring often, until the mushrooms give up their liquid. Cook until most of this liquid evaporates. Add the livers and seasonings and stir. Cook, stirring occasionally, about 10 minutes.

3. Pour and scrape this mixture into a food processor or blender. Add the cognac and blend to a fine purée.

4. Spoon and scrape the mousse into a small serving dish. Smooth the top. Serve slightly cooler than room temperature, with thinly sliced rye bread and chopped onion on the side.

    Yield: about 2 cups.

◆ ◆ ◆

Guacamole

    2 ripe, unblemished avocados, about 1 pound each
    ³/₄ cup finely chopped red onion
        Juice of 1 lime
    1 cup peeled and cubed tomato
    3 pickled serrano chilies or other small green chilies, finely
        chopped (about 1 tablespoon)
    ¹/₂ teaspoon ground cumin
        Salt to taste if desired
        Freshly ground pepper to taste

1. Peel the avocados. Cut them in half and discard the pits. Cut the avocados lengthwise into thin slices and finely dice them. There should be about 3 cups.

2. Put 1 cup avocado. ¹/₂ cup onion, and the juice of ¹/₂ lime in a mixing bowl. Mix well and mash enough to blend thoroughly.

3. Add the remaining avocado and onion and the tomato, chilies, and cumin. Add more lime juice if desired. Add salt and pepper to taste. Stir to blend.

    Yield: 4 to 6 servings, or about 3 cups.

Artichokes Vinaigrette

    4 artichokes (about ³/₄ pound each), prepared for poaching
        (see page 20)
        Salt to taste
    1 tablespoon imported mustard, preferably Dijon-style
    2 tablespoons red-wine vinegar
        Freshly ground pepper to taste
    ³/₄ cup peanut, vegetable, or corn oil
        Finely chopped parsley

1. Place the prepared artichokes in a kettle with cold water to cover. Add salt to taste. Fit a clean cloth snugly over the artichokes in the pot and bring to a

PREPARING ARTICHOKES FOR POACHING

1. Cut the stem at the base of the artichoke with a sharp knife, leaving the bottom flat so it can stand upright. Remove any tough outer leaves from the bottom of the artichoke.

3. Lay the artichoke on its side and chop off 1 inch from the top.

2. Using kitchen shears, work around the artichoke from top to bottom, trimming about ¼ inch from the top of each leaf to remove the sharp tip.

4. Place a thick lemon slice under the artichoke bottom. Tie the lemon to the artichoke with kitchen string. This preserves the artichoke color when cooking.

boil. Simmer 45 minutes or until tender. Do not overcook. Drain well and let stand until ready to serve.

2. Put the mustard, salt, vinegar, and pepper in a small mixing bowl. Beat vigorously with a wire whisk. Gradually add the oil, beating constantly. Add the parsley.

3. Serve the artichokes with the sauce on the side.

Yield: 4 servings.

Mixed Green Salad with Blue Cheese Dressing

   2 tablespoons red-wine vinegar
  ¹/₄ teaspoon finely minced garlic
  1 tablespoon Dijon-style mustard
  ¹/₂ cup crumbled blue cheese such as Roquefort, Saga, or
      Danish blue
  6 tablespoons vegetable oil
      Salt to taste if desired
      Freshly ground pepper to taste
  10 cups loosely packed bite-size pieces of watercress, red-leaf lettuce,
      and Belgian endive

1. Combine the vinegar, garlic, mustard, and cheese in a mixing bowl. Blend well. Add the oil, salt, and pepper and blend well with a wire whisk.

2. Place the salad greens in a bowl and toss well with the dressing.

    Yield: 4 to 6 servings.

Broccoli and Avocado Salad

  1 small bunch broccoli
      Salt to taste if desired
  1 large avocado
  ¹/₂ lemon
  1 teaspoon Dijon-style mustard
  2 tablespoons lemon juice
  3 tablespoons olive oil
      Freshly ground pepper to taste

1. Cut the broccoli into florets. If the pieces are large, split them at the bottom and cut them in half. Rinse and drain. Put the stems aside for another use.

2. Drop the broccoli into boiling salted water to cover. Bring to a boil. Drain and run briefly under cold water. Drain again and chill.

3. Cut the avocado in half. Peel each half and remove the pit. Cut each half into 8 lengthwise strips. Squeeze the lemon half over the strips to prevent discoloration. Arrange the broccoli and avocado alternately on each of 4 serving plates.

4. Blend the remaining ingredients in a bowl and pour over the broccoli and avocado. Serve immediately.

Yield: 4 servings.

Lentil Salad with Kielbasa

8 cups water
1 pound dried lentils
4 carrots, scraped and diced (about 1¼ cups)
1 stalk celery, diced (about ½ cup)
1 bay leaf
Salt to taste if desired
4 kielbasas (Polish sausages) (about ¾ pound), sliced diagonally
1 tablespoon plus 1 cup corn oil
1 cup chopped onion
1 clove garlic, chopped
1 tablespoon Dijon-style mustard
¼ cup red-wine vinegar
1 cup chopped parsley
Freshly ground pepper to taste

1. Put the water in a large saucepan. Wash the lentils in a colander and add them to the pan. Add the carrots, celery, bay leaf, and pinch of salt and simmer, covered, 30 minutes.

2. When the lentils are cooked, drain the mixture and put it in a bowl. Remove the bay leaf. Sauté the kielbasa in 1 tablespoon oil over medium-high heat 1 minute. Add it to the lentils with the onion and garlic.

3. Put the mustard, vinegar, and remaining 1 cup oil in a bowl. Mix with a fork or whisk. Add the parsley, salt, and pepper to taste. Pour the dressing over the lentils and mix. Serve lukewarm or cold.

Yield: 6 servings.

Roasted Pepper and Snow Pea Salad

   2 red sweet peppers, about ³/₄ pound
      Salt to taste if desired
 ³/₄ pound snow peas
   1 small red onion, peeled
   1 tablespoon imported mustard
   2 tablespoons red-wine vinegar
 ¹/₂ teaspoon ground cumin
      Freshly ground pepper to taste
 ¹/₄ cup olive oil
 ¹/₄ cup finely chopped parsley

1. Preheat the broiler or prepare a charcoal grill. Place the peppers under the broiler or on the grill and cook them on all sides until the skin is well charred. When cool enough to handle, split the peppers in half, core them, and discard the charred skin.

2. Cut the peppers lengthwise into thin strips. There should be about 1 cup. Put the strips in a salad bowl.

3. Bring enough water to a boil to cover the snow peas. Add salt to taste. Add the snow peas and boil 2 minutes. Drain in a sieve. Run cold water briefly over the snow peas and drain. Add to the salad bowl.

4. Cut the onion in half, cut each half crosswise into thin slices, and add them to the bowl.

5. Put the mustard, vinegar, and cumin in a separate bowl and add salt and pepper. Beat vigorously with a whisk while adding the oil. Stir in the parsley.

6. Pour the dressing over the vegetables and toss.

   Yield: 4 servings.

Arugula and Red Onion Salad

   ½ **pound arugula**
   1 **cup chopped red onion**
   ½ **cup finely chopped parsley, preferably flat-leaf Italian parsley**
   1½ **tablespoons red-wine vinegar**
      Salt to taste if desired
      Freshly ground pepper to taste
   ¼ **cup olive oil**

1. Pick over the arugula and discard any tough stems. There should be about 6 loosely packed cups. Put the leaves in a salad bowl and add the onion and parsley.

2. Put the vinegar in a bowl and add salt and pepper. Beat while gradually adding the oil. Pour the dressing over the salad and toss to blend.

   Yield: 4 servings.

Soups

Cream of Leek Soup

    12 medium leeks
     4 tablespoons butter
     1 tablespoon finely minced garlic
     6 tablespoons flour
     8 cups fresh or canned chicken broth
     2 cups milk
       Salt and freshly ground pepper to taste
   $^1/_4$ teaspoon freshly grated nutmeg
     1 cup heavy cream
   $^1/_3$ cup chervil sprigs or 3 tablespoons chopped fresh chives

1. Trim the leeks and rinse them well. Quarter them lengthwise and cut them into $^1/_4$-inch pieces. There should be about 5 cups.

2. Heat the butter in a large heavy saucepan and add the leeks and garlic. Cook briefly, stirring often, over medium heat. Add the flour, blending it well with a wire whisk, and add the chicken broth, milk, salt, pepper, and nutmeg. Bring to a simmer and cook for 30 minutes.

3. Spoon and scrape the mixture into a blender or food processor and purée.

4. Just before serving, add the cream. The soup can be served cold or brought to a simmer and served hot. Garnish each serving with the chervil or chives.

   Yield: 10 to 12 servings.

Cold Cucumber and Yogurt Soup with Fresh Mint

This cold summer soup slightly resembles the Indian side dish called raita, *a traditional antidote to fiery curry dishes.*

   The base is yogurt, sliced cucumbers, garlic, and mint. I add curry powder and a little freshly ground white pepper to give some zip. This soup requires minimal cooking, so it is especially welcome on sweltering summer days.

1 tablespoon butter
1 cup chopped onion
1 teaspoon finely chopped garlic
4 cups peeled, seeded, and sliced cucumbers
2 teaspoons curry powder
2 cups fresh or canned chicken broth
Salt and freshly ground pepper to taste
2 cups plain yogurt
1 cup peeled, seeded, and cubed cucumbers
2 tablespoons chopped fresh mint
Garlic Croutons (recipe follows)

1. Heat the butter in a saucepan and add the onion and garlic. Cook, stirring, over medium heat until wilted; do not brown. Add the sliced cucumbers, curry powder, broth, salt, and pepper. Bring to a simmer and cook for 5 minutes, stirring occasionally.

2. Put the mixture in a food processor and pulse to blend to a fine texture. Pour the mixture into a bowl. Chill thoroughly.

3. Stir in the yogurt, cubed cucumber, and mint. Blend well and serve in chilled bowls with the croutons.

Yield: 4 servings.

Garlic Croutons

1 loaf French or Italian bread
2 cloves garlic, peeled
1/4 cup olive oil
Freshly ground pepper to taste

1. Preheat the broiler.

2. Rub the crust of the bread with the garlic cloves. Cut the bread into 1/4-inch slices. Sprinkle one side of the slices with oil, then grind some pepper over it.

3. Put the slices on a baking sheet and place them under the broiler until golden brown. Turn and broil on the other side until golden brown.

Yield: 6 servings.

Gazpacho with Crab Meat

One of my first cooking rituals when the tomato crop comes in is to make my own version of gazpacho, to which I add fresh lump crab meat. The base is easy to make with a food processor or blender. Do not overblend, though, because you want the soup to have a pulpy texture. If you like your gazpacho spicier, add more jalapeño pepper. Lemon or lime juice adds a refreshing touch. If you cannot find fresh lump crab meat, lobster or shrimp can be substituted. Steamed lobster meat should be sliced very thin before adding it to the soup. If shrimp are used, place them in a pot, cover with water, and add some onion, a clove, thyme, a bay leaf, and black pepper. Bring the water to a boil, then turn off the flame. Remove the shrimp, peel them, and then devein and slice them before adding them to the soup.

- 3 pounds tomatoes, peeled, seeded, and chopped (about 6 cups)
- 1 cup chopped red onion
- 1 red sweet pepper, chopped
- 1 tablespoon chopped garlic
- 2 teaspoons chopped jalapeño pepper or to taste
- 6 tablespoons coarsely chopped fresh coriander
- 1/4 cup olive oil
- 3 tablespoons red-wine vinegar
- 3 tablespoons fresh lime or lemon juice
- Salt and freshly ground pepper to taste
- 1 1/2 cups peeled, seeded, and cubed cucumbers
- 1 pound lump crab meat, picked over

1. Combine all the ingredients except 2 tablespoons coriander, the cucumbers, and crab meat in a food processor and pulse to blend to a semi-coarse texture. Pour and scrape the mixture into a bowl. Cover with plastic wrap and refrigerate until cold.

2. Stir in the cucumbers and crab meat just before serving. Serve in chilled bowls and sprinkle with the remaining 2 tablespoons coriander.

Yield: 4 to 6 servings.

Spanish White Bean Soup

Cuisines around the world abound with dishes based on beans and peas. There is the cassoulet *of southwestern France, the* dal *of India, the black bean soup and* feijoada *of Brazil, Mexican refried beans and chickpea soup, Middle Eastern hummus (chickpea purée), Spanish* cocido *(boiled beef and chickpeas), Italian* fagioli Toscana *(bean and pasta soup), and, of course, New England baked beans. Dried beans are an excellent source of protein and extremely versatile—not to mention inexpensive. Here is one of my favorite cold weather soups, a Spanish staple made with ham hocks, leeks, and white beans.*

> 1 pound dried white beans
> 16 cups water
> 2½ pounds ham hocks (4 hocks)
> 1¼ cups diced leeks
> 2 cups chopped onions
> 1 tablespoon chopped garlic
> ½ teaspoon dry thyme
> 1 tablespoon olive oil
> 1½ cups chopped carrots
> 1½ cups cubed turnips
> ¼ cup chopped fresh coriander

1. Inspect the beans for imperfections or stones and rinse them under cold water. Place in a soup pot with 4 cups water. Bring to a boil and cook 10 minutes. Remove from the heat and cool 30 minutes.

2. Drain the beans and return them to the soup pot with the remaining 12 cups water. Add the ham hocks, cover, and bring to a boil. Reduce to a simmer.

3. Meanwhile, sauté the leeks, onions, garlic, and thyme in the olive oil over medium heat until wilted, about 5 minutes. Add to the soup pot.

4. Cook, covered, 1½ hours. Add the carrots and turnips and cook 30 minutes.

5. Remove the hocks and cool. When cool enough to handle, remove the meat from the bones, discarding the fat. Add the meat to the pot.

6. Add the coriander and serve.

   Yield: 8 to 10 servings.

Veal and Macaroni Soup

  1 pound lean veal from the shoulder or loin
  2 tablespoons butter
  1 cup finely chopped onion
    Salt to taste if desired
    Freshly ground pepper to taste
  ¼ cup flour
  3 cups fresh or canned chicken broth
  ½ cup small tubular macaroni such as imported tubetti
  ½ cup heavy cream
  1 cup milk
  2 egg yolks
  ½ cup freshly grated Parmesan cheese

1. Cut the veal into small cubes, about ½ inch or slightly smaller.

2. Heat the butter in a heavy saucepan or small kettle and add the onion. Cook over medium heat, stirring, until wilted and add the veal, salt, and pepper.

3. Sprinkle with the flour and stir to coat the pieces. Add the broth and bring to a boil, stirring. Simmer about 30 minutes.

4. Meanwhile, cook the macaroni in boiling salted water until tender, about 10 minutes. Drain.

5. Combine the cream and milk in a mixing bowl. Add the yolks and stir with a wire whisk to blend. Beat thoroughly.

6. Add the cream mixture to the veal mixture and cook over very low heat, stirring constantly with a wooden spoon, until the moment the soup starts to boil. Remove from the heat immediately. You must not let this soup boil for more than a few seconds or the eggs will curdle the liquid.

7. Add the macaroni and stir. Serve immediately with grated Parmesan cheese on the side.

   Yield: 4 to 6 servings.

Chicken and Winter-Vegetable Soup

1 pound skinless, boneless chicken breast
³/₄ pound potatoes, peeled
¹/₄ pound turnips, peeled
¹/₄ pound carrots, trimmed and scraped
1 parsnip (about ¹/₄ pound), trimmed and scraped
1 large leek, trimmed
2 tablespoons butter
1 cup finely chopped onion
1 teaspoon chopped garlic
5 cups fresh or canned chicken broth
2 sprigs fresh thyme or ¹/₂ teaspoon dry
1 bay leaf
Salt to taste if desired
Freshly ground pepper to taste

1. Cut the chicken breast into 1-inch cubes.

2. Cut the potatoes into ¹/₄-inch slices. Cut the slices into ¹/₄-inch strips. Cut the strips into ¹/₄-inch dice. There should be about 2 cups. Put the potatoes in cold water and set aside until ready to use.

3. Cut the turnips, carrots, and parsnip into dice of approximately the same size as the potatoes. There should be about 2 cups turnips, 1¹/₂ cups carrots, and 1 cup parsnips.

4. Split the leek down the center and rinse well between the leaves. Pat dry. Cut the leek into very fine dice. There should be about 1½ cups.

5. Heat the butter in a heavy saucepan or small kettle and add the onion and garlic. Cook over medium heat, stirring, until wilted. Add the chicken and stir. Add the turnips, carrots, parsnip, potatoes, and leek and cook, stirring, about 2 minutes.

6. Add the broth, thyme, bay leaf, salt, and pepper and bring to a boil. Simmer about 30 minutes. Remove the bay leaf.

   Yield: 4 to 6 servings.

Harira

(MOROCCAN LAMB AND CHICKPEA SOUP)

> ½ cup dried chickpeas or 1 cup drained, canned chickpeas
> 2 tablespoons butter
> 1 pound lean lamb, cut into ½-inch cubes
> 1½ teaspoons turmeric
> 1 teaspoon ground cinnamon
> 1½ teaspoons freshly ground pepper
> ½ teaspoon stem saffron
> ½ teaspoon ground ginger
> ¾ cup finely chopped celery, including a few leaves
> 1 cup finely chopped onion
> ½ cup finely chopped parsley
> 3½ cups peeled and finely chopped tomatoes
> ¾ cup dried lentils
> 2 quarts cold water
> Salt to taste if desired
> 8 small white onions, peeled
> ¼ cup very fine egg noodles
> 2 eggs, well beaten
> 2 tablespoons lemon juice
> 8 thin lemon slices or wedges

1. If dried chickpeas are used, put them in a bowl and add cold water to cover. Let stand overnight.

2. Heat the butter in a kettle over medium heat and add the lamb. Cook, stirring, until it loses its raw look. Add the turmeric, cinnamon, pepper, saffron, and ginger and stir to blend well.

3. Add the celery, onion, and parsley and cook, stirring often, for about 5 minutes.

4. Add the tomatoes and stir. Cook for 15 minutes.

5. Rinse the lentils well under cold running water. Add them to the kettle. Add the water and bring to a boil. If soaked dried chickpeas are to be used, drain and add them. Add salt to taste. Bring to a boil and cook for 1½ hours.

6. Add the white onions. If canned chickpeas are to be used, add them now. Simmer for 30 minutes longer.

7. Add the noodles and simmer for 3 to 5 minutes or until the noodles are tender.

8. Beat the eggs with the lemon juice. Add this to the soup and turn off the heat immediately. Stir carefully in one motion with a spoon or fork so that the egg remains in strands. Serve in hot bowls with a lemon slice as a garnish.

   Yield: 8 servings.

Pozole

(MEXICAN PORK AND HOMINY STEW)

I have a fondness for many of the foods of Mexico, including some of the simpler preparations such as stuffed chilies and the various moles *(pronounced MO-lay). One of the soups I love on brisk winter days is called* pozole, *and it is made of pork and hominy (dried corn kernels). It is served with the cooking liquid plus assorted garnishes including chopped onion, ground hot chilies, sliced radishes, shredded lettuce, and lime wedges. Traditionally, in Mexico, a small, fiery dried chili known as* pequin *is crumbled and served with this dish.*

- 4 pork chops, about 1½ pounds
- 2 chicken legs plus thighs, about 1½ pounds
- 6 cups water
- 1 onion (about ¼ pound), peeled and quartered
- 1 large clove garlic, peeled
  Salt to taste if desired
- 2 tablespoons chopped green hot peppers, optional
- 12 black peppercorns
- 2½ cups drained canned hominy (see Note)
- 1 small head iceberg lettuce, shredded
- 12 radishes, sliced
- 1 lime, quartered
- ½ cup finely chopped Bermuda onion

1. Cut the bones from the chops but reserve both the meat and the bones. Cut the meat into 1-inch cubes. Put the meat and bones in a small kettle and add the chicken. Add the water, quartered onion, garlic, salt, peppers, and peppercorns. Bring to a boil and cook, uncovered, 45 minutes or until the meat is quite tender. Remove the pork and chicken.

2. When cool enough to handle, remove and discard the skin and bones from the chicken. Cut the meat into bite-size pieces.

3. Strain the broth into another small kettle or saucepan. Add the meats and hominy and bring to a boil.

4. Serve with the lettuce, radishes, lime, and Bermuda onion on the side.

Yield: 4 servings.

NOTE: Hominy is available in shops and supermarkets that sell Spanish or Puerto Rican foods.

❖ ❖ ❖

Manhattan Clam Chowder

24 chowder clams
6 strips bacon, cut into ¼-inch cubes
1½ cups finely chopped onions
1 cup finely chopped green sweet pepper
1½ cups finely chopped carrots
1 cup finely chopped celery
3 cups crushed canned imported tomatoes with liquid
3 cups water
1 bay leaf
4 sprigs fresh thyme or 1 teaspoon dry
Salt to taste if desired
Freshly ground pepper to taste
1 pound potatoes, peeled and cut into ¼-inch cubes
(about 1½ cups)
½ cup finely chopped parsley

1. Chop the clams and reserve the juice. You should have about 3 cups juice; if not, add water to reach that volume.

2. Put the bacon in a deep saucepan and cook over medium-high heat until slightly crisp.

3. Add the onions and cook, stirring, until they are wilted. Add the green pepper, carrots, and celery, and cook, stirring, about 1 minute.

4. Add the clams, tomatoes, reserved clam juice, water, bay leaf, thyme, salt, and pepper. Bring to a boil and add the potatoes. Simmer, skimming the surface to remove all trace of foam, 20 to 30 minutes or until the potatoes are tender. Remove the bay leaf. Check the seasonings. Sprinkle with the parsley and serve.

Yield: 10 servings.

Japanese-Style Fish and Shellfish Soup

Fundamental changes in the way fresh seafood is prepared, sparked in part by a rising tide of interest in Japanese and other Eastern cuisines, have added a bright new stripe to America's culinary spinnaker.

If you have a good basic fish stock around the house—and it freezes well—all sorts of healthful and delicious seafood soups and stews can be made with little effort. This recipe was inspired by Tatany, a Japanese restaurant in Manhattan that serves a variety of glistening oceanic soups laced with translucent cellophane noodles. This vitamin-packed soup has three types of seafood plus carrots, scallions, celery, dried mushrooms, and herbs. It makes a rousing tonic that can be dramatically served in stark Japanese lacquered bowls. If you dare, serve it with chopsticks and let your guests slurp to their health's content, Japanese style.

    3 dozen mussels, well cleaned
    1 tablespoon minced shallot
    1 cup dry white wine
    8 cups Fish Stock (recipe follows)
  $1/8$ teaspoon loosely packed saffron threads
  $2/3$ cup thinly sliced carrots
    1 cup finely chopped celery
    2 ounces fresh angel hair pasta or cellophane noodles,
        cut into 2-inch lengths
   10 dried shiitake mushrooms, stemmed, rinsed, and
        soaked for 30 minutes
    1 pound monkfish fillets, cut into bite-size cubes
  $3/4$ pound medium shrimp, shelled and deveined
  $1/3$ cup chopped scallions

1. Combine the mussels, shallot, and white wine in a large pot over medium-high heat, and steam, covered, until all the mussels open, about 5 minutes. Strain the mussels, discarding any that remain closed. Remove the mussel meat from the shells, reserving 12 mussels on the half shell for the garnish. Reserve the cooking liquid. There should be about $2^{1}/2$ cups.

2. Combine the fish stock with 2 cups mussel broth in a large pot over high heat. Add the saffron, carrots, celery, pasta, and mushrooms and bring to a boil. Reduce the heat and simmer for 3 minutes.

3. Add the monkfish, return to a boil, and simmer for 1 minute. Add the shrimp, scallions, and mussels and cook for 1 minute.

4. Place 2 mussels on the half shell in each of 6 bowls. Ladle the soup over the mussels and serve immediately.

   Yield: 6 servings.

Fish Stock

Bones and head from 1 flounder, sole, or other non-oily fish, gills removed (available at your local fish shop)
8 cups water
1 cup dry white wine

1. Combine all the ingredients in a large pot over high heat and bring to a boil. (If you are making one of the recipes that calls for shrimp, reserve the shells and add them to the stock for extra flavor.) Reduce the heat and simmer for 15 minutes.

2. Strain the stock and set aside until ready to use.

   Yield: 4 cups.

Billi-Bi au Safran

(CREAM OF MUSSEL SOUP WITH SAFFRON)

Over the years I have offered a number of variations on this favorite seafood soup. It is essentially a cream of mussel soup that has both American and French roots. The story goes that a wealthy American named William B. Leeds lived for years, off and on, in Paris and that his favorite restaurant was Maxim's, among the most celebrated dining spots in the city. The menu listed a cream of mussel soup, and this was his choice on almost every visit. Mr. Leeds was a great favorite of the owner and as a result of his passion for the soup it was dubbed Billi-Bi, a version, of course, of Billy B.

Basically Billi-Bi is made with mussels that are steamed in the shell with a little wine, a few vegetables, and seasonings. Once the mussels are opened, the soup is finished with the addition of cream. This version calls for saffron. Because of saffron's high cost, however, you may want to omit it; the soup will still be delectable. This soup could be served hot or chilled.

  2 tablespoons butter
  3 tablespoons coarsely chopped shallots
  3 tablespoons coarsely chopped onion
  $\frac{1}{2}$ clove garlic, finely minced
  $1\frac{1}{2}$ teaspoons stem saffron, optional
  $1\frac{1}{2}$ quarts mussels, well scrubbed (see page 40)
    Tabasco sauce to taste
  $\frac{1}{4}$ cup finely chopped parsley
  1 cup dry white wine
  1 cup heavy cream
  1 cup half-and-half
    Salt to taste if desired
    Freshly ground pepper to taste
    Parmesan Cheese Bread (recipe follows)

1. Heat the butter in a deep saucepan or kettle and add the shallots, onion, garlic, and saffron. Cook, stirring, about 3 minutes and add the mussels.

2. Add the Tabasco, parsley, and wine. Cover and cook until the mussels open, 5 minutes or longer. Discard any unopened mussels.

3. Add the cream and half-and-half and bring to a boil. Add salt and pepper. Do not strain the soup. The mussels may be left in the shell, but it is preferable if they are served in the soup on the half shell. Serve the soup piping hot or chilled, along with the bread.

   Yield: 4 or more servings.

Parmesan Cheese Bread

  1 large loaf French or Italian bread
  $\frac{1}{4}$ cup olive oil
  6 tablespoons freshly grated Parmesan cheese
  $\frac{1}{2}$ teaspoon finely minced garlic, optional

CLEANING MUSSELS

1. Use a clam knife or other blunt-edged knife to scrape the barnacles and sand off the shells.

2. Remove the small "beard" protruding from the shell by grabbing it securely and tearing it out.

3. Place the scraped mussels in a bowl. The size depends on the number of mussels, but the bowl should be only about a third full. Pour enough cold water over the mussels to just cover. With one hand, briskly stir the mussels using a washing machine motion for 30 to 60 seconds. The grit will sink to the bottom. Remove the mussels to another bowl and repeat several times until the water is clean.

1. Preheat the oven to 450 degrees.

2. Split the loaf of bread in half lengthwise.

3. Brush the split sides with equal quantities of oil. Sprinkle with the cheese. If the garlic is to be used, add it to the oil before brushing the bread.

4. Arrange the halves split side up in a baking dish. Place in the oven and bake 10 minutes.

   Yield: 4 servings.

Vietnamese-Style Mussel Soup

2 tomatoes, about ³/₄ pound
¹/₄ cup olive oil
1 tablespoon finely minced garlic
1¹/₂ tablespoons grated fresh ginger
³/₄ cup finely chopped scallions
5 pounds mussels, well scrubbed (see opposite page)
1 teaspoon or more finely chopped red or green hot pepper
¹/₄ cup chopped fresh basil or 1 tablespoon dry
¹/₄ cup chopped parsley
2 tablespoons chopped fresh coriander
1 cup dry white wine

1. Cut the tomatoes into ¹/₄-inch cubes.

2. Heat the oil in a skillet and add the garlic, ginger, and scallions. Cook, stirring, about 1 minute.

3. Add the tomatoes and mussels and scatter the hot pepper, basil, parsley, and coriander over all. Add the wine, cover, and cook over high heat, stirring occasionally and shaking the kettle so as to redistribute the mussels, about 5 minutes or until all the mussels open. Discard any unopened mussels. Serve the mussels and liquid in soup bowls.

   Yield: 4 servings.

Crab and Shrimp Gumbo

There are many versions of gumbo in Louisiana, including one called gumbo z'herbes that is made with neither meat nor seafood but with seven greens including spinach, turnip greens, beet tops, collards, lettuce, mustard greens, and cabbage. The interesting thing is that many authentic recipes for gumbo do not call for okra, even though the word gumbo *is an African tribal word for okra, originally spelled* ngumbo.

This quick version of gumbo includes crab, shrimp, and sausage. I prepare the stock with shrimp shells rather than using a more complicated and time-consuming fish stock.

Ideally this stew is made with fresh okra, which is available in most sections of the country in warm weather. To my mind gumbo is a perfect dish for cooler weather, and I find that frozen okra is a perfectly acceptable substitute, although the texture is a bit less firm than the fresh.

1 pound raw unshelled shrimp
½ pound kielbasa (Polish sausage)
¼ pound cooked ham
2 tablespoons vegetable oil
1 tablespoon finely minced garlic
1 cup finely chopped onion
¾ cup finely chopped scallions or green onions
1 cup finely chopped green sweet pepper
1 cup finely chopped celery
1 pound small fresh okra or a 10-ounce package frozen okra
1 cup crushed imported tomatoes
1 bay leaf
3 cups Shrimp Broth (recipe follows) or water
½ to 1 teaspoon Tabasco sauce
1 teaspoon Worcestershire sauce
  Salt and freshly ground pepper to taste
2 tablespoons flour
4 thin lemon slices
¾ to 1 pound lump crab meat

1. Peel and devein the shrimp. Save the shells for the broth.

2. Cut the sausage diagonally into thin rounds, each about ¼-inch thick.

3. Cut the ham into ½-inch cubes.

4. Heat 1 tablespoon oil in a casserole and add the sausage. Cook, stirring often, until the sausage is lightly browned. Add the ham and stir. Cook about 1 minute. Transfer the meats to a bowl. Pour off the fat from the casserole.

5. Add the garlic, onion, scallions, green pepper, and celery to the casserole. Cook over medium heat, stirring, until the vegetables are wilted.

6. If fresh okra is used, trim off any tough stems. Cut the okra into small rounds. There should be about 1 cup. Add the fresh or frozen okra to the

casserole and stir. Continue cooking until the vegetables become fairly dry, about 5 minutes.

7. Add the tomatoes, bay leaf, 2½ cups shrimp broth, Tabasco, Worcestershire, salt, and pepper. Add the ham and sausage mixture. Bring to a boil.

8. Heat the remaining 1 tablespoon oil in a small skillet and add the flour, stirring constantly with a wooden spoon. Cook, stirring, until the flour is browned. Take care not to burn the flour or it will be bitter.

9. Add the remaining ½ cup shrimp broth while stirring rapidly with a wire whisk. Stir this sauce into the gumbo.

10. Add the shrimp and lemon slices and cook about 10 minutes. Add the crab meat. Stir gently to prevent breaking up the lumps. Cook about 5 minutes. Serve with plain boiled rice.

   Yield: 6 servings.

Shrimp Broth

  Shells from 1 pound shrimp
  3 **cups water**
  6 **black peppercorns**
  ½ **cup coarsely chopped onion**
  1 **stalk celery, coarsely chopped**
  1 **bay leaf**
  Salt to taste if desired

1. Put all the ingredients in a saucepan and bring to a boil. Simmer about 20 minutes.

2. Strain the broth, discarding the solids.

   Yield: about 3 cups.

Provençal Seafood Stew

³/₄ pound non-oily, firm-fleshed fish such as monkfish, tilefish, blackfish, or red snapper
1 pound tomatoes (preferably plum tomatoes), cored
3 tablespoons olive oil
2 teaspoons minced garlic
¹/₂ cup finely chopped onion
¹/₂ teaspoon turmeric
1 cup dry white wine
2 sprigs fresh thyme or ¹/₂ teaspoon dry
1 bay leaf
¹/₂ teaspoon finely minced green hot pepper such as jalapeño or ¹/₄ teaspoon red pepper flakes
2 tablespoons Ricard (see Note)
Salt to taste if desired
Freshly ground pepper to taste
¹/₂ pound sea scallops
2 tablespoons finely chopped parsley

1. Cut the fish into 1-inch cubes. There should be about 2 cups.

2. Cut the tomatoes into ¹/₂-inch cubes. There should be about 3 cups.

3. Heat the oil in a heavy skillet or casserole and add the garlic, onion, and turmeric. Cook over medium heat, stirring, until the onion is wilted. Add the wine.

4. Cook briefly and add the tomatoes, thyme, bay leaf, hot pepper, salt, and pepper. Bring to a boil and cover tightly. Simmer about 5 minutes.

5. Add the scallops and fish and stir. Cover and cook about 5 minutes. Add the Ricard and stir. Remove the bay leaf. Sprinkle with the parsley and serve.

Yield: 4 servings.

NOTE: Ricard is a brand name for a popular French aperitif from Provence. The flavor is akin to licorice, anise, and absinthe. Other brand names include Pernod (less sweet than Ricard) and the Greek drink ouzo.

Marseilles-Style Fish Soup

When I serve a fish soup at home, guests frequently ask whether it could be called *bouillabaisse*. I usually say, ''No, you can only find a genuine *bouillabaisse* in Provence'' —or at least where the fish of that region can be procured. Popular varieties include Saint-Pierre and *rascasse* or *devilfish*, which is sometimes referred to as the soul of *bouillabaisse*. It is not a common fish, but I am told *rascasse* can be found in American waters, where it is sometimes called *sculpin* or *red scorpion*. I think the whole argument is a bit specious, however. If the soup—by whatever name—is good, dine well and be happy.

I find that a good fish soup can come out of any kettle and can be made in much less than an hour. The most important consideration, more important than the variety of fish and shellfish, has to do with freshness. You cannot make a decent soup, no matter what denomination, if you don't have the freshest of ingredients.

The liquid of a good fish soup, at least in my own kitchen, generally contains white wine and tomatoes, and it may or may not be seasoned with saffron, an expensive addition that is good but not essential. You prepare the liquid first, add the seafood, and cook briefly.

- 1¼ pounds skinless, boneless sea bass
- 1 pound skinless, boneless halibut
- 4 cups canned imported tomatoes
- ½ pound raw unshelled shrimp
- ¼ cup olive oil
- 1½ cups finely chopped onions
- 1 cup finely diced celery
- 1 cup finely diced green sweet pepper
- 1 cup dry white wine
- 1 bay leaf
- 1 teaspoon dry thyme
- 1 small dried red hot pepper, broken in half
- Salt to taste if desired
- Freshly ground pepper to taste
- 1 pound mussels, well scrubbed (see page 40)
- 1 teaspoon finely minced garlic
- ¼ cup finely chopped parsley

1. Cut the bass and halibut into 1½-inch cubes.

2. Put the tomatoes and their liquid in a food processor and process until fine. Or put them through a food mill.

3. Shell and devein the shrimp.

4. Heat the oil in a deep skillet or small kettle and add the onions. Cook over medium heat, stirring, until wilted. Add the celery and green pepper. Cook, stirring, about 5 minutes, and add the wine and bay leaf. Cook about 1 minute. Add the tomatoes, thyme, and hot pepper. Add salt and pepper. Simmer about 12 minutes.

5. Add the fish and mussels. Push the solids down into the sauce. Cook over high heat about 3 minutes. Add the shrimp and immerse them in the sauce. Cook about 1 minute and sprinkle with the garlic and parsley. Stir and simmer about 3 minutes longer. Discard any unopened mussels.

Yield: 4 to 6 servings.

Lyonnaise Oyster Stew

Although hundreds of "new" recipes are created yearly in professional and home kitchens around the world, each is probably based on an old precept. The best example of this is vichyssoise, the creation of the great French chef Louis Diat of the Ritz-Carlton Hotel.

To prepare it, he remembered a simple leek and potato soup his mother served him as a child in Montmarault in central France. He altered the original recipe, made with milk and served hot, by adding cream and serving it cold. Vichyssoise was created for the midsummer opening of the hotel's roof garden, which was not air-conditioned.

The soup came to mind when I had one of the finest and most easily made oyster stews I have ever sampled. The dish, served at Paul Bocuse's great restaurant in Lyons, was a cream soup made with puréed leeks and potatoes. It arrived at my table piping hot with delectably tender and sweet fresh oysters added before it was removed from the fire.

Wonderful accompaniments are crisp bread croutons and a small helping of grated Gruyère cheese.

2 or 3 large, unblemished leeks, about 1½ pounds
3 medium potatoes, about 1¼ pounds
3 tablespoons butter
6 cups water
Salt and freshly ground pepper to taste

¼ pound cheese, preferably Gruyère or Swiss
¼ cup vegetable oil
3 cups crustless cubed white bread
1 cup heavy cream
⅛ teaspoon freshly grated nutmeg
1 pint shucked oysters with their liquor
¼ cup finely chopped parsley

1. Trim off the root ends and most of the green part of the leeks. Reserve the white part of the leeks plus a small part of the green. Split the white part in half and rinse thoroughly between the leaves.

2. Cut the leeks lengthwise into thin strips and then crosswise into very small cubes. There should be about 5 cups.

3. Peel the potatoes and cut them lengthwise in half. Cut each half crosswise into very thin slices. There should be about 4 cups.

4. Heat 2 tablespoons butter in a large saucepan and add the chopped leek. Cook, stirring often, about 5 minutes. Add the potatoes and water and bring to a boil. Add salt and pepper. Simmer 20 minutes. Drain in a colander. Reserve both the liquid and solids.

5. Meanwhile, finely grate the cheese. There should be about 1 cup.

6. Heat the oil and remaining 1 tablespoon butter in a heavy skillet and add the bread cubes. Cook, shaking the skillet and stirring, until the cubes are golden brown. Drain in a sieve.

7. Put the leek and potato solids in a food processor or blender. Blend thoroughly while adding small amounts of the reserved cooking liquid. Add only enough liquid to make a fine purée.

8. Combine the purée with the remaining liquid in a kettle and bring to a simmer. Add the cream and salt and pepper to taste. Add the nutmeg and heat thoroughly.

9. Add the oysters with their liquor and cook briefly or just until the oysters curl. Serve sprinkled with the parsley and with the croutons and cheese on the side.

Yield: 6 to 8 servings.

Quick Fish Stew with Vegetables

1 pound sea scallops
1 pound shrimp, shelled and deveined
1 cup oysters with their liquor
  Salt to taste if desired
  Freshly ground pepper to taste
1 tomato, about ½ pound
2 stalks celery
1 small carrot, trimmed and scraped
2 -inch length of leek
2 tablespoons olive oil
½ cup finely chopped onion
1 teaspoon finely minced garlic
½ teaspoon turmeric
½ cup dry white wine
1 cup fish broth or bottled clam juice
2 teaspoons tomato paste
2 teaspoons grated fresh ginger
3 tablespoons finely chopped parsley

1. Cut the scallops into quarters or halves, depending on size. Sprinkle the scallops, shrimp, and oysters with a small amount of salt and pepper.

2. Peel the tomato and remove the seeds. Cut into ¼-inch cubes. There should be about ¾ cup.

3. Cut the celery crosswise into thin pieces. There should be about ½ cup.

4. Cut the carrot crosswise into 1½-inch lengths. Cut the pieces lengthwise into very thin julienne strips. There should be about 1 cup.

5. Cut the leek into very thin julienne strips. There should be about ½ cup.

6. Heat the oil in skillet and add the onion and garlic. Cook, stirring, until the onion is wilted. Add the celery, carrot, and leek. Sprinkle with the turmeric. Cook, stirring, about 2 minutes.

7. Add the wine and fish broth. Stir in the tomato paste and ginger. Cook about 5 minutes.

8. Add the tomato and scallops and bring to a boil. Cook about 1 minute and add the oysters in their liquor and shrimp. Cook about 2½ minutes. Stir in the parsley and serve.

    Yield: 4 servings.

◆ ◆ ◆

Seafood

Sautéed Black Sea Bass with Red Peppers

Black sea bass is more popular than ever in restaurants and fish markets, especially since striped bass fishing has been banned in many areas because of water pollution. The black sea bass, while much smaller than the striped bass, has mild-flavored white meat that is well suited to simple dishes made with fresh herbs.

I recently found fresh black sea bass in a local market and prepared fillets with a red pepper sauce. Whether I sauté, broil, or grill meaty fish like bass, I leave the skin on; it adds flavor to the dish and holds the flesh together during cooking. (This is particularly important when you grill fish.)

For a sauce, I sautéed some red pepper cubes with shallots, then seasoned them with lemon juice and fresh basil.

4 sea bass fillets with skin on, each 6 ounces
   Salt and freshly ground pepper to taste
3 tablespoons milk
2 tablespoons flour
2 tablespoons olive oil
2 red sweet peppers (about 1 pound), cored, seeded, and cut into
      ¹/₂-inch cubes
2 tablespoons finely chopped shallots
1 teaspoon chopped fresh oregano or ¹/₂ teaspoon dry
2 tablespoons butter
2 tablespoons lemon juice
¹/₄ cup coarsely chopped fresh basil or parsley

1. Sprinkle the fillets with salt and pepper.

2. Pour the milk into a shallow bowl and put the flour in a flat dish. Dip each fillet in the milk and then dredge it in the flour, making sure the flour adheres.

3. Heat the oil in a nonstick skillet large enough to hold the fillets in one layer. Add the fillets, skin side down, and cook them over medium-high heat about 3 minutes or until golden brown on one side. Fast cooking is important.

4. Turn the fish and cook until golden brown, about 2 to 3 minutes.

5. Transfer the fish to a warm serving dish. Add the red pepper cubes to skillet and salt and pepper to taste. Cook and stir over medium heat for about 3 minutes. Add the shallots and oregano and cook briefly but do not brown. Add the butter and cook, stirring. Add the lemon juice and stir. Pour the sauce over the fish. Sprinkle with the basil and serve immediately.

Yield: 4 servings.

Fillets of Sea Bass with Basil and Tomatoes

> 4 sea bass fillets, about 1½ pounds with the skin
> Salt and freshly ground pepper to taste
> 2 ripe tomatoes, about ¾ pound
> 2 tablespoons milk
> 3 tablespoons flour
> 3 tablespoons vegetable oil
> 3 tablespoons olive oil
> ¼ cup chopped scallions or green onions
> 1 tablespoon chopped fresh rosemary or 1 teaspoon dry
> 2 tablespoons lemon juice
> ¼ cup basil leaves, cut into very thin strips

1. Carefully cut away and discard any bones that may remain on the sea bass. Sprinkle the fillets with salt and pepper on both sides.

2. Drop the tomatoes into boiling water and simmer exactly 10 seconds. Drain the tomatoes and cut away the cores. Pull away and discard the skin. Cut the tomatoes crosswise in half and discard the seeds in each half. Dice the tomatoes. There should be about 1½ cups.

3. Dip the fillets in the milk to coat well. Dip the fillets in the flour to coat both sides and shake off the excess.

4. Heat 2 tablespoons vegetable oil in a nonstick skillet over medium-high heat and add half of the fillets, skin side up. Cook about 4 minutes. Turn the fillets and cook about 3 minutes on the other side. Remove the fillets to a warm platter. Cook the remaining fillets in the same fashion for the same length of time, adding a little more oil as necessary.

5. Pour off any fat remaining in the skillet. Wipe out the skillet with paper towels.

6. Heat the olive oil in the skillet and add the tomatoes, scallions, and rosemary. Add the lemon juice, basil, salt, and pepper. Cook, shaking the skillet and stirring, about 4 minutes.

7. Spoon the tomato mixture over the fish fillets and serve.

   Yield: 4 servings.

Poached Cod with Lemon-Butter Sauce

In all seafood cookery one fish that is among the easiest to prepare—and one of the best bargains—is poached cod. It is also a dish that can rival many of the more elaborate fish creations. The technique is simple: Cut the cod fillets into serving pieces, put them in a pan, and add cold water, milk, and seasonings such as cloves, peppercorns, parsley, and bay leaf. Bring the liquid to a boil and let the fish simmer gently about two minutes or slightly longer, depending on the thickness of the pieces. Then drain and serve.

I have such a liking for poached cod I would settle for a simple sauce of melted butter and lemon juice. But, as I said, this fish can be transformed into many different dishes; just a change in the sauce will do the trick. Guests in my home have been delighted, for example, with a light butter sauce flavored with garlic, shallots, lemon, and parsley.

1 or 2 cod fillets, about 1³/₄ pounds
1 cup milk
¹/₈ teaspoon cayenne pepper
1¹/₂ cups water
1 bay leaf
4 sprigs fresh parsley plus 2 tablespoons finely minced parsley
4 whole peppercorns
Salt to taste if desired
2 whole cloves
4 tablespoons butter
¹/₂ teaspoon finely minced garlic
3 tablespoons finely chopped shallots
Juice of ¹/₂ lemon
Freshly ground pepper to taste

1. Cut the fillets crosswise into 4 equal pieces.

2. Arrange the cod pieces in one layer in a skillet and add the milk, cayenne pepper, and water. The fish should be barely covered with liquid. If necessary, add a little more water. Add the bay leaf, parsley sprigs, peppercorns, salt, and cloves.

3. Bring to a simmer and cover. Cook gently about 2 to 4 minutes. Cooking time will depend on the thickness of the fish. Cook only until the fish flakes easily when tested with a fork.

4. Heat 1 tablespoon butter in a saucepan and add the garlic and shallots. Cook briefly, stirring.

5. Remove ¹/₄ cup cooking liquid from the fish and add it to the saucepan, stirring.

6. Bring to a boil and simmer for 3 minutes. Add the lemon juice. Swirl in the remaining 3 tablespoons butter. Remove from the heat and add the minced parsley, salt, and pepper.

7. Drain the fish and serve hot with the melted butter sauce.

   Yield: 4 servings.

Fillets of Flounder with Parsley-Mustard Sauce

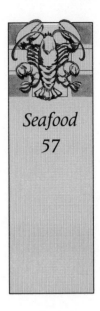

Butter for greasing the pan
Salt and freshly ground pepper to taste
4 **flounder fillets, about 1¼ pounds**
½ **cup plus 1 tablespoon dry white wine**
2 **cups loosely packed parsley leaves, stems removed**
2 **tablespoons finely chopped shallots**
½ **cup heavy cream**
2 **teaspoons Dijon-style mustard**

1. Preheat the oven to 500 degrees.

2. Select a rimmed pan or skillet large enough to hold the fillets in one layer. Generously butter the bottom and sides of the pan. Sprinkle the bottom with salt and pepper.

3. Arrange the fillets close together over the pan bottom. Sprinkle with salt and pepper and brush the tops with 1 tablespoon wine.

4. Bring enough water to a boil in a saucepan to cover the parsley leaves when added. Add the parsley leaves and cook about 1 minute, no longer. Drain thoroughly and run under cold water. Drain. Put the parsley in a clean square of cheesecloth and squeeze to extract the excess liquid. Put the parsley on flat surface and chop it fine.

5. Place the fish in the oven and bake 5 minutes.

6. Meanwhile, pour the remaining ½ cup wine in a saucepan and add the shallots. Cook until the wine is almost evaporated. Add the parsley, cream, and mustard. Stir and bring to a boil. Add to the sauce any liquid that accumulates around the fish. Add salt and pepper. Spoon the sauce over the fish and serve.

Yield: 4 servings.

◆ ◆ ◆

Flounder Fillets à l'Anglaise

It is amusing to note that when French chefs were passing out names for dishes in the days of Escoffier, they often named the simplest of dishes à l'anglaise, meaning "in the English style." The term was used for foods that were simply boiled in water or stock, like mutton, chicken, or potatoes. It was also applied to foods that were breaded and cooked in a little oil until golden brown.

8 small flounder fillets, about 1¼ pounds
Salt to taste if desired
Freshly ground pepper to taste
½ cup flour
1 egg
2 tablespoons water
2 cups fine fresh bread crumbs
2 tablespoons vegetable oil
3 tablespoons butter
2 tablespoons lemon juice

1. Sprinkle the flounder fillets on both sides with salt and pepper.

2. Dip the fillets in the flour to coat them on both sides. Shake off the excess. Beat the egg with the water. Dip the flour-coated pieces in the egg to coat them well and then dip them in the bread crumbs. Pat the fillets on both sides with the flat side of a knife to make the crumbs adhere.

3. Heat the oil in a nonstick skillet over high heat and add a few fillets in one layer—just enough so they do not touch. Cook 1 to 1½ minutes on one side or until golden brown. Turn and cook about 1 minute on the other side or until golden brown. As the pieces are cooked, transfer them to a warm platter. Continue cooking, adding a little more oil as necessary, until fillets are cooked on both sides.

4. Pour off the oil from the skillet and add the butter. Cook until it is lightly browned. Add the lemon juice and pour the sauce over the fish.

   Yield: 4 servings.

Fish Fillets in Beer Batter

When beer is added to a batter it acts like a leavening agent, resulting in a lighter coating for the fish.

THE BATTER:

1 cup flour
Salt to taste if desired
2 eggs, separated
1 cup beer, preferably at room temperature
2 tablespoons corn or vegetable oil
1/4 teaspoon Tabasco sauce
1/2 cup finely chopped scallions or green onions

8 small fish fillets, such as flounder, fluke, or sole, about 1 1/2 pounds
Salt and freshly ground pepper to taste
6 cups corn or vegetable oil
Sweet Red Pepper Mayonnaise (recipe follows)
2 lemons, cut into 8 wedges

1. To make the batter, put the flour and salt in a mixing bowl and add the egg yolks. Start beating with a whisk. Stir in the beer, oil, and Tabasco. Cover and let stand until ready to use.

2. Beat the egg whites until stiff and fold them in. Fold in the scallions.

3. Cut the fish fillets in half. If there is a small bone line down each fillet, trim it away. Sprinkle with salt and pepper.

4. Heat the oil in a deep fryer to 380 degrees.

5. Dip the pieces of fish, 1 at a time, in the batter and add them to the hot oil. Cook, carefully turning the pieces once or twice, about 2 1/2 minutes or until golden brown and crisp all over.

6. As the pieces are cooked, transfer them to paper towels to drain. Continue until all the fillets are cooked. Serve with the sauce and lemon wedges.

Yield: 4 servings.

Sweet Red Pepper Mayonnaise

    1 red sweet pepper, about ¹/₂ pound
    1 cup mayonnaise, preferably homemade (see page 289)
    1 hard-boiled egg
    3 tablespoons finely chopped shallots
    3 tablespoons finely chopped parsley
    Salt to taste if desired
    Freshly ground pepper to taste

1. Preheat the broiler or a charcoal grill.

2. Place the pepper under the broiler or on the grill and cook it on all sides until the entire skin is well charred. When cool enough to handle, split it in half. Remove and discard the seeds and veins. Pull off and discard the charred skin.

3. Put the pepper through a food mill or blend it thoroughly in a food processor or blender.

4. Put the mayonnaise in a mixing bowl and add the puréed pepper.

5. Put the egg through a fine sieve and add it to the mayonnaise. Add the shallots, parsley, salt, and pepper. Serve cold or at room temperature.

    Yield: about 2 cups.

Poached Halibut with Maître d'Hôtel Butter

Fresh halibut is sweet-fleshed and tender, with a taste vaguely reminiscent of turbot. But it begs to be dressed with a sauce whose flavor can act as a foil, enhancing the character of the fish.

    Any number of sauces will do. I particularly like maître d'hôtel butter. The butter consists basically of beating butter with parsley and lemon juice. Home cooks may vary this by substituting vinegar for the lemon and by adding Dijon-style mustard.

4 halibut steaks, each 1 inch thick and about ³/₄ pound
¹/₂ cup milk
   Salt to taste if desired
10 peppercorns
 1 bay leaf
 2 whole cloves
¹/₄ teaspoon Tabasco sauce
 2 sprigs fresh thyme or ¹/₂ teaspoon dry
 6 sprigs fresh parsley
   Maître d'Hôtel Butter with Mustard (recipe follows)

1. Arrange the halibut steaks in one layer in a large skillet. Add cold water to cover to a depth of about 1 inch above the top of the fish. Add the milk, salt, peppercorns, bay leaf, cloves, Tabasco, thyme, and parsley.

2. Bring to a boil and simmer 5 to 7 minutes or until the fish flakes easily when tested with a fork. Drain. Serve hot with the butter.

   Yield: 4 servings.

Maître d'Hôtel Butter with Mustard

2 tablespoons finely chopped shallots
¹/₂ cup dry white wine
6 tablespoons butter at room temperature
2 teaspoons Dijon-style mustard
1 tablespoon finely chopped parsley
   Salt to taste if desired
   Freshly ground pepper to taste
1 teaspoon fresh lemon juice

1. Combine the shallots and wine in a saucepan and cook until the wine is almost but not quite completely evaporated. Scrape the mixture into a small mixing bowl and cool.

2. Combine the butter, mustard, parsley, salt, pepper, and lemon juice in a bowl. Start blending with a wire whisk and add the shallot mixture. Blend thoroughly.

   Yield: about ³/₄ cup.

Halibut Fillets with Leeks and Linguine

There are nearly a dozen varieties of fish in the sole family, including Dover sole, English sole, Rex sole, sand sole, and at least fifteen varieties of the type of sole known as flounder, ranging from plaice to turbot. One of my favorite flounders is the one commonly known as halibut. (To make things even more confusing, there are at least four kinds of halibut—Atlantic, California, Greenland, and Pacific.) Its delicate flavor and meaty texture give halibut a special quality.

There are countless classic ways to prepare halibut: in a white-wine sauce, for example, in a béchamel sauce, or with grapes. I often make a quick, delicious dish by poaching the halibut in a mixture of dry white wine and finely chopped shallots.

When the fish is cooked it is removed briefly from the cooking liquid. The liquid is then reduced and a little cream is added to it. The fish is then placed on a bed of leeks.

I serve the fish and leeks alongside a dish of freshly cooked linguine into which I have blended some of the cream sauce. This is an excellent fish for winter dining since halibut is available throughout the season.

> 2 leeks, about ³/₄ pound after trimming and cleaning
> 2 tablespoons butter
> 1 cup dry white wine
> 2 tablespoons finely chopped shallots or scallions
> 1¹/₂ pounds boneless, skinless halibut, cut into 4 equal pieces
>   Salt and freshly ground pepper to taste
> ¹/₂ cup heavy cream
> ¹/₄ teaspoon freshly grated nutmeg
>   Dash cayenne pepper or to taste
>   Linguine in Cream Sauce (recipe follows)

1. Rinse the leek leaves thoroughly and pat dry. Chop the leeks as finely as possible. There should be about 3¹/₂ cups.

2. Heat 1 tablespoon butter in a saucepan and add the leeks. Cook, stirring often from the bottom, about 3 minutes. Add ¹/₂ cup wine and stir. Bring to a boil and cover. Cook 10 minutes. Keep warm.

3. Meanwhile, using the remaining 1 tablespoon butter, grease the bottom of a heavy skillet large enough to hold the fish pieces in one layer without crowding. Sprinkle the bottom of the skillet with the shallots and arrange the fish pieces over it. Sprinkle with salt and pepper to taste. Pour the remaining ¹/₂

cup wine over the fish. Bring the wine to a boil and cover the skillet tightly. Cook 4 minutes or until the fish just loses its raw look.

4. Transfer the fish pieces to a warm serving platter. Cover tightly with foil and keep warm. Briefly cook down the skillet liquid to ½ cup and then pour it into a saucepan. Add the cream, nutmeg, and cayenne. Bring to a boil and cook over medium-high heat about 4 minutes or until reduced to ¾ cup. Set aside 6 tablespoons sauce to be added to the linguine.

6. Spoon 4 equal portions of the cooked leeks onto 4 individual serving dishes. Top each portion with 1 piece of fish. Spoon all but the reserved 6 table-spoons sauce over the fish.

7. Serve the linguine in cream sauce on the side.

Yield: 4 servings.

Linguine in Cream Sauce

> 10 cups water
>   Salt to taste if desired
> ½ pound fresh or dried linguine
> 2 tablespoons butter
> 6 tablespoons cream sauce from the Halibut Fillets with Leeks

1. The cooking time will vary depending on whether you use fresh or dried linguine. Bring the water to a boil and add the salt. Add the linguine and cook until tender. Fresh linguine should require about 1 to 1½ minutes. Dried linguine will require about 7 to 9 minutes. Drain.

2. Add the butter and cream sauce to the linguine and toss.

Yield: 4 servings.

◆ ◆ ◆

Monkfish in Red-Wine Sauce

5 tablespoons butter
¼ cup coarsely chopped shallots
1 tablespoon chopped garlic
½ teaspoon dry thyme
4 sprigs parsley
1 bay leaf
2 whole cloves
3 tablespoons flour
1 bottle dry red wine
2 cups fish stock or bottled clam juice
12 small red potatoes, peeled
2 cups pearl onions
12 ounces button mushrooms (about 4 cups)
1 teaspoon finely chopped garlic
¼ cup finely chopped shallots
   Salt and pepper to taste
4 pounds monkfish, cut into 1-inch cubes
2 tablespoons cognac
½ cup chopped parsley

1. Heat 3 tablespoons butter in a saucepan over medium heat. Add the coarsely chopped shallots and chopped garlic. Cook, stirring, until wilted. Add the thyme, parsley sprigs, bay leaf, and cloves. Sprinkle with the flour and stir well. Add the wine and fish stock. Bring the sauce to a boil and simmer for 20 minutes.

2. Meanwhile, cook the potatoes in salted water for about 15 minutes. Blanch the pearl onions in boiling water for 5 minutes. Drain.

3. Heat the remaining 2 tablespoons butter in a large kettle and sauté the pearl onions, mushrooms, finely chopped garlic, and finely chopped shallots over medium heat for 3 to 4 minutes. Season with salt and pepper. Add the fish and cook for 3 minutes, stirring often. Deglaze the pot with the cognac and add the red-wine sauce. Bring to a boil and simmer for 5 minutes. Add the potatoes, sprinkle with the chopped parsley, and serve immediately.

   Yield: 8 to 10 servings.

Lotte au Poivre

(MONKFISH COATED WITH CRUSHED PEPPER)

Lotte au poivre *is a precursor of the ubiquitous blackened redfish popularized in New Orleans. Benoit, a stylish family-run bistro in the fourth arrondissement of Paris, serves a spirited version that is spicy but not as blackened as Cajun redfish. The whole fillet is coated with crushed peppercorns before sautéing it in a pan over high heat. The accompanying white-wine sauce is simple and quick to make.*

> 4 monkfish fillets, about 1¼ pounds
> 2 teaspoons crushed white peppercorns or coarse black pepper
>   Salt to taste
> 2 tablespoons olive oil
> 2 tablespoons finely chopped shallots
> ¼ cup dry white wine
> 4 tablespoons butter
>   Chervil or dill sprigs for garnish

1. Coat the fish on both sides with the pepper. Sprinkle with salt to taste.

2. Heat the oil in a black cast-iron skillet over medium heat. Add the fish and cook about 2 minutes or until lightly browned. Turn the fish, cover tightly, and lower the heat. Cook for 3 minutes. Transfer the fish to a plate and keep warm.

3. Add the shallots to the skillet and cook over medium heat until wilted. Add the wine and bring to a boil, stirring. Reduce by half, add the butter, and blend well. Spoon the sauce over the fish. Garnish with the chervil.

   Yield: 4 servings.

Brochette of Salmon with Bacon

1½ pounds skinless, boneless salmon fillets
   Salt and freshly ground pepper to taste
2 teaspoons ground cumin
1 large red sweet pepper
6 slices bacon
1 red onion
1 tablespoon olive oil
3 tablespoons butter
1 tablespoon lemon juice
3 tablespoons chopped fresh dill

1. Preheat a charcoal grill or broiler. Soak 8 wooden skewers in cold water until ready to use.

2. Cut the salmon into 1½-inch cubes. There should be 24 pieces. Sprinkle the pieces with salt, pepper, and cumin.

3. Cut away and discard the pepper core and veins. Discard the seeds. Cut the pepper into 16 equal pieces.

4. Cut the bacon into 16 equal rectangles.

5. Cut the onion into 16 ½-inch cubes. Put any remaining onion to another use.

6. Heat a nonstick skillet and add the bacon pieces in one layer. Scatter the pepper and onion cubes over the bacon. Cook, shaking the pieces and stirring, for about 1 minute. Drain and cook slightly longer.

7. Drain the bacon mixture again.

8. Arrange the various ingredients on each of the skewers as follows: 1 sweet pepper cube, 1 piece of bacon, 1 piece of salmon, 1 cube of onion, 1 piece of salmon, 1 cube of onion, 1 piece of bacon, 1 piece of salmon, and 1 cube of pepper. Brush the brochettes all over with the olive oil. Sprinkle with salt and pepper.

9. If the brochettes are to be cooked under the broiler, arrange them on a rack about 4 inches from the heat; leave the door slightly ajar. Cook 3 minutes on

one side and turn the brochettes. Cook 2 minutes. If the brochettes are to be cooked on a grill, place them on the grill and cook 3 minutes. Turn and cook on the other side about 2 minutes.

10. Meanwhile, heat the butter and add the lemon juice and dill. Stir and brush the sauce over the brochettes.

   Yield: 4 servings.

Salmon Baked in Foil Packages

Cooking fish in foil has two distinct advantages: It helps retain moisture and meld the flavors of herbs and spices; it also is a neat and convenient way to cook. Such dishes can be assembled ahead of time and popped in the oven at the last minute.

  1½ pounds skinless, boneless salmon fillets cut into 4 equal pieces
   4 carrots, about ¾ pound
   1 zucchini, about ¼ pound
  ½ pound mushrooms
   2 tablespoons butter
     Juice of ½ lemon
  ½ cup trimmed scallions, cut into 2-inch lengths
     Salt to taste if desired
   1 tablespoon finely chopped fresh tarragon or ½ teaspoon dry
   6 tablespoons melted butter or oil for greasing the paper or foil
     rounds
   8 teaspoons finely chopped shallots
   4 teaspoons lemon-flavored vodka (such as Absolute Citron) or dry
     white wine
     Freshly ground pepper to taste

1. Preheat the oven to 525 degrees or the hottest temperature possible. Place a baking sheet in the oven and heat it at least 5 minutes.

2. Holding the knife at an angle, cut the salmon into very thin slices as if you were slicing smoked salmon.

3. Spread a length of foil (not heavy-duty or it will not puff up) or nonstick parchment on a flat surface. Invert a 12-inch round baking dish, such as a

cake pan, on the foil and trace around the pan with a sharp knife to cut away 1 round. Continue until you have 4 foil rounds.

4. Scrape and trim the carrots and cut them crosswise into 1-inch lengths. Cut each length into thin slices. Stack the slices and cut them into very thin matchlike strips. There should be about 3 cups. Trim the zucchini and slice into $^{1}/_{4}$-inch rounds. There should be about $1^{1}/_{2}$ cups.

5. Cut off and discard the bottom of each mushroom. Cut the caps crosswise into thin slices. There should be about 2 cups.

6. Heat the 2 tablespoons butter in a saucepan and add the mushrooms. Sprinkle with the lemon juice. Cook, shaking the skillet and stirring, about 1 minute. Add the carrots, zucchini, scallions, and salt. Cover and cook 7 to 8 minutes. Add the tarragon and stir. Cover and set aside.

7. Place each foil round on a flat surface and brush all over with the melted butter. Spoon an equal portion of the vegetable mixture slightly off center on each round, leaving an ample margin for folding over.

8. Cover the vegetable mixture with slices of raw salmon, leaving them slightly overlapping but making a compact row that just covers the vegetables. Sprinkle each serving with 2 teaspoons shallots and 1 teaspoon vodka or wine. Sprinkle with salt and pepper.

9. Fold over each foil round to completely enclose the filling. Fold and pleat the edges over and over to seal the filling as tightly as possible.

10. Arrange the packages neatly in one layer on the preheated baking sheet. Place in the oven and bake 7 minutes.

   Yield: 4 servings.

◆ ◆ ◆

Peppered Salmon with Onion Compote

1 center-cut boneless salmon fillet with the skin left intact, about
    1¼ pounds
4 red onions, about 1½ pounds
5 tablespoons butter
2 tablespoons red-wine vinegar
1 whole clove
¼ teaspoon Tabasco sauce
2 tablespoons honey
   Salt to taste if desired
2 tablespoons olive oil
2 teaspoons coarsely cracked black pepper
2 tablespoons lemon juice
1 tablespoon finely chopped fresh sweet herb such as dill, parsley,
   or basil

1. Cut the salmon fillet slightly on the bias into 4 equal pieces.

2. Peel the onions and cut them crosswise in half. Cut the halves into quarters. Cut the quarters into 1-inch cubes. There should be about 5½ cups.

3. Heat 2 tablespoons butter in a heavy casserole and add the onion pieces. Cover. Cook over medium-high heat, stirring occasionally, about 15 minutes. The onions will start to brown. Uncover and add the vinegar, clove, and Tabasco. Cook briefly until the vinegar is almost evaporated and stir in the honey. Cover tightly. Cook 10 minutes.

4. Sprinkle the salmon pieces with salt. Coat the pieces with the oil and coarsely cracked black pepper.

5. Preheat a charcoal grill or the broiler. If the fish is to be broiled, place the pieces, skin side down, on a baking sheet. Place the baking sheet under the broiler with the fish about 4 inches from the heat. Leave the door partly open. Cook 3 minutes and turn the pieces; continue cooking about 3 minutes more. If the salmon is to be grilled, place the pieces on the grill, skin

side down. Cook about 3 minutes and turn the pieces; cook about 3 minutes more. Transfer the fish to a warm platter.

6. Heat the remaining 3 tablespoons butter in a small saucepan and add the lemon juice and herb. When the mixture starts to bubble, pour it over the salmon pieces. Serve the salmon with the onions.

Yield: 4 servings.

Salmon Burgers with Brown Butter Sauce

1¼ pounds skinless, boneless salmon
1¼ cups fine fresh bread crumbs
    Salt and freshly ground pepper to taste
¼ teaspoon freshly grated nutmeg
¼ teaspoon ground cumin
¼ teaspoon Tabasco sauce
⅓ cup milk
⅓ cup sour cream
¼ cup chopped fresh coriander
1 tablespoon corn or vegetable oil
4 tablespoons butter
1 tablespoon lemon juice

1. Chop the salmon coarsely with a very heavy sharp knife or with a food processor.

2. Place the salmon in a mixing bowl and add ½ cup bread crumbs, the salt, pepper, nutmeg, cumin, Tabasco sauce, and milk. Stir briefly with a wooden spoon. Add the sour cream and coriander and stir rapidly until well blended.

3. Divide the mixture into 8 patties and lay them on a sheet of wax paper. They should be about ¾ inch thick. Coat the patties on all sides with the remaining ¾ cup bread crumbs.

4. Heat the oil in a nonstick skillet large enough to hold the patties in one layer. Cook on one side over medium heat about 4 minutes or until golden brown. Turn and cook about 3 to 4 minutes longer or until golden brown on the second side. Transfer the patties to a warm serving platter.

5. Wipe out the skillet and add the butter. Cook, shaking the skillet, until the butter starts to brown. Add the lemon juice and blend. Pour over the patties and serve immediately.

   Yield: 4 servings.

Grilled Herbed Salmon with Shrimp

1½ pounds boneless salmon fillet with the skin left intact
8 large shrimp, about ½ pound
¼ cup olive oil
  Salt and freshly ground pepper to taste
1 tablespoon chopped fresh thyme or ½ teaspoon dry
1 tablespoon chopped fresh marjoram or 1 teaspoon dry
¼ teaspoon red pepper flakes
¼ cup dry white wine
1 tablespoon fresh lemon juice
2 tablespoons melted butter
2 tablespoons finely chopped parsley

1. Preheat a charcoal grill or the broiler.

2. Cut the salmon into 4 equal pieces.

3. Place each shrimp on a flat surface and cut through the back of the shell, leaving the shell and underside feelers intact. Open each shrimp butterfly-fashion and devein it.

4. Pour the oil into a flat dish and add the shrimp and salmon. Turn the pieces to coat them on all sides. Sprinkle all over with the salt, pepper, thyme, mar-

joram, pepper flakes, wine, and lemon juice. Cover with plastic wrap and let stand at room temperature about 10 to 15 minutes.

5. When ready to cook, remove the seafood from the marinade. Pour the marinade into a small saucepan. If using a broiler, arrange the salmon, skin side up, on a baking sheet. Place under the broiler about 4 inches from the heat. Leave the door partly open. Broil 1½ minutes on one side and turn. Arrange the shrimp, shell side down, around the salmon and broil 2 minutes. Leave the door totally open. Turn the shrimp and continue cooking 1 minute.

6. If using a grill, place the salmon pieces, skin side down, on the grill and cook about 1½ minutes. Turn the salmon and add the shrimp, shell side down. Continue cooking 2 minutes, turning the shrimp occasionally.

7. Transfer the pieces to a heated platter. Add the melted butter to the reserved marinade and bring to a boil. Pour the butter mixture over the seafood. Sprinkle with the chopped parsley and serve.

Yield: 4 servings.

Matelote of Salmon and Shellfish

In French the term matelote, *which originated in my home region of Burgundy, generally refers to a stewlike dish made with freshwater fish and red wine. The following recipe is made with salmon.*

   8 jumbo shrimp, about ½ pound
½ pound skinless, boneless salmon fillets
½ pint bay or sea scallops
½ pound mushrooms
   4 tablespoons butter
½ cup finely chopped onion
¼ cup finely chopped shallots
¼ cup finely diced carrot
¼ cup finely diced celery
¼ teaspoon dry thyme
½ teaspoon peppercorns

1 small bay leaf
¼ teaspoon finely minced garlic
3 sprigs parsley
2 tablespoons flour
1½ cups dry red wine
1 cup fish broth or bottled clam juice
  Salt to taste if desired
  Freshly ground pepper to taste
2 tablespoons cognac
2 tablespoons finely chopped parsley

1. Peel and devein the shrimp, reserving the shells.

2. Cut the salmon into 1-inch cubes.

3. If sea scallops are used, cut them into quarters.

4. If the mushrooms are small, leave them whole. If they are large, cut them into quarters.

5. Heat 1 tablespoon butter in a saucepan and add the onion, shallots, carrot, celery, thyme, peppercorns, bay leaf, garlic, and parsley sprigs. Cook, stirring, until the onions are wilted. Add the shrimp shells and stir. Add the flour and stir. Add the wine, stirring with a wire whisk. Add the fish broth and bring to a boil. Simmer 20 minutes or until reduced to about 1½ cups when strained. Strain the sauce, discarding the solids.

6. Heat 2 tablespoons butter in a casserole and add the mushrooms, salt, and pepper. Cook, stirring, about 5 minutes.

7. Add the cognac and strained sauce and bring to a boil. Simmer about 5 minutes. Add the shrimp, scallops, and salmon. Cook, stirring gently, so that the fish and seafood are coated with the sauce. Simmer about 3 minutes. Do not overcook. Swirl in the remaining 1 tablespoon butter. Sprinkle with the chopped parsley and serve.

   Yield: 4 servings.

◆ ◆ ◆

Sesame-Coated Fish Fillets

4 skinless, boneless fish fillets such as weakfish, red snapper,
    blackfish, or other non-oily fish
1/4 cup fresh lemon or lime juice
1/4 teaspoon Tabasco sauce
2 tablespoons Worcestershire sauce
1 egg, lightly beaten
1 tablespoon milk
    Salt to taste if desired
    Freshly ground pepper to taste
3/4 cup sesame seeds
3/4 cup freshly grated Parmesan cheese
1/3 cup flour
1/4 cup olive oil
1 tablespoon butter
    Lemon wedges for garnish

1. Put the fish fillets in a dish and add the lemon juice, Tabasco, and Worcester-shire sauce. Turn the fillets in the mixture and let them stand until ready to cook.

2. Put the beaten egg, milk, salt, and pepper in a flat dish and stir to blend. Put the sesame seeds and cheese in a separate dish and blend. Put the flour in a third dish.

3. Lift the fillets, 1 at a time, and with your fingers wipe off most, but not all, of the marinating liquid. Dip the fillets, 1 at a time, in the flour to coat well. Dip the pieces in the egg mixture to coat on both sides. Dip in the sesame seed mixture to coat well.

4. Heat the oil and butter in a nonstick skillet over high heat and add the fish fillets. (It may be necessary to cook the fish in 2 batches if the skillet is not large enough, but the amount of oil and butter indicated should be suffi-cient.) Cook 2 minutes and turn carefully with a pancake turner or spatula. Cook about 2 minutes on the second side. If all the fillets have not been cooked, add a second batch to the skillet and cook in the same manner. Transfer the fillets to a warm platter. Pour the pan drippings over all. Gar-nish with the lemon wedges.

    Yield: 4 servings.

Skate with Black Butter Sauce

Americans are eating more varieties of seafood than ever, including some excellent but uncommon varieties formerly called ''trash fish'' because they used to be thrown back by fishermen who had no market for them. The list of trash fish includes tilefish, monkfish, and skate, which is known in France as raie. *I recall that ten or fifteen years ago only one French restaurant in New York City regularly offered skate on the menu. Today, it is familiar on many menus.*

To my mind skate may be the best and most interesting of all these fish. It has fins in the form of wings that contain many long bones, but the bones are easily removed. The fish can be cooked in many ways and served with any of a number of sauces, from melted butter to hollandaise. It can also be fried or served au gratin. By far the best-known preparation for skate is with a black butter sauce that includes capers and a touch of vinegar to give it piquancy.

> 4 pieces of skinless, boneless skate, each about ½ inch thick at the thickest part
> ¼ cup white vinegar
>   Salt to taste if desired
> 1 bay leaf
> 8 peppercorns
> 2 whole cloves
> 4 sprigs fresh thyme or ½ teaspoon dry
> 6 tablespoons butter
> ½ cup drained capers
> 2 tablespoons red-wine vinegar
> ¼ cup finely chopped parsley

1. Arrange the fish pieces in one layer, slightly overlapping, in a skillet or casserole. Add water to cover, the white vinegar, salt, bay leaf, peppercorns, cloves, and thyme.

2. Bring to a boil and simmer over low heat about 2 minutes or less. Turn off the heat and let stand until ready to serve. Do not let stand for more than a very few minutes. Transfer the fish pieces to a layer of paper towels and then to a heated serving dish.

3. Heat a heavy skillet, preferably of cast iron, almost to smoking. Add the butter; when it melts and starts to darken, add the capers. Cook, shaking the skillet and stirring, about 1 minute or until the butter starts to blacken. Add the red-wine vinegar and parsley, swirling it around, and pour the sauce over the fish.

   Yield: 4 servings.

Red Snapper Fillets with Pine Nut Coating

1³/₄ pounds skinless, boneless red snapper fillets (see Note)
Salt to taste if desired
Freshly ground pepper to taste
¹/₂ cup pine nuts, about 2 ounces
¹/₄ cup corn or vegetable oil
2 teaspoons plus 4 tablespoons butter
¹/₂ cup drained capers
2 tablespoons lemon juice
2 tablespoons finely chopped parsley

1. Cut the fish into 4 equal portions. Salt and pepper the pieces on both sides.

2. Chop the pine nuts finely with a knife or mini-chopper. Do not purée them. You want a nutty texture.

3. Dredge the fish on both sides in the nuts and press lightly with your fingers to make them adhere.

4. In a nonstick skillet heat 2 tablespoons oil and 1 teaspoon butter over medium-high heat. Add half the fish and cook until golden brown on one side, about 5 minutes. Baste the fish as it cooks. Turn the pieces and cook about 3 minutes. Cover and cook about 2 minutes longer. Repeat with a second batch.

5. Transfer fish to a warm platter.

6. Heat the remaining 4 tablespoons butter in a clean skillet and, when it starts to brown, add the capers and cook over high heat, shaking the skillet and stirring, about 1 minute. Add the lemon juice and pour over the fish. Sprinkle with the parsley and serve.

Yield: 4 servings.

NOTE: This recipe also works with fluke, sea bass, flounder, or other mild, white-fleshed fish fillets.

Grilled Swordfish with Ginger-Butter Sauce

I have always been partial to fresh swordfish steaks, simply broiled or grilled. I am an ardent fisherman and spend many hours each year fishing off the east coast of Long Island, but I have never hauled in a swordfish. Most swordfish taken for commercial purposes are harpooned. A swordfish steak—which has a meaty texture that is not equaled by other fish from salt or fresh water—is easy to cook and is delectable served with a simple butter and lemon sauce or, as I do often, with a more exotic sauce.

As any good cook knows, one of the finest sauces in the French kitchen is what is known as a beurre blanc, *or white butter sauce. This is made by cooking finely chopped shallots with white wine and/or vinegar until the liquid is almost completely reduced. Some butter is then whisked in. You can vary the flavor of this sauce in many ways. One day I had a small portion of gingerroot left over, so I grated it and added it to the sauce, along with a few chopped tomatoes.*

    2 swordfish steaks (about 2¼ pounds), each about 1 inch thick
      Salt and freshly ground pepper to taste
    1 tablespoon chopped fresh rosemary or 1 teaspoon dry
    2 tablespoons corn, peanut, or vegetable oil
      Basil leaves for garnish
    ¾ cup Ginger-Butter Sauce (recipe follows)

1. Preheat the broiler. Preheat the broiler rack.

2. Sprinkle the swordfish on both sides with salt, pepper, and rosemary. Brush all over with the oil.

3. Brush the broiler rack with oil. Place the swordfish on the rack and place under the broiler. The top of the fish should be about 2 to 3 inches from the heat. Let the door remain partly open. Broil about 7 minutes and carefully turn with a spatula. Broil about 3 minutes on the second side. Transfer the steaks to a warm serving platter. Garnish with basil leaves and serve, if desired, with the sauce.

   Yield: 4 or more servings.

◆ ◆ ◆

Ginger-Butter Sauce

¼ cup finely chopped shallots
2 tablespoons finely chopped fresh ginger
¼ cup dry white wine
2 tablespoons white vinegar
¼ cup heavy cream
6 tablespoons cold butter, cut into small cubes
¼ cup finely diced, peeled, and seeded tomato

1. Combine the shallots, ginger, wine, and vinegar in a saucepan and cook over medium-high heat until the liquid is almost completely reduced.

2. Add the cream and cook about 1 minute. Gradually add the butter, stirring constantly, cooking only until the sauce is thickened and the butter is totally melted.

3. Strain the sauce through a fine sieve, preferably of the sort known in French kitchens as a chinois. Return the sauce to the saucepan. Add the tomato and reheat gently.

Yield: about ¾ cup.

Sautéed Trout with Lime

A New York Times *reader once asked me how to prepare* truite au bleu, *or blue trout, a dish he had had in Switzerland. The trout was curled and served with the skin on and hollandaise sauce on the side. For this dish it's necessary to start with live trout, which is stunned with a blow to the head, quickly eviscerated, and dropped into a simmering seasoned liquid containing vinegar. When the trout hits the boiling liquid it curls.*

That letter whetted my appetite for trout, and, although I could not get any live, I was able to find some very fresh ones at my local seafood market. Trout must be cooked quickly because, if it is overcooked, it becomes unpalatably dry. I prepared it in the meunière *style—dipped in a little milk, coated in flour, and cooked briefly in oil. Once the fish was browned all over and cooked through, I poured browned butter over it. I garnished the fish, for a contrast in flavors, with small lime sections, a bit of lime juice, and quickly sautéed mushrooms.*

4 cleaned trout, about ½ pound each
2 tablespoons milk
¼ teaspoon cayenne pepper
   Salt and freshly ground pepper to taste
4 large mushrooms, about ¼ pound
2 limes
¼ cup flour
¼ cup vegetable oil
4 tablespoons butter
2 tablespoons chopped parsley

1. Place the trout in a dish and add the milk, cayenne, salt, and pepper. Turn the fish in the milk to coat well.

2. Cut the mushrooms into thin slices. There should be about 2 cups.

3. Peel the limes. Cut the flesh from the white pulpy sections to make wedges.

4. Remove the fish from the milk without patting it dry. Dip the fish in the flour to coat on all sides. Shake off the excess.

5. Heat the oil in a nonstick skillet large enough to hold the fish in one layer. Add the fish and cook over medium-high heat 2 to 3 minutes or until golden brown on one side. Turn and cook on the second side, basting often, 4 to 5 minutes more.

6. Transfer the fish to a hot serving platter.

7. Meanwhile, heat 1 tablespoon butter in a skillet and add the mushroom slices. Cook, shaking the skillet and stirring, until the mushrooms wilt. Cook until the liquid evaporates. Continue cooking until browned, about 3 minutes in all.

8. Arrange the mushroom slices neatly over the trout. Arrange the lime wedges between the mushroom slices. Sprinkle any accumulated lime juice over the trout.

9. Heat the remaining 3 tablespoons butter in a skillet until it melts. Continue cooking until the butter is lightly browned. Pour this over the trout. Sprinkle with the parsley and serve.

   Yield: 4 servings.

Sea Trout with Anchovies and Tomatoes

4 sea trout fillets with skin left on, about 1½ pounds
Salt and freshly ground pepper to taste
5 ripe plum tomatoes, about 1 pound
¼ cup olive oil
2 teaspoons minced garlic
3 sprigs fresh thyme or ½ teaspoon dry
8 flat anchovy fillets
¼ cup finely chopped fresh basil

1. Sprinkle the fish with salt and pepper. Lightly score the skin of each fillet at ½-inch intervals.

2. Bring to a boil enough water to cover the tomatoes. Add the tomatoes, remove from the heat, and let stand about 10 seconds. Drain and peel the tomatoes, then cut them into ½-inch cubes. There should be about 3 cups.

3. Heat 1 tablespoon oil in a saucepan over medium-high heat and add the garlic, thyme, tomatoes, salt, and pepper. Cook about 10 minutes.

4. Meanwhile, heat the remaining 3 tablespoons oil in a skillet and add the fillets, skin side down. Cook over high heat about 3 minutes on one side. Turn the fillets and cook about 2 minutes longer. Arrange the fillets, skin side up, on a warm serving platter. Garnish each fillet with 2 anchovy fillets, crossing one over the other. Spoon 1½ teaspoons cooking oil over each fillet.

5. Spoon equal portions of the tomatoes over each fillet. Sprinkle with the chopped basil and serve.

   Yield: 4 servings.

Tuna Niçoise

    4 tuna steaks (about 1½ pounds) each 1 inch thick
   ½ cup plus 2 tablespoons olive oil
    6 sprigs fresh thyme or ½ teaspoon dry
    2 sprigs fresh rosemary or ½ teaspoon dry
    1 clove garlic, sliced thinly
       Salt and freshly ground pepper to taste
    2 tablespoons finely chopped green onions or scallions
    1 tablespoon finely chopped stuffed olives
    1 tablespoon finely chopped capers
    2 tablespoons balsamic vinegar
    1 teaspoon finely chopped anchovy fillets or anchovy paste
    2 tablespoons finely chopped parsley

1. Place the tuna in a mixing bowl and add 2 tablespoons oil, the thyme, rosemary, garlic, salt, and pepper. Turn the steaks to coat well. Cover with plastic wrap and let stand in a cool place (not the refrigerator) for about 15 minutes.

2. Heat a nonstick skillet large enough to hold the steaks in one layer. Add the steaks and cook about 3 minutes. Turn and cook 3 minutes on the other side.

3. As the tuna cooks, prepare the sauce. Put onions, olives, and capers in a mixing bowl and stir in the vinegar and pepper to taste. Beat in the anchovy and remaining ½ cup oil and stir in the parsley.

4. When the steaks have cooked, transfer them to a warm serving dish. Spoon half the sauce over them, smoothing it. Serve the remaining sauce on the side.

   Yield: 4 servings.

◆ ◆ ◆

Broiled Tuna Provençal

4 tuna steaks (about 2 pounds), each about 1 inch thick
Salt to taste if desired
Freshly ground pepper to taste
1 tablespoon freshly grated ginger
1 teaspoon paprika
½ teaspoon ground cumin
1 tablespoon lemon juice
2 tablespoons olive oil
Provençal Sauce (recipe follows)

1. Preheat the broiler or a charcoal grill.

2. Place tuna steaks on a plate and sprinkle each side with salt and pepper. Rub the ginger, paprika, and cumin on both sides of each steak and sprinkle evenly with the lemon juice and oil. Cover tightly with foil and let stand until ready to broil.

3. If broiling, arrange the steaks on a rack and place under the broiler about 6 inches from the heat. Broil 5 minutes with the door partly open. Turn the steaks. Continue broiling, leaving the door open, about 5 minutes.

4. If grilling, put the steaks on a hot grill and cover the grill. Cook 5 minutes. Turn the fish, cover the grill, and continue cooking about 5 minutes. Serve with the sauce on the side.

Yield: 4 servings.

Provençal Sauce

2 ripe tomatoes, about ¾ pound
2 tablespoons red-wine vinegar
¼ cup olive oil
¼ cup finely chopped shallots
1 teaspoon finely minced garlic
1 tablespoon chopped fresh marjoram or 1 teaspoon dry
¼ cup finely chopped fresh basil or parsley
½ teaspoon grated lemon rind
Salt and freshly ground pepper to taste

1. Put the tomatoes in boiling water for about 10 seconds. Drain and pull away the skin; cut away and discard the core. Cut the tomatoes crosswise in half. Remove and discard the seeds. Cut into ¼-inch cubes. There should be about ¾ cup.

2. Put the vinegar in a mixing bowl and add the oil, shallots, garlic, marjoram, basil, and tomato. Add the lemon rind, salt, and pepper. Blend well with a whisk. Cook, stirring, for 3 minutes.

   Yield: about 1¼ cup.

Grilled Tuna with Mediterranean Salad

  2 tuna steaks (about 1¼ pounds), each 1 inch thick
  2 tablespoons olive oil
    Salt and freshly ground pepper to taste
  4 sprigs fresh thyme
  ¼ teaspoon red pepper flakes
    Mediterranean Salad with Tomato Dressing (recipe follows)

1. Preheat charcoal grill or the broiler.

2. Put the tuna on a flat surface and cut away and discard the dark center streak or bones. Spoon the oil over the fish and sprinkle with the salt, pepper, thyme, and pepper flakes.

3. If a grill is used, rub the rack lightly with olive oil. Place the fish on the grill. If the broiler is used, place the fish on a rack about 4 inches from the heat. Cook 3 minutes and turn; cook for another 3 minutes for rare. If you wish the fish to be well done, cook 5 minutes on each side.

4. Remove the fish and cut it into thin diagonal slices.

5. Arrange ¼ of the salad greens on each of 4 large plates. Arrange an equal number of fish slices on each plate, placing them in the center of the greens.

6. Spoon equal amounts of the dressing over the salad greens and around the fish. Serve any remaining dressing on the side. Serve while the fish is still warm.

Yield: 4 servings.

Mediterranean Salad with Tomato Dressing

  1 red sweet pepper, about ½ pound
½ red onion, about ¼ pound
  2 ripe plum tomatoes, about ¼ pound
½ jalapeño pepper, cored, seeded, and coarsely chopped
  8 pitted green olives
  1 large clove garlic, peeled and thinly sliced
  2 tablespoons Dijon-style mustard, preferably with seeds
½ cup plus 2 tablespoons olive oil
  7 tablespoons red-wine vinegar
  1 tablespoon coarsely chopped fresh coriander leaves
    Salt to taste if desired
    Freshly ground pepper to taste
½ pound bibb lettuce
¼ pound red-leaf lettuce
¼ pound arugula, ends trimmed

1. Put the red pepper on a grill over a flame or under the broiler. Cook, turning often, so that it browns evenly. Cook until the skin is charred. Run the pepper under cold water and remove the charred peel. Cut away the core and discard. Cut the pepper into quarters and remove the seeds and white veins. Cut the pepper into ½-inch cubes. There should be about ¾ cup.

2. Peel and cut the onion into coarse chunks. There should be about ¾ cup.

3. Cut away and discard the core of each tomato. Cut the tomatoes into ½-inch cubes. There should be about ¾ cup.

4. Put the red pepper, onion, tomatoes, jalapeño pepper, olives, garlic, mustard, ½ cup olive oil, 6 tablespoons vinegar, and coriander in a food proces-

sor or blender. Add salt and pepper. Blend thoroughly. There should be about 2 cups dressing.

5. Rinse the lettuces well and pat dry. There should be about 6 cups bibb lettuce, 3 cups red-leaf lettuce, and 2 cups arugula.

6. Put the salad greens in a large bowl and add the remaining 2 tablespoons olive oil and 1 tablespoon vinegar and toss well.

   Yield: 4 servings.

Grilled Tuna with Fresh Thyme

    4 tuna steaks (about 1¾ pounds), each about 1 inch thick
      Salt to taste if desired
      Freshly ground pepper to taste
    2 tablespoons olive oil
    4 sprigs fresh thyme or ½ teaspoon dry
    2 teaspoons minced garlic
    2 teaspoons lemon juice
    1 teaspoon grated lemon rind
   ¼ teaspoon red pepper flakes
    2 tablespoons melted butter

1. Preheat a charcoal grill or the broiler.

2. Sprinkle the tuna with salt and pepper on both sides. Place the oil in a flat dish and add the thyme, garlic, lemon juice, lemon rind, and pepper flakes. Place the tuna in the marinade and coat well on both sides. Cover with plastic wrap and let stand in a cool place (not the refrigerator) for 15 minutes.

3. Remove tuna from the marinade. Add the butter to the marinade and set aside.

4. If the tuna is to be cooked on a grill, place it directly on the grill, fatty side down, and cook, turning often, 5 to 6 minutes. If it is to be cooked under a

broiler, arrange the tuna on a rack, fatty side up. Broil about 2 inches from the heat, leaving the door partly open. Cook 3 minutes and turn; continue cooking 2 minutes for rare tuna. If you want it medium-rare, cook another minute on each side. Transfer the tuna to the marinade. Turn the tuna to coat it on both sides. Cut it into thin slices and serve.

Yield: 4 servings.

Cornmeal-Coated Shrimp, Scallops, and Clams

    ³/₄ pound shrimp, about 30
    ¹/₂ pound bay or sea scallops
    ³/₄ pound shucked soft-shell clams
    1 egg
    ¹/₄ cup flour
    ¹/₂ teaspoon chopped fresh oregano or ¹/₄ teaspoon dry
    1 teaspoon chopped fresh thyme or ¹/₂ teaspoon dry
    ¹/₂ cup milk
        Salt to taste if desired
        Freshly ground pepper to taste
  2¹/₂ cups cornmeal, preferably stone-ground
    3 cups corn or vegetable oil
  1¹/₃ cups Spicy Mayonnaise (recipe follows)

1. Peel the shrimp. If bay scallops are used, leave them whole. If sea scallops are used, cut them into quarters. If the clams are sandy, rinse and drain them.

2. Combine the egg, flour, oregano, and thyme and beat in the milk, using a wire whisk. Add the salt and pepper. Put the cornmeal in a separate shallow bowl.

3. Heat the oil in a skillet or wok to 365 degrees.

4. Dip the shrimp in the batter and coat well. Then dredge them in the corn-meal, coating thoroughly and shaking off the excess. Set aside.

5. Add the clams to the batter and coat well. Drain in a sieve, allowing the bat-ter to fall back into a bowl. Empty the clams into the cornmeal and coat well. Shake off the excess. Set aside separately.

6. Add the scallops to the batter and coat well. As with the clams, drain the scallops in a sieve and empty them into the cornmeal. Coat well. Shake off the excess. Set aside.

7. Add the shrimp to the hot oil and cook until golden brown and crisp, about $2^1/_2$ to 3 minutes. Drain on paper towels. Repeat with the clams and then with the scallops. Serve with the mayonnaise on the side.

Yield: 6 servings.

Mayonnaise with Scallions

> 1 egg
> 1 tablespoon Dijon-style mustard, preferably with seeds
> 1 tablespoon white vinegar
> 1 tablespoon lemon juice
> $1/_2$ cup vegetable oil
> Salt to taste if desired
> Freshly ground pepper to taste
> $1/_4$ cup finely chopped scallions
> 1 tablespoon sweet relish

1. Put the egg in a mixing bowl and add the mustard, vinegar, and lemon juice. Start beating while gradually adding the oil. Add the salt and pepper. Beat in the scallions and relish and serve.

Yield: about $1^1/_3$ cups.

❖ ❖ ❖

Georges Perrier's Crab Cakes with Shrimp

Crab meat is available in three grades: lump, flake, and claw. Lump is the choicest, flake comes in smaller pieces, and claw meat has a somewhat brownish cast. Lump crab meat is so expensive because of the labor involved in extracting the meat from the shell.

The traditional recipe for crab cakes calls for crab meat seasoned with mayonnaise, dry or prepared mustard, Worcestershire sauce, Tabasco sauce, and fresh or dried herbs.

I remember watching a colleague and friend, Georges Perrier, owner-chef of Le Bec-Fin restaurant in Philadelphia, demonstrate a new recipe for crab cakes. Using a food processor, he prepared a mousse-like combination of shrimp, egg, and cream. Then he gently blended in the lump crab meat. The mixture was shaped into patties, cooked in oil until golden brown on both sides, and served with a parsley butter sauce. This made a delectable luncheon dish and might serve as a first course to a more complex meal. The crab mixture could be made at least two or three hours in advance and refrigerated until ready to cook. It might even be shaped into patties and wrapped in plastic wrap before chilling.

- 1 pound lump crab meat
- ³/₄ pound unshelled shrimp
- 1 whole egg
- ³/₄ cup heavy cream
  Salt and freshly ground pepper to taste
- ¹/₂ cup finely chopped green onions or scallions
- 1 tablespoon Dijon-style mustard
- 1 teaspoon Worcestershire sauce
- ¹/₄ teaspoon Tabasco sauce
- ¹/₂ cup vegetable oil
  Parsley Butter Sauce (recipe follows)

1. Pick over the crab meat to remove any cartilage or shell. Leave the lumps as large as possible.

2. Shell and devein the shrimp. Put the shrimp in a food processor or blender and add the egg, cream, salt, and pepper. Blend as finely as possible. Pour and scrape the mixture into a mixing bowl.

3. Add the crab meat, green onions, mustard, Worcestershire sauce, and Tabasco sauce. Blend gently but thoroughly. Shape the mixture into 10 cakes.

4. Heat 2 teaspoons oil in a nonstick skillet and add the cakes, several at a time. Cook over medium heat about 3 minutes on each side or until golden brown. Transfer the cakes to a warm platter as they are cooked. Continue adding oil as necessary. Serve with the sauce spooned over.

Yield: 5 servings.

Parsley Butter Sauce

   3 tablespoons finely chopped shallots
   2 tablespoons sherry vinegar
  1/4 cup dry white wine
  1/2 cup fish broth or bottled clam juice
  1/2 cup heavy cream
   3 tablespoons butter
    Salt to taste if desired
    Freshly ground pepper to taste
   1 tablespoon coarse or Meaux mustard
  1/4 cup finely chopped parsley

1. Combine the shallots, vinegar, and wine in a saucepan and bring to a boil. Cook until reduced by half. Add the broth and cream and bring to a boil. Cook at a rolling boil about 45 seconds.

2. Swirl in the butter. Add the salt and pepper and stir in the mustard and parsley.

Yield: about 3/4 cup.

◆ ◆ ◆

Crab Meat and Spinach au Gratin

One of my favorite dishes is crab with spinach in Mornay sauce, a white sauce to which cheese has been added. The dish is usually sprinkled with freshly grated Parmesan before baking.

 1 pound crab meat, preferably lump
1¼ pounds fresh spinach
 4 tablespoons butter
 3 tablespoons flour
  Salt to taste if desired
  Freshly ground pepper to taste
 ⅛ teaspoon cayenne pepper
1¾ cups milk
 ⅓ cup heavy cream
 ⅛ teaspoon freshly grated nutmeg
 1 egg yolk
 2 tablespoons finely diced cheese, preferably Gruyère or Swiss
 2 tablespoons finely chopped shallots
 2 tablespoons freshly grated Parmesan cheese

1. Preheat the oven to 350 degrees.

2. Pick over the crab meat carefully to remove and discard pieces of shell or cartilage. Do not break up the pieces of crab; leave them as whole as possible.

3. Pick over the spinach to remove tough stems or blemished leaves. Rinse well and drain.

4. Heat 3 tablespoons butter in a saucepan and add the flour, stirring rapidly with a whisk. Add the salt, pepper, and cayenne. When blended, stir in milk, cream, and nutmeg. Simmer, stirring often from the bottom, about 10 minutes. Beat in the egg yolk with a wire whisk. Add the diced cheese and stir until melted. Remove from the heat.

5. Put the spinach in a deep skillet or casserole without water. Cook, stirring often, unti the leaves wilt. Drain. Press or squeeze to extract as much liquid as possible from the leaves. Chop the spinach until it is medium-fine.

6. Heat the remaining 1 tablespoon butter in a skillet and add 1 tablespoon

shallots. Cook briefly, stirring, and add the spinach. Add salt and pepper. Spoon the mixture into a baking dish (an oval dish measuring 14 by 8 by 2 inches is ideal).

7. Spoon the crab into a smaller ovenproof dish and sprinkle it with the remaining 1 tablespoon shallot. Place in the oven and bake 5 minutes. Scatter the crab meat over the spinach and smooth it to make an even layer. Spoon the cheese sauce over all and smooth it. Sprinkle the Parmesan cheese evenly on top.

8. Place dish in the oven and bake 10 minutes. Heat the broiler. Broil, leaving the door partly ajar, about 2 minutes or until nicely glazed on top.

Yield: 4 servings.

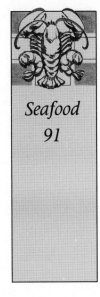
Baked Lobster with Tarragon-Cream Sauce

Considering the price of fresh lobster, extra care should be taken not to overcook it. As a rule of thumb, I cook a 1-pound lobster 7 minutes, a 1½-pound lobster 10 minutes, and a 5-pound lobster 25 minutes. I remove the kettle from the heat and let it stand about 5 minutes before draining.

I have also had great success with a new technique. I parboil a 1½-pound lobster for 2 minutes, then drain it. I put it in a baking pan and then in a 500-degree oven for 12 minutes. It emerges tender and moist.

To serve, I split the lobster in half and serve it with a butter sauce containing the lobster coral. The sauce is cooked briefly with finely chopped shallot and a little heavy cream. This is strained and thickened slightly with butter and flavored with finely chopped tarragon.

4 live lobsters, 1½ pounds each

8 cups water

2 tablespoons chopped shallots

½ cup heavy cream

   Salt to taste if desired

   Freshly ground pepper to taste

   Dash Tabasco sauce

2 tablespoons lemon juice

2 tablespoons butter

1 tablespoon chopped fresh tarragon or 1 teaspoon dry

1. Preheat the oven to 500 degrees.

2. Remove and discard the rubber or wood claw holders from the lobsters.

3. Bring the water to a vigorous boil in a large kettle and drop the lobsters in to kill them quickly. When the water returns to a boil, cook the lobsters for exactly 2 minutes and drain. Arrange the lobsters, shell side up, in one layer in a baking pan. Place in the oven and bake exactly 12 minutes.

4. Scoop out the soft mass (coral, liver, and so on) from the inside of each lobster. Spoon and scrape this into a saucepan. Save any juices and add these to the saucepan. Cut up the lobster.

5. Arrange the lobster halves, shell side down, in one layer in a serving dish. Pull and discard the upper half of each claw shell. Add the remaining claws to the dish.

6. Add the shallots to the saucepan and boil, stirring, for 1 minute.

7. Add the cream, salt, pepper, and Tabasco and bring to a boil. Add the lemon juice. Cook about 2 minutes.

8. Line a saucepan with a sieve and pour the sauce through the sieve. Rub with a rubber spatula to extract as much liquid as possible. There should be about 1 cup. Discard the solids.

9. Put the sauce on the stove and bring to a simmer. Swirl in the butter and tarragon.

10. Spoon the sauce over the cut portions of the lobsters and serve.

Yield: 4 servings.

Lobster Américaine

 4 live lobsters, about 1¼ pounds each
 3 tablespoons vegetable oil
   Salt to taste
 4 tablespoons butter
 1 teaspoon minced garlic
 ½ cup minced shallots
 2 teaspoons freshly ground pepper
 ½ cup diced carrots
 ¼ cup plus 2 tablespoons brandy
 1 cup white wine
 4 cups imported canned tomatoes
 2 tablespoons tomato paste
 1 cup water
 ¼ cup chopped fresh tarragon
 1 bay leaf
 ½ teaspoon dry thyme
 ½ teaspoon cayenne pepper
 1 tablespoon flour
 1 tablespoon chopped fresh chervil

1. Prepare the lobster for cooking (see page 94).

2. Heat the oil in a Dutch oven over high heat. Place all the lobster pieces and salt in the pot and toss them gently for about 2 minutes. Pour off the oil and return the pot to the heat.

3. Add 1 tablespoon butter, the garlic, shallots, pepper, carrots, ¼ cup brandy, wine, tomatoes, tomato paste, water, 2 tablespoons tarragon, bay leaf, thyme, and cayenne pepper. Cover and cook over high heat for 10 minutes.

4. Remove the lobster pieces and cool slightly. When they are cool enough to handle, remove as much meat as possible and keep it warm. Save all the shells and juices.

5. Pour the juices from the pot through a fine strainer. Place all the shells and other juices in the strainer and press to extract as much juice as possible.

6. Place all the juice in a saucepan and reduce over high heat to about 3 cups.

Cuisine
Rapide
94

CUTTING UP LOBSTER

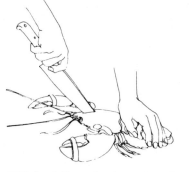

1. Kill the lobster by inserting the tip of a large chef's knife between the eyes as illustrated.

2. Reverse the lobster and run the knife through the body toward the tail.

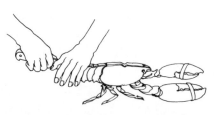

3. Hold one hand on top of the tail as you run the knife through it to completely cut the lobster in half.

4. Pull away and discard the tough sac at the head end of the lobster.

5. Remove the intestine that runs along one or both sides of the body. Remove the dark green coral and set it aside in a small bowl. Cut each lobster half into 3 pieces.

6. Remove the claws and rubber bands.

While the juice is reducing, add 2 tablespoons butter and the flour to the reserved lobster coral. Stir well until all are bound together.

7. When the juices are reduced add the coral mixture to the pot along with the remaining 2 tablespoons tarragon and the chervil. Add the remaining tablespoon butter and 2 tablespoons brandy. Put the lobster meat back in the sauce and heat just to warm. Serve with rice or noodles.

Yield: 4 servings.

Cold Lobster with Hot-Mustard Sauce

This recipe can be made quickly on the stove or grill. When steaming lobster, make sure the water under the steamer rack has reached a fast boil and that the lid is secure. (If you're not using a rack, place the lobsters directly in a shallow pool of boiling water.) Four lobsters, each about a pound and a half, should cook in ten to twelve minutes. Overcooking causes the meat to become rubbery.

I often use sea water when steaming lobsters. If you don't have access to clean ocean water, use tap water and salt it well to bring out the flavor.

The quick blender sauce here can be prepared a day or more in advance. Add the fresh basil just before serving. Some of the sauce can be saved to use as an all-around condiment sauce for fish and grilled poultry.

    Salt to taste
4 live lobsters, about 1½ pounds each
1 egg yolk
2 tablespoons Dijon-style mustard
2 tablespoons red-wine vinegar
    Freshly ground pepper to taste
¼ teaspoon jalapeño pepper, chopped, cored, and seeded
1 clove garlic, peeled
1 large red sweet pepper, cored, seeded, and cut into large pieces
½ cup olive or vegetable oil
12 fresh basil leaves

1. Pour about 2 inches of water in the bottom of a large steamer. Add salt. Bring to a boil.

2. Place the lobsters on the steamer rack and cover the pot. Cook over high heat for 10 to 12 minutes. Remove the lobsters from the steamer and cool.

3. Split the lobsters in half lengthwise and crack the claws. Remove and discard the small sac near the eyes as well as the intestine that runs through the middle of the tail.

4. Combine all the remaining ingredients with salt to taste in a blender or food processor and blend to a fine texture. Serve the sauce with the lobsters.

   Yield: 4 servings.

Sea Scallops with Watercress Sauce

1¼ pounds sea scallops
½ pound medium shrimp
1 bunch watercress, about ½ pound
½ pound mushrooms
1 tablespoon butter
2 tablespoons finely chopped shallots
½ cup dry white wine
   Salt to taste if desired
   Freshly ground pepper to taste
¾ cup heavy cream
¼ teaspoon cayenne pepper
1 tablespoon Ricard (anise-flavored liqueur)
   Turmeric Rice (see page 282)

1. If the scallops are exceptionally large, cut each in half crosswise. There should be about 3 cups.

2. Shell and devein the shrimp.

3. Discard all the large, tough watercress stems. There should be about 6 loosely packed cups.

4. Rinse the mushrooms, pat them dry, and cut into quarters. There should be about 2 cups.

5. Bring enough water to a boil to cover the watercress. Add the watercress and cook, stirring, 2 minutes or until wilted. Drain well and rinse under cold water. Squeeze to extract most of the excess liquid and chop. There should be $1/2$ cup.

6. Heat the butter in a skillet over high heat and add the mushrooms. Cook, stirring, 1 minute. Add the shallots and stir. Cook 1 minute. Add the wine and cook about 5 minutes or until it is almost reduced.

7. Add the scallops and stir. Sprinkle with salt and pepper and stir. Cook 1 minute, stirring occasionally, and add the shrimp. Stir briefly and cook $1^1/2$ minutes.

8. Line a mixing bowl with a sieve and drain the seafood mixture. Reserve the cooking liquid. There should be $1/2$ cup. Remove the mushrooms and set aside.

9. Put the cooking liquid in a skillet and cook over high heat 1 minute. Add $1/2$ cup cream and cook 2 minutes. Stir in the watercress, salt, and pepper. Cook 1 minute.

10. Pour the mixture into a blender or a food processor. Blend thoroughly. Add the mushrooms and continue blending.

11. Put the scallop and shrimp mixture in a skillet and pour in the watercress and mushroom sauce. Stir in the remaining $1/4$ cup cream. Bring to a simmer and cook until piping hot. Add the cayenne and Ricard and serve with Turmeric Rice.

Yield: 4 servings.

Scallops with Endive in Saffron Sauce

This elegant scallop dish calls for half a teaspoon of saffron. If saffron is unavailable, you can simulate the color with turmeric.

1¼ pounds bay or sea scallops
2 large Belgian endive, about ½ pound
1 tablespoon butter
3 tablespoons finely chopped shallots
Juice of ½ lemon
½ cup dry white wine
1 cup heavy cream
½ teaspoon stem saffron
⅛ teaspoon red pepper flakes
Salt to taste if desired
Freshly ground pepper to taste

1. If extra-large sea scallops are used, cut them into quarters.

2. Trim off the ends of the endive. Cut the endive crosswise into 1-inch pieces. There should be about 4 loosely packed cups.

3. Heat the butter in a skillet and add the shallots. Cook briefly and add the endive and lemon juice. Cook, stirring, until wilted. Add the wine and bring to a boil. Cover tightly and simmer 10 minutes.

4. Add ¾ cup cream, the saffron, pepper flakes, salt, and pepper and cook, uncovered, over high heat, stirring often, about 5 minutes.

5. Add the scallops and cook, stirring, about 2 minutes. Add the remaining ¼ cup cream, salt, and pepper. Cook about 3 minutes or until the scallops have lost their raw look. Do not overcook.

Yield: 4 servings.

◆ ◆ ◆

Scallops Américaine

      2 tablespoons olive oil
      2 tablespoons finely chopped shallots
      1 tablespoon finely chopped onion
    ½ teaspoon finely minced garlic
    ½ cup dry white wine
    ¼ cup coarsely chopped fresh tarragon or 1 teaspoon dry
    ½ cup fish stock or bottled clam juice
      2 cups crushed canned tomatoes
    ⅛ teaspoon cayenne pepper
      Salt to taste if desired
      Freshly ground pepper to taste
      2 tablespoons butter
  1½ pounds medium-size sea scallops (if using large sea scallops, slice
      them in half widthwise)
      2 tablespoons cognac

1. Heat 1 tablespoon oil in a saucepan and add the shallots, onion, and garlic. Cook, stirring, until wilted. Add the wine and 2 tablespoons tarragon and bring to a boil. Cook until the wine is reduced by half.

2. Add the stock, tomatoes, cayenne, salt, and pepper. Bring to a boil and simmer 5 minutes.

3. Line a saucepan with a sieve and strain the sauce through it. Stir to extract as much liquid as possible from the pulp and herbs. Discard the solids. There should be about 1½ cups sauce.

4. Meanwhile, heat the remaining tablespoon oil and 1 tablespoon butter and add the scallops. Cook, stirring, about 1 minute and add the cognac. Cook about 30 seconds and add the tomato sauce. Stir to blend and bring to a boil. Stir in the remaining 2 tablespoons tarragon and 1 tablespoon butter.

    Yield: 4 servings.

◆ ◆ ◆

Scallop and Zucchini Brochettes

28 sea scallops, about 1¼ pounds
   Salt and freshly ground pepper to taste
¼ cup olive oil
¼ teaspoon red pepper flakes
 1 teaspoon Dijon-style mustard, preferably with seeds
 1 teaspoon finely chopped fresh thyme
 2 teaspoons minced garlic
 1 zucchini, about ½ pound
   Vegetable oil for greasing the grill

1. Preheat charcoal grill.

2. Place the scallops in a dish and add the salt, pepper, 3 tablespoons olive oil, pepper flakes, mustard, thyme, and garlic.

3. Trim off the ends of the zucchini and cut it crosswise into 16 slices about ¼ inch thick. Add to the scallops in the dish and blend the ingredients.

4. Place 1 piece of zucchini on a skewer and add 2 scallops. Add another piece of zucchini and 2 more scallops. Add a third slice of zucchini, 3 more scallops, and a final slice of zucchini. Repeat, using 3 more skewers and the remaining scallops and zucchini.

5. Brush the grill with a light coating of oil. Place the skewers on the grill and cook about 1 minute. Turn and cook 1 minute. Cook on the 2 other sides about 1 minute each. Continue cooking about 2 minutes longer for a total cooking time of about 6 minutes. This cooking time will produce scallops that are medium-well done. Cook the scallops about 2 minutes longer if you wish them well done. Brush with the remaining tablespoon olive oil and serve hot.

   Yield: 4 servings.

Broiled Shrimp with Lemon-Garlic Butter

20 to 24 medium to large shrimp, about 1½ pounds
Salt and freshly ground pepper to taste
2 tablespoons olive oil
2 tablespoons lemon juice
2 tablespoons dry white wine
1 tablespoon chopped fresh rosemary or 2 teaspoons dry
1 tablespoon finely minced garlic
6 tablespoons cold butter
2 tablespoons finely chopped chives

1. Preheat a charcoal grill or the broiler.

2. Using a sharp knife and starting at the back of the shell, cut the shrimp partly open butterfly-fashion. Sprinkle the cut portions with salt and pepper and brush with the oil. Turn the shrimp, cut side down.

3. Combine the lemon juice, wine, rosemary, and garlic in a small saucepan. Cut the butter into 12 pieces. Bring the liquid to a boil and gradually add the butter, stirring with a wire whisk. When all the butter is added and melted, remove the sauce from the heat.

4. If the shrimp are to be broiled, place them about 4 inches from the heat. Cook about 1½ minutes and turn them, cut side up. Cook about 1½ minutes longer. If the shrimp are to be grilled, arrange them, cut side down, on the grill. Cook about 45 to 60 seconds on one side and turn them, cut side up. Cook about 45 to 60 seconds and remove from the grill.

5. Add the chives to the hot butter. Arrange the shrimp, cut side up, on serving plates and spoon the sauce over them.

Yield: 4 servings.

◆ ◆ ◆

Grilled Shrimp in Lemon-Basil Marinade

1½ teaspoons finely minced garlic
1½ teaspoons finely chopped shallots
1½ teaspoons Dijon-style mustard
⅓ cup dry white wine
⅓ cup fresh lemon juice
¼ teaspoon cayenne pepper
½ cup olive oil
⅓ cup finely chopped fresh basil
24 jumbo shrimp (about 1¼ pounds), shelled and deveined

1. Combine the garlic, shallots, mustard, wine, lemon juice, cayenne pepper, olive oil, and basil in a bowl. Stir to blend. Add the shrimp and stir to coat. Let stand until ready to cook.

2. When ready to cook, preheat charcoal grill or the broiler.

3. Remove the shrimp from the marinade and pour the marinade into a small saucepan. Arrange the shrimp, 6 to a skewer, pushing the skewer through the tail section, then the head section, so it will lie flat. Arrange them barely touching and without crowding.

4. Place the skewers on the grill or on a rack under the broiler about 6 inches from the heat. Cook about 3 minutes or until the shrimp can be lifted from the grill or rack without sticking. Turn the skewers and cook about 2 minutes longer.

5. Meanwhile, bring the marinade to a boil and simmer about 2 minutes.

6. Remove the shrimp from the skewers and arrange them on 4 plates. Spoon the sauce over the shrimp and serve.

   Yield: 4 servings.

◆ ◆ ◆

Shrimp with Mushrooms and Paprika Sauce

24 large shrimp, about 1½ pounds
½ pound mushrooms
2 tablespoons butter
3 tablespoons finely chopped shallots
  Salt and freshly ground pepper to taste
2 teaspoons paprika
¾ cup dry white wine
¾ cup heavy cream
¼ teaspoon red pepper flakes
¼ cup sour cream
2 tablespoons lemon juice

1. Peel and devein the shrimp.

2. Cut the mushrooms into thin slices. There should be about 2 cups.

3. Heat the butter in a skillet and add the shallots, mushrooms, salt, and pepper. Sprinkle with the paprika and stir. Cook, stirring, about 1 minute. Add the wine and stir. Cook, stirring, over high heat about 5 minutes or until the wine is almost completely evaporated. Add the cream and stir. Cook about 1 minute. Add the pepper flakes.

4. Add the shrimp and stir. Cook, stirring gently, about 1 minute. Stir in the sour cream and lemon juice and bring to a boil. Remove from the heat and let stand about 5 minutes. Serve hot.

   Yield: 4 servings.

◆ ◆ ◆

Szechuan-Style Shrimp with Peppercorns

1½ pounds medium shrimp
½ pound onions, peeled
1 pound red and green sweet peppers
3 plum tomatoes, about ½ pound
¼ cup olive oil
1 tablespoon finely minced garlic
1 bay leaf
½ teaspoon dry thyme
2 teaspoons seasoned salt or to taste (see Note)
¼ teaspoon red pepper flakes
¼ cup dry white wine
¼ cup white-wine vinegar
½ cup finely shredded fresh basil

1. Shell and devein the shrimp.

2. Cut the onions in half lengthwise. Place each half, cut side down, on a flat surface and slice thinly. There should be about 2½ cups.

3. Cut away and discard the cores from the peppers. Cut the peppers in half lengthwise. Remove and discard the seeds and veins. Place each pepper half on a flat surface and cut each half crosswise into thin strips. There should be about 4 cups.

4. Cut away and discard the cores of the tomatoes. Cut the tomatoes into small cubes. There should be about 2 cups.

5. Heat the oil in a heavy skillet and add the onion and garlic. Cook, stirring, until wilted. Add the pepper strips, bay leaf, thyme, seasoned salt, and pepper flakes and stir. Cook about 2 minutes, stirring, and add the tomatoes. Cook 1 minute and add the wine and vinegar. Cover and cook 5 minutes.

6. Add the shrimp and stir. Cover and cook about 2 minutes. Stir in the basil and serve.

   Yield: 4 servings.

NOTE: To make the seasoned salt, heat 1/3 cup Szechuan peppercorns in a dry skillet over medium-high heat, stirring, for about 2 minutes or until they start to smoke. Place the peppercorns in a spice grinder and add 6 tablespoons salt. Blend thoroughly. Keep in a tightly sealed container.

Cabbage Packets Stuffed with Shrimp and Salmon

THE CABBAGE PACKETS:

- 1 medium head green or Savoy cabbage, cored and trimmed of loose outer leaves
- 1/2 pound skinless salmon fillet
- 1 pound medium shrimp, shelled, deveined, and chilled
- 1/8 teaspoon Tabasco sauce
  Salt and freshly ground white pepper to taste
- 1/8 teaspoon freshly grated nutmeg
- 1 teaspoon freshly grated ginger
- 1 egg yolk
- 4 egg whites
- 1/2 cup fish stock or bottled clam juice
- 1/3 cup chopped scallions

THE SAUCE:

- 1 tablespoon unsalted butter
- 1 tablespoon olive oil
- 2 tablespoons minced shallots
- 3 tablespoons minced onion
- 2 sprigs fresh thyme or a pinch dry
- 3/4 pound plum tomatoes, cubed
- 1/2 teaspoon minced garlic
- 1 bay leaf
- 2 whole cloves
- 1 cup dry white wine
- 1 1/2 cups fresh or canned chicken stock
  Salt and freshly ground white pepper to taste

WORKING WITH CABBAGE

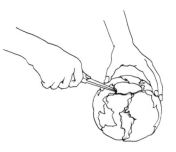

1. Core a cabbage before boiling. Dig down deeply to get all the hard core out.

2. Remove the hard stems before making the packets.

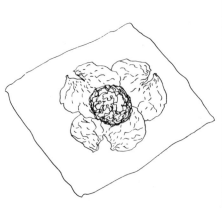

3. Arrange the cabbage leaves over cheesecloth with the mousse filling in the center. Note that the stem sides face out.

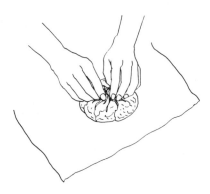

4. Fold the cabbage leaves over the filling to form packets.

5. Fold the cheesecloth and twist it to shape, firming the packets.

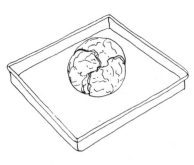

6. Finished product.

1. Bring a large pot of lightly salted water to a boil and immerse the cabbage head. After a few minutes the outer leaves will begin to soften and separate. As they do, remove them from the water with a wooden fork and drain them in a colander. Continue cooking until all the leaves are loose, about 10 minutes. Rinse the cabbage leaves under cool water and drain.

2. Cut the salmon fillet into 8 strips, each about $\frac{1}{2}$ inch wide and 2 inches long.

3. Combine the shrimp, Tabasco sauce, salt, pepper, nutmeg, ginger, and egg yolk in a food processor or blender and purée for 5 seconds. Add the egg whites and purée for about 45 seconds or until smooth. Add $\frac{1}{2}$ cup fish stock in a steady stream while puréeing and continue blending for 1 minute or until the mousse is very smooth. (You can test the consistency by dropping a teaspoonful of the mousse into simmering salted water and poaching it for 1 minute. If the texture is too watery, add more shrimp; if too firm and tough, add more fish stock.) Stir in the scallions. There should be about 2 cups of mousse.

4. To assemble the cabbage packets, place 3 medium cabbage leaves in a circular pattern on a thin cotton cloth or a double-layer of cheesecloth. The top edges of the leaves should overlap and the 3 stem sides should face away from the center. Cut out the tough white stem sections. Salt and pepper the cabbage generously. Place $\frac{1}{3}$ cup mousse in the center of each set of leaves and lay a strip of salmon over each mound of mousse.

5. Carefully fold the cabbage leaves over the filling, overlapping them to form a complete seal. Lift the edges of the cloth to encircle the packet and over the sink very slowly twist the cloth, exerting a gentle pressure on the cabbage packet. The pressure should be sufficient to squeeze liquid from the cabbage packet without breaking the leaves. Carefully open the cloth and set aside the packet, seam side down. Repeat to make a total of 8 packets.

6. To make the sauce, combine the butter, oil, shallots, and onion in a pot over high heat and cook for 1 minute, stirring well. Add the remaining ingredients and cook for 1 minute, stirring occasionally.

7. Gently place the cabbage packets in the pot, seam side down. Salt and pepper them generously, cover, and braise over medium-high heat for 10 minutes. To serve, place 2 cabbage packets on each of 4 plates and spoon some sauce around them.

    Yield: 4 servings.

Warm Shrimp Salad

1¼ pounds medium-size shrimp

16 large, firm, unblemished spinach leaves, trimmed of tough stems, rinsed well and patted dry

16 white, trimmed, unblemished endive leaves

1 small head Boston lettuce, trimmed and cut into bite-size pieces (about 3 to 4 cups)

4 thin slices red onions, broken into rings

¾ cup olive oil

Salt to taste if desired

Freshly ground pepper to taste

½ cup green pea pods, trimmed, optional

¼ teaspoon dried red hot pepper flakes

¼ cup red-wine vinegar

2 tablespoons finely chopped fresh dill

3 tablespoons finely chopped chives

1. Peel and devein the shrimp and set aside.

2. Arrange 4 spinach leaves on each of 4 individual serving dishes. Dinner plates are recommended. Arrange alternate leaves of endive between the spinach leaves.

3. Arrange equal portions of Boston lettuce and then onion rings in the center of each serving.

4. Heat the oil in a skillet and add the shrimp. Add salt and pepper. Cook, stirring, about 30 seconds. Add the pea pods and pepper flakes. Cook, stirring, about 1½ minutes.

5. Add the vinegar and cook about 30 seconds. Add the dill and toss. Spoon the shrimp and the sauce over the salad greens. Sprinkle with chopped chives and serve.

   Yield: 4 servings.

◆ ◆ ◆

Poultry & Game

Breaded Chicken Breasts with Parmesan Cheese

4 skinless, boneless chicken breast halves, about 1¼ pounds
Salt to taste if desired
Freshly ground pepper to taste
2 tablespoons flour
1 large egg, beaten
2 tablespoons water
1 cup fine fresh bread crumbs
2 tablespoons minced fresh rosemary or 2 teaspoons dry
¼ cup freshly grated Parmesan cheese
1 tablespoon vegetable oil
2 tablespoons butter
1 tablespoon minced fresh tarragon or 1 teaspoon dry
2 tablespoons lemon juice

1. If the chicken breasts are connected, separate the fillets and cut away any membranes or fat. Sprinkle with salt and pepper.

2. Put the flour in a shallow dish. Dip the breasts in the flour. Coat well and shake off the excess.

3. Combine the egg with the water and salt and pepper in another shallow dish and blend.

4. Combine the bread crumbs, rosemary, and Parmesan cheese in a third dish and blend.

5. Dip the breasts in the egg mixture, coating thoroughly. Drain off the excess. Dip the pieces in the bread crumb mixture, also coating thoroughly. Pat the pieces lightly with the flat side of a large knife to make the crumbs adhere.

6. Heat the oil in a nonstick skillet (large enough to hold the breasts in one layer) over medium-high heat. Add the breasts. Cook until golden brown on one side, 3 to 4 minutes. Turn and cook 3 to 4 minutes or until golden brown on the second side.

7. Transfer the chicken to a warm platter; discard the fat from the skillet.

8. Add the butter to the skillet and cook until bubbling. Add the tarragon and lemon juice; blend. Pour the sauce over the chicken.

Yield: 4 servings.

Chicken Breasts with Garlic and Balsamic Vinegar

Balsamic vinegar, imported from Italy and widely available in specialty food stores, adds a sharp but subtle touch to many dishes. The best brands are made from the cooked must of white Trebbiano grapes, and the color is slightly caramel. It is aged and produced like sherry and has a sweet taste

This vinegar is excellent in salads but is also highly appealing as an ingredient in sauces. I use it in the preparation of quickly cooked chicken breasts with whole cloves of peeled garlic. The vinegar is diluted with a good chicken broth. If this is not done it seems a bit too strong.

> 4 skinless, boneless chicken breast halves, about 1¼ pounds
> Salt to taste if desired
> Freshly ground pepper to taste
> ³/₄ pound small to medium mushrooms
> 2 tablespoons flour
> 2 tablespoons olive oil
> 6 cloves garlic, peeled
> ¼ cup balsamic vinegar
> ³/₄ cup fresh or canned chicken broth
> 1 bay leaf
> ½ teaspoon minced fresh thyme or ¼ teaspoon dry
> 1 tablespoon butter

1. If the chicken breasts are connected, separate the fillets and cut away any membranes or fat. Sprinkle with salt and pepper.

2. Rinse the mushrooms; drain and pat dry.

3. Season the flour with salt and pepper and dredge the chicken breasts in the mixture. Shake off the excess.

4. Heat the oil in a heavy skillet over medium-high heat and cook the chicken breasts until nicely browned on one side, about 3 minutes. Add the garlic cloves.

5. Turn the chicken pieces and scatter the mushrooms over them. Continue cooking, shaking the skillet and redistributing the mushrooms so that they cook evenly. Cook about 3 minutes and add the balsamic vinegar, broth, bay leaf, and thyme.

6. Cover tightly and cook over medium-low heat 10 minutes. Turn the pieces occasionally as they cook.

7. Transfer the pieces to a warm serving platter and cover with foil. Cook the sauce with the mushrooms, uncovered, over medium-high heat about 7 minutes. Swirl in the butter.

8. Discard the bay leaf. Pour the mushrooms and sauce over the chicken and serve.

   Yield: 4 servings.

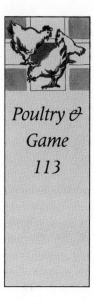
Lime-Marinated Grilled Chicken Breasts

During my childhood in France, my mother cooked many foods in our fireplace in the front room of the house. I was accustomed to the sweet, smoky flavor imparted to foods by the burning of apple and cherry twigs or vine cuttings from nearby Chablis.

I was reminded of this when I saw that vine cuttings are now available commercially. The ones I saw were labeled "Château Vignes du Cuisinier—Vintage 1984."

The cuttings are easy to use, requiring only a half hour or so of soaking in water before they are spread evenly over hot charcoals or briquettes. (Apple and cherry tree cuttings, which are more widely available, are equally appropriate for the grill and enhance the taste of barbecued foods as delightfully now as they did those years ago in France.) For this experiment, I barbecued marinated skinless, boneless chicken breasts. My marinade is very simple, consisting of assorted spices (including turmeric and rosemary), garlic, lime juice, and olive oil.

6 skinless, boneless chicken breast halves, about 1½ pounds
2 tablespoons olive oil
3 tablespoons fresh lime or lemon juice
½ teaspoon chili powder
½ teaspoon turmeric
½ teaspoon ground cumin
2 tablespoons chopped fresh rosemary or 1 tablespoon dry
1 teaspoon finely minced garlic
   Salt and freshly ground pepper to taste
2 tablespoons hot melted butter

1. Preheat a charcoal grill or broiler.

2. Cut the breasts lengthwise down the center. Cut away and discard any fat and membranes.

3. Put the oil in a mixing bowl with the lime juice, chili powder, turmeric, cumin, rosemary, garlic, salt, and pepper. Stir to blend well and add the chicken pieces. Turn them in the marinade to coat well. Cover and set aside until ready to cook. If they are to be marinated for a long period, refrigerate them.

4. Place the chicken pieces on the grill or on a rack under the broiler. Cover the grill or close the door to the broiler. Cook about 2 to 3 minutes and turn the pieces. Continue cooking until done, about 2 to 3 minutes on the grill, possibly a little longer under the broiler.

5. Remove the pieces and brush the tops with the melted butter.

   Yield: 4 to 6 servings.

◆ ◆ ◆

Poulet Noelle

(SAUTÉED CHICKEN BREASTS WITH ARTICHOKES)

8 skinless, boneless chicken breasts, about 2 pounds
Salt to taste if desired
Freshly ground pepper to taste
2 red sweet peppers, about $^3/_4$ pound
4 tablespoons butter
$^1/_2$ pound mushrooms, thinly sliced (about 3 cups)
2 tablespoons chopped shallots
$^1/_4$ cup dry white wine
$^1/_2$ cup heavy cream
$^1/_4$ pound medium egg noodles
4 Buttered Artichoke Bottoms (recipe follows)
2 tablespoons chopped parsley

1. Sprinkle the chicken breasts with salt and pepper.

2. Core the peppers. Cut them lengthwise into quarters; discard the inner veins and seeds. Put the pieces of pepper in a saucepan with water to cover and bring to a boil. Simmer about 8 minutes. Drain. Blend the pepper to a fine purée in a food processor or blender. Pour the purée into a small skillet and cook about 5 minutes to reduce it. Stir in 1 tablespoon butter.

3. Heat 2 tablespoons butter in a large skillet and add the chicken. Cook about 1$^1/_2$ minutes, loosening the pieces if they stick. Turn the pieces and scatter the mushrooms over them. Continue cooking for 5 minutes, stirring occasionally. Sprinkle with the shallots and cook about 1 minute more or until done.

4. Transfer the chicken pieces to a warm serving dish. Cover tightly with foil.

5. Sprinkle the wine over the ingredients left in the skillet. Bring to a boil. Cook, uncovered, about 3 minutes. Add the cream and continue cooking, stirring occasionally, about 3 minutes. Add to the skillet any liquid that accumulates around the chicken. Add salt and pepper to taste.

6. Put the noodles into 2 quarts boiling water and add salt if desired. Boil about

5 minutes or until tender. Drain well and return the noodles to the pot. Add the remaining 1 tablespoon butter and stir.

7. Pour the noodles onto a large serving dish and arrange the chicken pieces neatly over them. Arrange the artichoke bottoms around the chicken. Spoon equal portions of the pepper purée into the center of each artichoke bottom.

8. Spoon the mushroom sauce over the chicken. Sprinkle with the parsley.

   Yield: 4 servings.

Buttered Artichoke Bottoms

          1 tablespoon flour
       1¹/₂ cups water
          1 tablespoon lemon juice
             Salt to taste if desired
          1 tablespoon butter
          4 small artichokes (about ¹/₂ pound each),
                trimmed into bottoms (see opposite page)

1. Put the flour in a small sieve and hold the sieve over a small saucepan. Pour the water over the flour, stirring to dissolve the flour. Add the lemon juice and salt to taste.

2. Put the artichoke bottoms in the saucepan and bring to a boil, uncovered. Simmer 20 minutes or until tender but not mushy. Remove from the heat.

3. When cool enough to handle, remove the fuzzy ''choke'' in the center of each artichoke bottom using your fingers or a spoon.

4. Melt the butter in a small skillet and add the artichoke bottoms. Cook, turning the bottoms in the hot butter, about 2 minutes or until very lightly browned on all sides.

   Yield: 4 servings.

PREPARING ARTICHOKE BOTTOMS

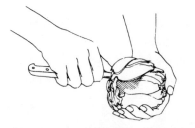

1. Place each artichoke on its side on a flat surface and cut away the stem. Cut away the bottom leaves with a sharp knife.

2. This should leave a clean, leafless base.

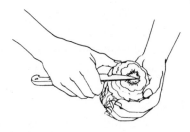

3. Trim all the green part off the artichoke bottom.

4. Sever the leaves from the base of the artichoke.

5. Trim the top of the artichoke to round off the edges.

6. Rub the artichoke bottom all over with the juice from a halved lemon.

◆ ◆ ◆

Suprêmes de Volaille aux Sesames

(SESAME-COATED CHICKEN BREASTS)

Sesame seeds make an excellent coating for fish and poultry—they lend a diverting crunchy texture and nicely nutty flavor. The chicken recipe below is a good example. It is easy to do, too, involving nothing more than coating the breast halves with the seeds and sautéeing them briefly in butter. The final touch is a light sauce made of hazelnut butter to which a dash of lemon juice has been added.

8 skinless, boneless chicken breast halves, about ¼ pound each (2
    pounds total weight)
Salt to taste if desired
Freshly ground pepper to taste
¾ cup sesame seeds
2 tablespoons vegetable oil
4 tablespoons butter
Juice of 1 lemon

1. Place each chicken breast half between sheets of plastic wrap. Pound the chicken lightly with a mallet or meat pounder. Remove the chicken breasts from the plastic wrap.

2. Sprinkle the chicken with salt and pepper. Dredge the pieces on all sides in the sesame seeds.

3. Heat the oil in a large nonstick skillet and add the breasts in one layer. Cook over medium heat for about 5 minutes on one side. Turn and cook on the second side about 5 minutes. Transfer the chicken to a heated serving dish. Pour off the fat from the skillet and wipe it clean with a paper towel.

4. Melt the butter in the skillet. Swirl the butter around until it is hazelnut brown. Stir in the lemon juice. Pour the sauce over the chicken breasts and serve hot.

    Yield: 4 servings.

◆ ◆ ◆

Chicken Burgers with Chive Sauce

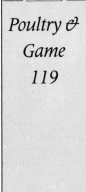

Chicken Pojarski is a traditional Russian dish made with ground meats (in this recipe I use chicken, which is less expensive) blended with cream and bread crumbs. The dish is said to have been created, perhaps with game and beef, in old Russia by a tavernkeeper named Pojarski.

When I prepare the dish I add a trace of ground cumin, a minor change that makes a major transformation in taste. I serve the dish with a butter sauce flavored with chopped chives. The original recipe does not call for a sauce.

    4 skinless, boneless chicken breast halves, about 1 pound
 1½ cups fine fresh bread crumbs
  ½ cup fresh or canned chicken broth
  ¼ cup heavy cream
    2 tablespoons finely minced onion (see page 120)
  ½ teaspoon ground cumin
  ⅛ teaspoon freshly grated nutmeg
    Salt to taste if desired
    Freshly ground pepper to taste
    2 dashes Tabasco sauce
    2 tablespoons corn, peanut, or vegetable oil
    4 tablespoons butter
    2 tablespoons finely chopped chives

1. Cut the chicken into 1-inch cubes. (If you do not use it right away, refrigerate it. The mixture binds better when the meat is cold.)

2. Put the chicken in a food processor or blender and chop to a medium-coarse texture. Scrape the chicken into a mixing bowl and add ½ cup bread

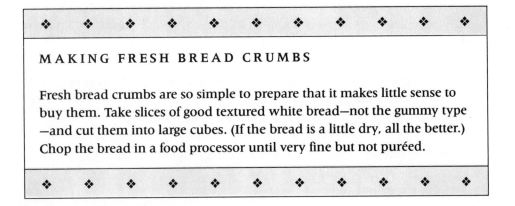

MAKING FRESH BREAD CRUMBS

Fresh bread crumbs are so simple to prepare that it makes little sense to buy them. Take slices of good textured white bread—not the gummy type —and cut them into large cubes. (If the bread is a little dry, all the better.) Chop the bread in a food processor until very fine but not puréed.

MINCING AN ONION

1. Lay a halved onion on the board, cut side down, with the stem end as shown. Holding the stem end, slice the onion as thinly as possible starting your knife tip just in front of the stem and moving away to the other end. Leave the stem intact.

2. Place the knife in a horizontal position as shown and slice the onion toward the stem as shown.

3. Mince down across the onion as shown.

crumbs, ¼ cup chicken broth, the cream, onion, cumin, nutmeg, salt, pepper, and Tabasco. Use your fingers to blend well.

3. Spoon the remaining 1 cup bread crumbs onto a flat surface. Divide the chicken mixture into 4 portions; shape each into a ball and roll the balls in the bread crumbs to coat thoroughly but lightly. Flatten each ball into a patty about ¾ inch thick.

4. Heat the oil in a nonstick skillet. Add the chicken patties and cook over medium-low heat about 5 minutes or until nicely browned on one side. Turn the patties and cook about 5 minutes more. Transfer to a warm platter.

5. Heat 2 tablespoons butter in small saucepan and add the remaining ¼ cup broth. Bring to a boil, stirring with a wire whisk, and cook until reduced by half. Gradually add the remaining 2 tablespoons butter while whisking.

6. Stir in the chives and pour the sauce over the burgers.

Yield: 4 servings.

Cabbage Leaves Stuffed with Chicken and Ginger

1 cabbage (about 2 pounds), cored and trimmed of tough outer
    leaves
³/₄ pound skinless, boneless chicken breasts, cut into ¹/₂-inch cubes
    Salt to taste if desired
    Freshly ground pepper to taste
¹/₈ teaspoon cayenne pepper
¹/₃ cup fresh or canned chicken broth
1 teaspoon grated or finely chopped fresh ginger
1 egg
3 tablespoons finely chopped scallions or green onions
    Sweet-and-Sour Sauce (recipe follows)

1. In a large pot bring to a boil enough water to cover the cabbage. Add the cabbage and cook 7 to 10 minutes. As the outer leaves soften, break them off and set them aside on paper towels to drain. (The leaves should be soft but not thoroughly cooked.)

2. Put the chicken pieces in a food processor or blender. Add the salt, pepper, cayenne, broth, ginger, and egg. Blend to a medium-coarse texture. Add the scallions and blend quickly.

3. Meanwhile, bring about 2 inches of water to a simmer in the bottom of a steamer.

4. Arrange 4 of the largest cabbage leaves, curved side up, on a flat surface. Arrange 4 slightly smaller leaves overlapping on each larger leaf. Arrange 1 more layer of smaller leaves on each stack.

5. Drain the cabbage well and remove the small leaves from the center of the cabbage. Chop them to a fine texture. There should be about 1 cup. Distribute the chopped cabbage evenly over the large cabbage leaves.

6. Spoon equal portions of the chicken mixture on top of the chopped cabbage on each leaf stack. To form cabbage packets, lift the outer edges of the leaves to enclose the filling. Open up a piece of clean kitchen toweling or cheesecloth and place on a flat surface. Place one cabbage packet in the center.

Bring up the edges of the cloth and twist it tightly to make the packet compact.

7. Remove the packet from the cheesecloth and place it, seam side down, on a steamer rack. Repeat with 3 remaining packages. Place the rack over the simmering water and cover tightly. Steam 12 minutes. Remove from the heat and let stand 5 minutes. Serve hot with the sauce spooned over each packet.

   Yield: 4 servings.

Sweet-and-Sour Sauce

> 1 tablespoon sesame oil
> 1/4 cup finely chopped onion
> 1/2 teaspoon minced garlic
> 1 tablespoon red-wine vinegar
> 1 tablespoon honey
> 1 tablespoon crushed tomatoes
> 1 tablespoon prepared horseradish
> 1/3 cup fresh or canned chicken broth
> 1 tablespoon butter

1. Heat the sesame oil in a saucepan and add the onion and garlic. Cook briefly, stirring. Add the vinegar and honey. Simmer for about 3 minutes and add the tomatoes, horseradish, and broth. Cook about 5 minutes. There should be about 3/4 cup.

2. Swirl in the butter and serve hot.

   Yield: about 3/4 cup.

◆ ◆ ◆

Breast of Chicken with Capers and Corn

   4 skinless, boneless chicken breast halves, about 1½ pounds
      Salt to taste if desired
      Freshly ground pepper to taste
   2 ears of corn
   1 tablespoon butter
   1 tablespoon finely chopped shallots
   ¼ cup dry white wine
   3 tablespoons drained capers
   ½ cup heavy cream
   1 tablespoon finely chopped chives

1. If the chicken breasts are connected, separate the fillets and remove any membranes or fat. Sprinkle with salt and pepper.

2. Cut the kernels from the ears of corn. There should be a little more than 1 cup.

3. Melt the butter in a heavy nonstick skillet large enough to hold the chicken breasts in one layer. Add the chicken breasts and cook 2 minutes. Turn the chicken and sprinkle the shallots between the pieces. Add the wine and bring to a boil. Cover and cook about 3 minutes.

4. Sprinkle with the capers and cream. Stir to distribute the ingredients. Cover and cook 5 minutes.

5. Transfer the chicken pieces to a warm platter. Add the corn to the sauce and cook 1 minute. Add the chives and stir. There should be about 1 cup sauce.

6. Spoon the sauce over the chicken and serve.

   Yield: 4 servings.

❖   ❖   ❖

Chicken Goujonettes

What the French have been calling goujonettes *for centuries, Americans have recently come to call chicken nuggets, or some variation on the term. Strictly speaking,* goujonettes *refer to fish fillets, but the technique works equally well with chicken. I make the crisp and delicious chicken version by taking some chicken breasts and cutting the meat into small strips, each about half an inch wide. I then dip them in a blend of egg and melted butter, coat them well with fresh bread crumbs, and let them stand briefly. I heat a small amount of oil in a heavy skillet and sauté the pieces until they are golden brown. Then I pour a bit more hot melted butter over all and sprinkle them with chopped chives.*

> 4 skinless, boneless chicken breasts, about 1³/₄ pounds
> 1 egg
> 2 tablespoons lukewarm water
> ¹/₄ cup melted butter
> Salt to taste if desired
> Freshly ground pepper to taste
> 1¹/₂ cups fine fresh bread crumbs
> 3 to 4 tablespoons corn, peanut, or vegetable oil
> 2 tablespoons finely chopped chives
> 4 lemon wedges

1. Using a sharp knife, cut the fillets in half crosswise, then lengthwise into thin strips about ¹/₂ inch wide. There should be about 3 cups.

2. Beat the egg in a small bowl and add the water, butter, salt, and pepper. Blend well.

3. Pour the egg mixture into a shallow dish, add the chicken pieces, and stir to coat well. Drain briefly. (The chicken strips should be coated lightly.)

4. Put the bread crumbs in a flat dish and add the chicken pieces in one layer. Stir to coat, keeping each strip separate. Roll the chicken pieces, 1 at a time, between your palms to help the crumbs adhere. As the pieces are prepared, arrange them in one layer in a flat dish.

5. Heat the oil in a nonstick skillet over medium-high heat. Add about half the breaded chicken pieces in one layer, close together but not touching. Cook 2 to 3 minutes or until golden brown on one side. Turn the pieces and continue cooking on the second side about 2 to 3 minutes or until golden

brown. Using a slotted spoon, transfer the pieces to a warm serving dish. Repeat with the remaining chicken and, if necessary, add 1 more tablespoon oil to the skillet. When the second batch is browned, return the first batch of chicken to the skillet and sprinkle with the chives. Toss gently to blend. Serve with the lemon wedges.

Yield: 4 servings.

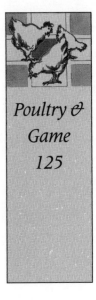

Chicken Nuggets with Herb Breading

> 4 skinless, boneless chicken breast halves, about 1¼ pounds
> 1 egg
> 2 tablespoons water
>   Salt and freshly ground pepper to taste
> 2 cups fine fresh bread crumbs
> 6 fresh sage leaves, chopped fine, or 2 teaspoons dry
> 4 sprigs fresh thyme, chopped fine, or 2 teaspoons dry
> 1 teaspoon ground cumin
> 1 cup corn or vegetable oil
>   Tomato-Horseradish Sauce (recipe follows)

1. Using a sharp knife, cut the chicken breast halves horizontally into half-inch-wide strips.

2. In a bowl combine the egg, water, salt, and pepper. Beat well to blend.

3. Place the bread crumbs on a large platter. Add the sage, thyme, cumin, and pepper to taste and blend.

4. Dip the chicken pieces in the egg mixture and coat well. Drain the excess. Toss the chicken in the bread crumbs, 1 piece at a time, coating thoroughly. As they are done place them in a dish.

5. Heat the oil in a deep fryer or cast-iron skillet to 360 degrees. Add about ⅓ of the chicken pieces. Do not crowd them in the pan. Cook, shaking and stir-

ring so they brown evenly, about 3 minutes. Remove with a slotted spoon and drain on paper towels.

6. Repeat with 2 more batches. Serve with the Tomato-Horseradish Sauce.

Yield: 4 servings.

Tomato-Horseradish Sauce with Basil

  1 tablespoon olive oil
  $\frac{1}{2}$ cup finely chopped onion
  2 teaspoons finely chopped garlic
  1 tablespoon red-wine vinegar
  2 tomatoes (about $\frac{3}{4}$ pound), skinned and cubed
  2 tablespoons tomato paste
   Salt and freshly ground pepper to taste
  10 fresh basil leaves, chopped, or, if not available, 1 dry bay leaf
  2 tablespoons horseradish, preferably freshly grated
  1 tablespoon butter

1. Heat the olive oil in a small saucepan. Add the onion and garlic. Cook until wilted and add the vinegar (if bay leaf is used, add it here). Reduce over high heat by half.

2. Add the tomatoes, tomato paste, salt, and pepper. Cook over medium heat, stirring often, for about 5 minutes. Add the fresh basil and horseradish and swirl in the butter.

Yield: about $1\frac{1}{4}$ cups.

Chicken Breasts with Blue Cheese Sauce

This dish, like so many I have created over the years, came about by accident. One day, while cooking with Craig Claiborne, I asked our kitchen assistant to hand me some cheese, thinking that we had some Gruyère. Instead, he handed me a quarter pound of blue cheese. My first reaction was negative, but on second thought I said, ''Why not?'' I was very pleased with the result.

   4 skinless, boneless chicken breast halves, about 1¼ pounds
     Salt to taste if desired
     Freshly ground pepper to taste
   3 tablespoons butter
   1 tablespoon flour
   ½ cup fresh or canned chicken broth
   ½ cup milk
   ¼ cup heavy cream
   ¼ pound blue cheese
   4 rectangles of thinly sliced cooked ham, about ¼ pound
   ¼ cup finely chopped onion
   ¼ cup dry white wine

1. Sprinkle the breast halves with salt and pepper.

2. Heat 2 tablespoons butter in a heavy skillet large enough to hold the chicken in one layer over medium-high heat. Add the chicken and brown lightly on one side. Turn and continue cooking about 5 minutes or until cooked through. Remove the pieces and keep warm.

3. Meanwhile, heat the remaining 1 tablespoon butter in a saucepan and add the flour, stirring rapidly with a wire whisk. Add the broth and milk, and continue stirring rapidly. Add the cream and cook, stirring often, about 5 minutes. Add the cheese and stir until melted.

4. Add the ham slices to the skillet in which the chicken pieces cooked and sauté briefly on both sides just to heat through. Transfer the slices to a heated serving dish and cover each slice with a piece of chicken breast.

5. Add the onion to the skillet and cook, stirring, until wilted. Add the wine and stir to dissolve the brown particles that cling to the bottom and sides of the skillet. Stir in the cheese sauce.

6. Place a sieve over a small saucepan and strain the sauce, stirring and pushing down with a plastic spatula to press through as much of it as possible. There should be about 1⅓ cups of sauce.

7. Pour the sauce over the chicken pieces and serve hot.

   Yield: 4 servings.

Breasts of Chicken Bonne Maman

4 whole skinless, boneless chicken breast halves, about 1¼ pounds
 Salt to taste if desired
 Freshly ground pepper to taste
26 small pearl onions, about ½ pound
 2 tablespoons olive oil
 1 teaspoon minced garlic
½ pound mushrooms, left whole if small, otherwise sliced or quartered
 4 sprigs fresh thyme or 1 teaspoon dry
 8 fresh basil leaves
¼ cup dry white wine
 1 tablespoon butter

1. Sprinkle the chicken breasts with salt and pepper.

2. Peel the onions and put them in a saucepan. Add cold water to cover and salt to taste. Bring to a boil and cook about 2 minutes. Drain.

3. Heat the oil in a large heavy nonstick skillet over medium heat and add the breast pieces. Cook about 30 seconds on each side. Add the onions and garlic.

4. Cook 10 minutes and turn the breast pieces. Scatter the mushrooms over all and cook about 3 minutes. Add the thyme, stir, and add the basil leaves, wine, and butter. Cover and cook about 3 minutes.

   Yield: 4 servings.

Chicken Breasts with Fresh Tomato and Garlic

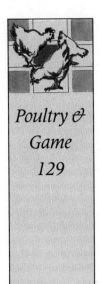

4 skinless, boneless chicken breast halves, about 1¼ pounds
 Salt to taste if desired
 Freshly ground pepper to taste
4 large tomatoes, about 1¼ pounds
2 tablespoons olive oil
4 large unpeeled cloves garlic, about 1 ounce
½ cup finely chopped onion
½ cup dry white wine
1 bay leaf
2 sprigs fresh thyme or ½ teaspoon dry

1. Sprinkle the chicken breasts with salt and pepper.

2. Drop the tomatoes into a pot of boiling water and let stand about 12 seconds. Drain and peel. Cut away and discard the cores. Cut the tomatoes into 1-inch cubes. There should be about 3 cups.

3. Heat the oil in a heavy casserole and add the chicken pieces. Scatter the garlic cloves around. Cook the chicken until golden brown on one side, about 2 minutes. Turn the chicken pieces and garlic. Scatter the onion around and cook briefly until wilted. Add the wine, cubed tomatoes, bay leaf, and thyme. Cover tightly and cook 15 minutes.

4. Remove the garlic cloves and, when cool enough to handle, peel them. Chop the cloves and mash them to a paste with the flat side of a knife. Return the mashed garlic to the casserole. Cover tightly and cook 5 minutes. Remove the bay leaf and serve.

   Yield: 4 servings.

◆ ◆ ◆

Chinese-Style Broiled Chicken Breasts

4 chicken breast halves (about 2 pounds), boned but unskinned
  and with wings attached
Salt to taste if desired
Freshly ground pepper to taste
2 tablespoons soy sauce
2 tablespoons maple syrup
1 tablespoon sesame or olive oil
1 teaspoon red-wine vinegar
1 teaspoon finely minced garlic
¼ teaspoon red pepper flakes

1. Sprinkle the chicken breasts with salt and pepper.

2. Combine the soy sauce, maple syrup, oil, vinegar, garlic, and pepper flakes in a dish large enough to hold the breasts in one layer. Blend well.

3. Add the chicken breast halves and coat them with the marinade. Arrange them, skin side up, in the dish and cover with plastic wrap. Let stand 15 minutes or until ready to cook.

4. Meanwhile, preheat the broiler or a charcoal grill.

5. Arrange the chicken breasts, skin side down, in one layer in a baking dish. Place the chicken under the broiler about 6 inches from the heat. Leave the door partly open. Cook about 5 minutes and turn the pieces. Cook, skin side up, about 2 minutes. Shift the pan to the lower rack so that the pieces are about 12 inches from the heat. Continue broiling, skin side up, with the broiler door partly open about 5 minutes longer.

6. Turn the pieces, skin side down, and broil 5 minutes longer on the bottom rack.

7. Turn the pieces, skin side up, and pour the remaining marinade over all. Place the chicken pieces about 6 inches from the heat and broil about 2 minutes. (If you barbecue, cook the chicken on the hot grill, covered. The cooking time is the same.)

   Yield: 4 servings.

Chicken Breasts with Mustard-Shallot Sauce

    4 skinless, boneless chicken breast halves, about 1¼ pounds
      Salt to taste if desired
      Freshly ground pepper to taste
    1 tablespoon butter
    3 tablespoons finely chopped shallots or green onions
    2 sprigs fresh thyme or ¼ teaspoon dry
    1 tablespoon balsamic or red-wine vinegar
    ¼ cup dry white wine
    1 teaspoon Worcestershire sauce
    ½ cup fresh or canned chicken broth
    2 teaspoons tomato paste
    ¼ cup heavy cream
    1 tablespoon Dijon-style mustard
    2 tablespoons finely chopped parsley

1. Sprinkle the chicken breasts with salt and pepper.

2. Melt the butter in a heavy nonstick skillet over medium-high heat and add the breasts, skin side down. Cook until lightly browned, about 6 minutes. Turn the pieces and cook about 6 minutes longer.

3. Remove the chicken pieces to a warm platter. Add the shallots and thyme to the skillet and cook briefly, stirring, until the shallot is wilted. Add the vinegar, wine, and Worcestershire sauce and bring to a boil. Add the chicken broth and return to a boil. Stir in the tomato paste. Cook until reduced by half and add the cream. Bring to a full rolling boil and stir in the mustard. There should be about ¾ cup.

4. Spoon the sauce over the chicken pieces and garnish, if desired, with parsley.

   Yield: 4 servings.

◆ ◆ ◆

Chicken Breasts Saltimbocca

Breast of chicken is one of the finest substitutes for veal. As much as I admire veal, it is at times prohibitively expensive. Recently I wound up with several leftover slices of freshly bought prosciutto. I decided that saltimbocca alla Romana, *a dish that I have enjoyed on many occasions, would be a nice use for the prosciutto.*

Traditionally, of course, this is made with scaloppine of veal. I decided to use skinless, boneless chicken breasts instead, and the result was excellent. It is a simple and a quick enough dish to prepare.

    4 skinless, boneless chicken breast halves, about 1¼ pounds
      Salt and freshly ground pepper to taste
½ cup flour
    2 tablespoons olive oil
    4 large thin slices prosciutto, about 2 ounces
    2 tablespoons butter
    1 tablespoon chopped fresh sage or 1 teaspoon dry
¾ cup Marsala wine
      Escarole with Garlic and Oil (see page 309)

1. Place a breast half between sheets of plastic wrap and pound it lightly and evenly with a flat mallet or meat pounder without breaking the flesh until the fillet is about ¼ inch thick. Repeat with the remaining halves.

2. Sprinkle the chicken with salt and pepper. Dredge lightly in the flour and shake off the excess.

3. Heat the oil in a heavy nonstick skillet large enough to hold the chicken pieces. Add the pieces in one layer and cook over high heat about 1 minute or until golden brown on one side. Turn and cook about 45 seconds on the other side. Remove and keep warm.

4. Sauté the prosciutto briefly, about 15 seconds; remove and set aside. Add the butter to the pan. Return the chicken to the pan. Lay a slice of prosciutto over each.

5. Sprinkle the sage over the prosciutto and pour the Marsala into the pan. Cover and cook about 1 minute.

6. Spoon equal portions of the escarole onto 4 hot serving plates. Top each with a serving of chicken and prosciutto.

Yield: 4 servings.

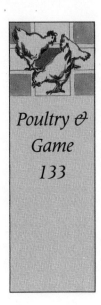
Bitoks

(RUSSIAN-STYLE CHICKEN BURGERS)

One of the most interesting quick dishes in Russian cooking is called bitok. *Properly made, it is one of the most delectable of ground meat dishes. It can consist of almost any ground or chopped meat—beef, veal, or chicken. Ground skinless, boneless chicken breasts make a fine, economical bitok. Chicken is much lighter and leaner than beef.*

The classic Russian sauce for a bitok *is a Stroganoff sauce, of which there are many versions. The one I prefer is made with sour cream and a touch of paprika and onion.*

   1½ pounds skinless, boneless chicken breasts
    1 cup fine fresh bread crumbs
   ½ cup light cream
   ¼ cup grated onion
      Pinch cayenne pepper
      Salt and freshly ground pepper to taste
   ⅛ teaspoon freshly grated nutmeg
    2 tablespoons corn, peanut, or vegetable oil
    4 tablespoons butter
    1 tablespoon lemon juice
      Dill sprigs for garnish

1. Cut away and discard any fat, tissue, and soft cartilage from the chicken breasts. Cut the chicken meat into 1-inch cubes. Put the cubes in a food processor and chop coarsely.

2. Scrape the meat into a mixing bowl. Add ½ cup bread crumbs, the cream, and the onion, and blend. Add the cayenne, salt, pepper, and nutmeg. Blend thoroughly with your hands.

3. Divide the mixture into 4 equal portions. Shape each portion into a patty. Roll each patty in the remaining ¹/₂ cup bread crumbs to coat thoroughly.

4. Heat the oil in a nonstick skillet large enough to hold the patties in one layer. Add the patties and cook until nicely browned on one side, 2 or 3 minutes. Turn and cook 10 minutes more. Remove to a warm serving platter.

5. Wipe the skillet with paper towels. Add the butter over medium-high heat and cook, stirring, until it turns light brown. Swirl in the lemon juice and pour immediately over the patties. Garnish with the dill.

Yield: 4 servings.

Quick Chicken Couscous

The term couscous actually refers to a stewlike dish traditionally made with lamb or mutton, cubed pork, ground pork (shaped into balls and flavored with cumin), and chicken. This North African staple also has an assortment of vegetables, including zucchini, turnips, green peppers, chickpeas, and carrots.

With these ingredients you prepare a stew and then steam the grain on top. The grain ordinarily requires more than an hour's preparation, but a quick-cooking imported version is widely available in supermarkets.

For cooks with limited time I have devised a basic chicken couscous. It is prepared with the usual vegetables and served with the quick-cooking grain stirred with butter. Traditionally, couscous is served with a spicy sauce called harissa, which is optional. I make my own harissa with peppers, garlic, and oil. You may also buy it in specialty foods shops.

    ³/₄ pound zucchini and/or yellow squash
    2 white turnips, about ³/₄ pound
    3 carrots, about ³/₄ pound
    1 red or green sweet pepper, about ¹/₂ pound
    1 large onion, about ³/₄ pound
    2 tablespoons corn oil or melted butter

1 chicken (3½ pounds), cut into serving pieces
9 cups water or chicken broth
½ cinnamon stick or ½ teaspoon ground
½ teaspoon ground cumin
¼ teaspoon turmeric
½ teaspoon stem saffron, optional
3 tablespoons honey, optional
   Salt to taste if desired
   Freshly ground pepper to taste
¼ cup raisins
1 cup drained canned chickpeas
2½ cups quick-cooking couscous
3 tablespoons butter
   Harissa (recipe follows), optional

1. Trim off the ends of the squash and cut them into quarters lengthwise. Cut the pieces crosswise into 1½-inch lengths. There should be 5 or 6 cups.

2. Peel the turnips and cut into quarters. Cut the quartered pieces crosswise into 1-inch pieces. There should be 2 cups.

3. Trim and scrape the carrots and cut them into 1-inch lengths. There should be 1½ cups.

4. Cut the pepper in half. Remove the core, veins, and seeds. Cut it into 1½-inch cubes.

5. Cut the onion into quarters. Cut the quarters crosswise into 1½-inch cubes.

6. Heat the oil in a kettle and add the onion. Cook, stirring, about 5 minutes. Add the chicken pieces and cook briefly until they lose their raw look. Add 5 cups of water, the cinnamon stick, cumin, turmeric, saffron, honey, salt, and pepper. Bring to a boil and cover. Cook 15 minutes.

7. Add the zucchini, turnips, carrots, pepper, raisins, and chickpeas and bring to a boil. Cover and cook 15 minutes.

8. Shortly before the stew is ready, bring the remaining 4 cups water to a boil in a saucepan. Add the couscous and bring to a boil. Simmer 2 minutes and remove from the heat. Cover and let stand 10 to 15 minutes. Stir in the butter.

9. Spoon the couscous into 4 heated soup bowls. Make a well in the center of each. Spoon the chicken, vegetables, and as much liquid as desired into each bowl. Serve with Harissa on the side.

Yield: 4 servings.

Harissa

> 12 green or red hot peppers
> 3 large cloves garlic, peeled
> ¼ cup olive oil
> ⅛ teaspoon ground cumin
> Tabasco or Louisiana hot sauce to taste, optional

1. Cut off the stems of the peppers. Cut away and discard the veins and the rest of the stems. Chop the peppers. There should be ½ cup.

2. Put the peppers, garlic, oil, and cumin in a blender. Blend at high speed to a fine liquid. Add the Tabasco or Louisiana hot sauce.

Yield: about ⅓ cup.

◆ ◆ ◆

Poulet au Vin Rouge

(CHICKEN IN RED WINE)

In my native Burgundy, wine is an integral part of cooking. The best-known wine dishes from France are boeuf Bourguignon—*beef Burgundy-style—and* coq au vin, *both of which are well-known in this country. My family always kept a wine cask in the cellar, and it was my duty as a child to descend those stairs to fill up the metal utensil kept next to the stove for cooking.*

I am often asked whether one should use a fine wine in everyday cooking. My answer is that the cost should not be the criterion for the wine you use but rather whether it is a wine that is acceptable for drinking. Generally speaking, if the wine is good to drink, it is good for cooking. The converse is true also. You should always taste the wine before cooking with it. If the wine is too acidic, or even slightly acidic rather than dry, then it should not be used.

One of the simplest and best wine dishes that I know of is chicken au vin rouge, *which is very much a part of my childhood. To prepare the dish, simply coat the chicken with flour, shaking off the excess. Then cook it, first in oil (which is poured off once the chicken is browned) and then with herbs, a small white onion, wine, and garlic. The total cooking time is twenty to thirty minutes. The acidity and alcohol of the wine (provided it was not too evident to begin with) dissipates as it cooks.*

   1 chicken (3½ pounds), cut into serving pieces
     Salt and freshly ground pepper to taste
 ¼ cup flour
 ¼ cup peanut or corn oil
 ½ pound small mushrooms, cleaned and stems removed
   8 small white onions (about ¼ pound), peeled
   1 teaspoon finely chopped garlic
1½ cups dry red wine (Burgundy-style preferred)
   2 sprigs fresh thyme or ½ teaspoon dry
   1 bay leaf
   2 tablespoons butter
   2 tablespoons finely chopped parsley

1. Sprinkle the chicken pieces with salt and pepper. Dredge lightly in the flour. Shake off the excess.

2. Heat the oil in a heavy skillet large enough to hold the chicken in one layer. Add the chicken pieces, skin side down, with the mushrooms, onions, and garlic. Cook until the chicken is nicely browned on one side, about 4 to

5 minutes. Turn the pieces and continue cooking about 4 minutes. Pour off the fat from the skillet. Add the wine, thyme, and bay leaf. Cover tightly and cook about 15 minutes.

3. Transfer the chicken, mushrooms, and onions to a serving dish. Discard the bay leaf. Reduce the sauce over high heat for about 1 minute. Remove from the heat, add the butter, and stir. Pour the sauce over the chicken and sprinkle with the parsley.

Yield: 4 servings.

Roast Chicken with Herbs

Roast chicken with French fries is a classic bistro meal. It is a relatively simple dinner to prepare well if you have a good grasp of the fundamental techniques. The single most common mistake home cooks make when roasting chicken is to use an insufficiently hot oven. The recipe below calls for a 425-degree oven, which yields a succulent golden skin. One hour should be sufficient for a three-pound chicken. To test for doneness, insert a knife into the thick part of the thigh; if the juices run clear, it is thoroughly cooked.

    1 bay leaf
    2 sprigs fresh thyme or $^1/_2$ teaspoon dry
    1 clove garlic, peeled
    1 roasting chicken (3 to $3^1/_2$ pounds) with giblets
       Salt and freshly ground pepper to taste
    1 tablespoon vegetable oil
    1 whole onion, peeled and halved
    2 tablespoons butter
$^1/_2$ cup fresh or canned chicken broth
$^1/_4$ cup water

TRUSSING POULTRY OR GAME

Proper trussing of a chicken is essential to get the best results from roasting. A well-trussed chicken holds its shape in the oven and is more attractive when served; it is also easier to carve. When a chicken is trussed securely, it cooks evenly and retains moisture well. This is especially critical for any stuffed bird.

TRUSSING POULTRY OR GAME

Kitchen twine and a trussing needle about 10½ inches long should be used for a three- to four-pound chicken. The basic technique is as illustrated.

1. Place the chicken on its back, tuck the wings under the body, and hold the legs upright. Insert the threaded needle into one side of the tail cavity and push it all the way through the thigh joint of the opposite leg. Leave some slack at the incision point for tying a knot.

2. Run the needle through the middle of the wing, passing through the skin of the neck to pierce the other wing. Pull the needle all the way through until the thread is taut.

3. Invert the chicken, pull the legs back, and run the needle through the thigh joint to the opposite side of the tail cavity.

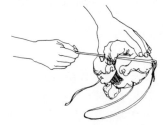

4. Press the legs down and push the needle through the skin under the breastbone. Pull it out the other side.

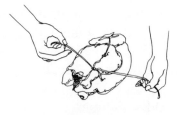

5. Flip the chicken on its side, pull the twine tightly, and tie a double knot.

6. The chicken is ready for roasting.

1. Preheat the oven to 425 degrees.

2. Place the bay leaf, thyme, and garlic inside the chicken cavity. Sprinkle inside and out with salt and pepper. Truss.

3. Place the chicken in a shallow roasting pan. Rub with the oil. Place the chicken on one side and scatter the neck, gizzard, liver, and onion halves around it.

4. Place the chicken in the oven and roast it 20 minutes, basting occasionally. Turn the chicken on the other side. Roast for 20 minutes, basting occasionally. Remove the fat from the roasting pan. Place the chicken on its back. Add the butter, stock, and water. Roast for 20 minutes longer, basting. When cooked, the chicken should be golden brown all over. When the joint between the thigh and leg is pierced, the juices should run clear. Lift the chicken with a large fork and let the juices flow into the pan. Baste the chicken with the juices.

5. Untruss the chicken. Remove and discard the bay leaf, thyme, and garlic. Carve the chicken into serving pieces. Place the roasting pan on top of the stove. Bring the pan gravy to a boil, stirring and scraping. Serve the chicken with the hot gravy and, if you like, French fries (see recipe on page 318).

Yield: 4 servings.

Chicken Fricassee with Leeks

There are several fundamental differences between a fricassee and a stew. First, a fricassee usually has a white sauce or broth base, whereas a stew is dark—hence, the meat in a fricassee is not browned as stew meats are before cooking. Second, a poultry fricassee generally uses younger, more tender birds; stews use older birds.

Fricassees go well with rice or, as provided here, a couscous mixture sweetened with raisins.

> 1 whole chicken (3½ pounds), cut into 10 serving pieces
> Salt to taste if desired
> Freshly ground pepper to taste
> 1 tablespoon butter

3 cups finely chopped leeks, well rinsed and drained
1 cup finely chopped onion
1 teaspoon turmeric
2 tablespoons flour
½ cup dry white wine
2 cups fresh or canned chicken broth
1 bay leaf
4 sprigs fresh thyme or ½ teaspoon dry
¾ pound baby carrots, trimmed and scraped
¼ cup heavy cream
Couscous with Raisins (recipe follows)

1. Sprinkle the chicken pieces with salt and pepper. Melt the butter over medium heat, in a skillet large enough to hold the pieces in one layer. Add the chicken, skin side down, and cook for about 5 minutes. The chicken should be lightly browned all over.

2. Add the leeks and onion and sprinkle with the turmeric and flour. Stir until the pieces are coated evenly. Add the wine, broth, bay leaf, and thyme. Stir and bring to a boil. Scatter the carrots over all and stir. Cover and cook about 30 minutes or until the carrots are tender.

3. Transfer the chicken and carrots to a warm platter. Carefully skim and discard the fat from the surface of the sauce. Stir in the cream. Return the chicken and carrots to the sauce. Bring to a boil. Remove the bay leaf and serve with the couscous.

Yield: 4 servings.

Couscous with Raisins

¼ cup raisins
2 tablespoons butter
¼ cup chopped onion
1½ cups boiling water
⅛ teaspoon ground cinnamon
¼ teaspoon ground cumin
1 cup quick-cooking couscous
Salt to taste if desired

CUTTING A CHICKEN INTO TEN SERVING PIECES

1. Place the chicken on a cutting surface, breast side up. Cut off the bony wing tips and discard them.

2. Pull each wing away from the body and cut through the middle joint. Reserve these wing sections.

3. Slice through the skin where the thighs join the body.

4. Pull away the thighs to expose the joints and cut around them to loosen them. Slice through the joints to remove the thighs.

5. Arrange the thighs and legs, skin side down, and look for the strip of yellow fat that covers the joints. Cut through the joints to sever the legs and thighs.

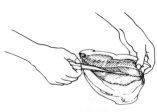

6. Make a long incision along one side of the backbone, beginning at the neck and running to the hind section. Repeat this action until this section of breast meat is removed.

CUTTING A CHICKEN INTO TEN SERVING PIECES

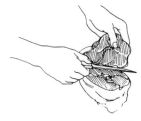

7. Cut through to sever the breast completely.

8. Reverse the chicken and cut away the other breast half, starting at the back end of the breast and running to the neck.

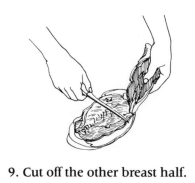

9. Cut off the other breast half.

10. Run a knife between the backbone and the breast to separate the remaining meat on top.

11. Cut crosswise through the remaining meat and center bone.

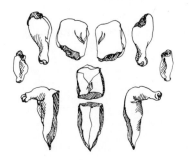

12. You have 10 pieces.

1. Put the raisins in a small bowl and cover with lukewarm water. Soak about 20 minutes. Drain.

2. Melt the butter in a saucepan over low heat and add the onion. Cook and stir until wilted but not brown. Add the water, raisins, cinnamon, and cumin. Bring to a boil, remove from the heat, and add the couscous. Add salt. Cover and let stand for 5 minutes. Uncover and fluff the couscous with a fork.

   Yield: 4 servings.

Mediterranean-Style Chicken

In the French cooking lexicon, a dish with tomatoes, garlic, olive oil, peppers, olives, and saffron is considered Mediterranean in tradition. Such dishes are gaining in popularity, and chicken is one of the easiest and most appropriate foods to cook Mediterranean style.

    1 whole chicken (3 1/2 pounds), cut into 10 serving pieces
       Salt to taste if desired
       Freshly ground pepper to taste
    2 tablespoons olive oil
    1 cup finely chopped onion
    2 teaspoons finely chopped garlic
 1/2 teaspoon loosely packed thread saffron, optional
 1/2 cup dry white wine
1 1/2 cups fresh or canned chicken broth
    2 cups coarsely chopped red sweet pepper
1 1/2 cups coarsely chopped fresh (or canned) tomatoes
    1 tablespoon tomato paste
   16 pitted green olives, about 3/4 cup
    1 teaspoon dry rosemary, crushed
 1/2 teaspoon red pepper flakes
    1 bay leaf
    2 small zucchini (about 1/2 pound), ends trimmed and cut into
       1/2-inch rounds

1. Season the chicken pieces with salt and pepper. Heat the oil in a heavy skillet and add the chicken pieces, skin side down. Cook until browned on one side, about 5 minutes, and turn. Continue cooking, turning pieces often, until browned on all sides, about 5 minutes.

2. Pour off and discard the fat from the skillet, add the onion, garlic, and saffron, and cook, stirring, about 1 minute. Add the wine and broth. Add the chopped pepper and tomatoes. Stir in the tomato paste and add the olives, rosemary, pepper flakes, and bay leaf.

3. Cover tightly and cook about 5 minutes. Add the zucchini, salt, and pepper and cook about 5 minutes longer. Uncover and cook about 5 minutes more.

   Yield: 4 servings.

Broiled Mustard-Brushed Chicken

  1 chicken (about 3½ pounds), halved for broiling
    Salt to taste if desired
    Freshly ground pepper to taste
  3 tablespoons olive oil
  2 tablespoons melted butter
  1 teaspoon Worcestershire sauce
 ¼ teaspoon Tabasco sauce
  2 teaspoons dry rosemary
  1 tablespoon mustard seeds
 ¼ teaspoon ground cumin
  1 tablespoon Dijon-style mustard
 ½ cup fresh or canned chicken broth
  1 tablespoon finely chopped parsley

1. Sprinkle the chicken with salt and pepper.

2. Place the chicken halves in a high-sided broiling pan, skin side up. Blend the oil, butter, Worcestershire sauce, Tabasco sauce, rosemary, mustard seeds, cumin, Dijon-style mustard, and a generous grinding of black pepper in a bowl.

3. Brush the chicken on all sides with the spice mixture. Let stand for 30 minutes or until ready to cook.

4. Ten minutes before you are ready to cook, preheat the broiler. Place the chicken about 6 inches from the heat and cook about 10 minutes.

5. Turn the chicken and place the pieces about 12 inches from the heat. Continue cooking about 10 minutes. Pour off the fat from the pan.

6. Add the broth to the pan, scrape and stir well, and return everything to the bottom rack of the oven for about 5 to 10 minutes or until the chicken is done, basting occasionally. Cut the chicken into 8 serving pieces, pour sauce over each piece, and sprinkle with the parsley.

    Yield: 4 servings.

Turkey Breast with Capers and Mushrooms

Lean and healthful slices of raw turkey meat are appearing with greater frequency at supermarkets. They are usually called turkey breast tenderloin steaks, which underscores their resemblance to lean veal—at less than half the price.

Turkey breast can be prepared in different ways to simulate all kinds of meats. One day at home I experimented with a dish of turkey slices with a sauce of capers and mushrooms. The meat slices—gently flattened with a flat mallet before cooking—were dredged in flour and prepared exactly as if they were veal. To tell the truth, no one at dinner guessed otherwise.

> 8 slices turkey breast tenderloin steaks, about 1½ pounds
> ½ pound mushrooms
> ¼ cup flour
>   Salt to taste if desired
>   Freshly ground pepper to taste
> 2 to 4 tablespoons olive oil
> 4 tablespoons butter
> ¼ cup drained capers
> ½ teaspoon finely minced garlic
> 2 tablespoons chicken broth
> ¼ cup finely chopped parsley

1. Place each turkey breast steak between sheets of clear plastic wrap and pound lightly and evenly with a flat mallet or meat pounder to make slices about ¼ inch thick.

2. Cut the mushrooms into thin slices. There should be about 3 cups.

3. Season the flour with salt and pepper. Dip the turkey slices in the flour to coat. Shake off excess.

4. Heat 2 tablespoons of the oil in a nonstick skillet. Add enough turkey slices to cover the bottom of the skillet without crowding. Cook until golden brown on one side, about 2 to 3 minutes, and turn. Cook until golden brown on the other side, about 2 minutes. Transfer the slices to a warm serving dish.

5. Add another tablespoon of oil to the skillet and repeat with a second batch

of slices. Continue cooking, adding more oil as necessary, until all slices are nicely browned.

6. In the same skillet, heat 1 tablespoon of butter. Add mushrooms and cook, shaking the skillet and stirring, about 5 minutes. Add capers and garlic, and toss to blend. Add chicken broth and cook about 1 minute. Swirl in the remaining butter.

7. Spoon the mushroom mixture over the turkey slices and sprinkle with parsley.

   Yield: 4 servings.

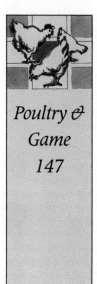
Turkey Breast with Prosciutto and Cheese

> 4 turkey breast steaks, about 1¹/₂ pounds
> Salt to taste if desired
> Freshly ground pepper to taste
> ¹/₄ pound Fontina, Gruyère, or Cheddar cheese
> 3 tablespoons butter
> 4 thin slices prosciutto or other ham, about 2 ounces
> 2 tablespoons chopped fresh rosemary or 2 teaspoons dry
> 1 tablespoon chopped shallots
> ¹/₄ pound mushrooms, thinly sliced
> ¹/₄ cup Madeira wine
> ¹/₄ cup fresh or canned chicken broth

1. Preheat the broiler.

2. Season the turkey pieces with salt and pepper.

3. Cut the cheese into thin slices to fit neatly on the turkey steaks.

4. Heat 2 tablespoons butter over medium-high heat in a heavy skillet large enough to hold the turkey steaks in one layer. Add the steaks and cook about 4 minutes or until nicely browned on one side. Turn the steaks. Lay a slice of prosciutto over each. Sprinkle evenly with the rosemary and cover tightly. Cook about 3 minutes.

5. Transfer the prosciutto-topped steaks to a serving dish. Add the remaining 1 tablespoon butter to the skillet and, when it is melted, add the shallots. Cook briefly, stirring, and add the mushrooms. Cook, stirring, about 2 minutes.

6. Add the Madeira wine and broth, stirring. Cook about 1 minute over medium-high heat.

7. Meanwhile, cover each prosciutto-topped steak with a slice of cheese. Run briefly under the broiler until the cheese melts. Pour the mushroom mixture over the cheese and serve hot.

   Yield: 4 servings.

Roast Breast of Turkey with Apple-Sausage Stuffing

    1 fresh turkey breast, with ribs (4 pounds)
    2 tablespoons peanut, corn, or vegetable oil
      Salt to taste if desired
      Freshly ground pepper to taste
    ¹/₂ teaspoon dry thyme
    1 onion (about ¹/₂ pound), peeled and halved
    1 clove garlic, peeled
    1 bay leaf
    ¹/₂ cup dry white wine
    1 cup fresh or canned chicken broth
      Apple-Sausage Stuffing (recipe follows)

1. Preheat the oven to 450 degrees.

2. Rub the turkey breast with the oil. Sprinkle with salt and pepper. Rub with the thyme inside and outside. Place the turkey breast, skin side up, in a roasting pan and place the onion, cut side down, around it. Place the garlic and bay leaf inside the breast and put the breast in the oven. Roast 30 minutes, then cover with foil.

3. Continue baking 15 minutes, basting. Remove the turkey from the roasting pan and pour off most of the fat.

4. Return the turkey breast to the pan, skin side up, and pour the wine and broth around it. Return to the oven and continue roasting 10 minutes, basting often. Remove from the oven and cover with foil. Let stand 10 to 15 minutes before carving. Carve and serve with the pan gravy and stuffing.

Yield: 6 to 8 servings.

Apple-Sausage Stuffing

    2 apples (preferably Granny Smith), about 1 pound
   ½ pound ground sausage meat
    2 cups finely chopped onions
    1 teaspoon finely minced garlic
    2 cups cubed bread, toasted
       Salt to taste if desired
       Freshly ground pepper to taste
    2 teaspoons finely chopped fresh sage
    1 cup fresh or canned chicken broth
   ½ cup finely chopped parsley
    2 tablespoons butter
    1 egg, well beaten

1. Peel the apples and remove and discard the stems and cores. Cut the apples into quarters. Cut the apple quarters crosswise into very thin slices. There should be about 3 cups.

2. Place the sausage in a skillet over medium heat and cook, breaking up any lumps, until the meat has lost its raw look, about 5 minutes.

3. Add the onions and garlic and cook, stirring, until wilted.

4. Add the apples to the skillet and stir. Add the toasted bread cubes, salt, pepper, sage, broth, and parsley. Add the butter and egg and blend well. Cover and cook over low heat about 10 minutes. Remove from the heat and keep warm until serving.

Yield: 6 to 8 servings.

Turkey Patties with Curry Sauce

1 tablespoon butter
$^1/_2$ cup finely chopped onion
1$^1/_2$ cups fine fresh bread crumbs
$^1/_2$ cup fresh or canned chicken broth
$^1/_8$ teaspoon freshly ground nutmeg
2 tablespoons finely chopped parsley
1 egg, lightly beaten
Salt to taste if desired
Freshly ground pepper to taste
1-pound package ground turkey
2 to 4 tablespoons corn, peanut, or vegetable oil
$^1/_2$ cup blanched slivered almonds
Curry Sauce (see page 292)

1. Heat the butter in a saucepan and add the onion. Cook, stirring occasionally, until wilted.

2. Put 1 cup bread crumbs in a mixing bowl and add the broth. Stir. Add the cooked onion, nutmeg, parsley, egg, salt, and pepper. Add the turkey and blend well. Divide the mixture into 8 equal portions.

3. Sprinkle the remaining $^1/_2$ cup bread crumbs on a flat surface and roll each portion in the bread crumbs. Flatten each portion into a round patty about $^3/_4$ inch thick.

4. Heat about 2 tablespoons oil in 1 or 2 skillets large enough to hold the patties without crowding. Add the patties and cook about 4 minutes on each side or until browned. Turn often as the patties cook.

5. Meanwhile put the almonds in another skillet and cook them, shaking the skillet and stirring, until they are browned. Remove from the heat and cool.

6. Spoon the Curry Sauce over the patties and sprinkle them with the almonds.

   Yield: 4 servings.

Poached Capon with Pistachio Stuffing

    1 capon (9 pounds), including the gizzard, liver, and heart
    4 cups coarsely chopped fresh bread crumbs
 1/4 cup chopped shallots
1 1/2 cups finely chopped onions
    2 teaspoons finely chopped garlic
 1/4 cup coarsely chopped Italian parsley
    2 tablespoons chopped fresh tarragon or 2 teaspoons dry
    1 egg
 1/4 cup milk
 1/2 cup pistachio nuts, shelled
      Salt and freshly ground pepper to taste
    4 cups fresh or canned chicken broth
    2 bay leaves
    3 sprigs fresh thyme or 1 teaspoon dry
    2 onions, coarsely chopped
   10 black peppercorns
    2 cloves garlic, peeled and chopped
    4 sprigs parsley, tied together
    3 leeks, cut lengthwise into 1/2-inch strips
    2 cups chopped celery
    2 cups whole baby carrots (about 24), scraped
   10 ounces Brussels sprouts, trimmed and rinsed
    1 cup orzo

1. Mince the gizzard, liver, and heart of the capon. Combine these in a mixing bowl with bread crumbs, shallots, finely chopped onions, garlic, parsley, tarragon, egg, milk, pistachios, salt, and pepper. Mix the stuffing well.

2. Rinse the inside of the capon and pat it dry. Fill the cavity with the stuffing and truss the capon securely.

3. Place the capon in a large kettle or stockpot. Add the broth and enough water to cover. Add the bay leaves, thyme, coarsely chopped onions, peppercorns, salt, garlic, and parsley sprigs. Bring to a boil, cover, and simmer for 1 hour.

4. Add the leeks, celery, carrots, and Brussels sprouts. Cook 30 minutes more,

uncovered. Add the orzo and cook 15 minutes more. The total cooking time should be 1³/₄ hours. Turn off the heat and let stand for 15 minutes. To serve, remove the capon and place it on a platter surrounded by the vegetables, orzo, and stuffing.

Yield: **8 to 10 servings.**

Faisan Sauté aux Herbes

(SAUTÉED PHEASANT WITH HERBS)

As recently as five years ago I rarely gave recipes for game in The New York Times *for the simple reason that it was not widely available to the average home cook. Today, however, I see supermarkets across the country featuring fresh pheasant, squabs, quail, and rabbit. Virtually all supermarket game is farm-raised and does not require hanging or aging.*

Pheasant is a fine introduction to game for the home cook. It is relatively mild-flavored and succulent when cooked properly. Always look for young pheasant. Like any bird or poultry, the older it is, the tougher the meat.

In this quick recipe I sauté the pheasant after it has been cut into serving pieces. I add a few seasonings and dry white wine and cook it for twenty minutes or so. A fine accompaniment to game is a root vegetable such as turnip or rutabaga purée (see page 320).

> 1 cleaned, ready-to-cook pheasant (about 2 pounds), cut into
> serving pieces
> Salt and freshly ground pepper to taste
> 4 tablespoons butter
> 2 cloves garlic, peeled
> 1 bay leaf
> 2 sprigs fresh thyme or ¹/₂ teaspoon dry
> ³/₄ cup dry white wine
> 2 tablespoons finely chopped parsley

1. Sprinkle the pheasant pieces with salt and pepper.

2. Melt 2 tablespoons butter in a skillet over medium-high heat and add the pheasant, skin side down. Sauté about 2 or 3 minutes or until the skin is golden brown. Turn the pieces and continue cooking about 3 minutes more.

3. Add the garlic, bay leaf, thyme, and wine. Cover and cook 20 minutes or until the pheasant is tender.

4. Transfer the pheasant pieces to a serving dish. Swirl the remaining 2 tablespoons butter into the sauce. Pour the sauce with the garlic and thyme sprig over the pheasant and sprinkle with the parsley.

   Yield: 4 servings.

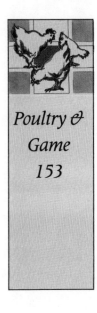
Pheasant in Beaujolais Sauce

    1 cleaned, ready-to-cook pheasant (2½ pounds), cut into 8 pieces,
       with the carcass and neck reserved
      Salt and freshly ground pepper to taste
    3 tablespoons butter
  ¼ cup minced shallots
    2 cloves garlic, finely chopped
    4 sprigs fresh thyme or ½ teaspoon dry
    1 bay leaf
    1 tablespoon flour
    3 tablespoons cognac
    1 bottle Beaujolais
    4 juniper berries
    1 whole clove
    4 parsley sprigs
    1 large leek, cut into thin strips
    1 chicken liver

1. Remove the excess fat from the pheasant pieces and sprinkle them lightly with salt and pepper.

2. Melt 1 tablespoon butter in a deep, heavy skillet over high heat and place the pheasant pieces in it, skin side down. Add the reserved carcass and neck. Brown the pieces over medium-high heat about 5 minutes on each side. Pour off the fat.

3. Return the skillet with the pheasant pieces to the heat and add the shallots, garlic, thyme, and bay leaf. Reduce the heat to medium. Sprinkle with the flour and stir well. Add 2 tablespoons cognac, tilt pan slightly, and ignite.

When the flame dies down add the Beaujolais and bring to a boil. Add the juniper berries, clove, and parsley. Boil for 1 minute. Cover and simmer over low heat for 45 minutes or until tender.

4. While the pheasant is cooking, sauté the leek in 1 tablespoon butter with salt and pepper for 3 minutes, stirring occasionally. Add the leek to the pheasant mixture 10 minutes before the pheasant is finished.

5. Purée the chicken liver in a food processor or blender and blend it well with ¼ cup of the sauce from the pheasant. Return this mixture to the sauce, increase the heat to high, and blend well.

6. Remove the bay leaf and thyme sprigs. Add the remaining 1 tablespoon cognac. Stir and adjust the seasonings. Stir in the remaining 1 tablespoon butter.

Yield: 3 to 4 servings.

ABOUT GAME

Aside from its special flavor, game is beneficial to home cooks for its healthful properties. According to the Federal Agriculture Department, venison has about two grams of fat in a four-ounce serving, compared with seven grams for rib roast. Wild duck has about five grams of fat per serving against twenty-five grams for domestic duck (assuming the fat is consumed). Pheasant and quail are roughly equivalent to chicken, about five grams with the skin and two without.

Several rules should be kept in mind when cooking game birds. Because wild birds have more muscle tissue than domesticated ones, special care must be taken not to overcook them. Also, their age is critical: A young bird will be tender and good for broiling or sautéing; an older one needs to be stewed to break down the muscle and fibers. To check the age of a pheasant, quail, duck, or partridge, grab the rear tip of the breastbone (not the backbone). If it is flexible the bird is young; if brittle it is old.

Pheasant in Onion Sauce

    1 cleaned, ready-to-cook pheasant, 2¹/₂ pounds
    Salt to taste if desired
    Freshly ground pepper to taste
    1 tablespoon vegetable oil
    2 sprigs fresh thyme or ¹/₄ teaspoon dry
    1 small bay leaf
    1 medium onion, chopped
    ¹/₄ cup dry white wine
    ³/₄ cup heavy cream
    3 tablespoons lemon juice

1. Preheat the oven to 425 degrees.

2. Sprinkle the cavity of the pheasant with salt and pepper. Rub the pheasant with the oil. Sprinkle the outside with salt and pepper. Put the thyme and bay leaf inside and truss the bird well.

3. Place the pheasant in a roasting pan. Roast in the oven for 15 minutes on one side. Turn and roast for 15 minutes more. Turn breast side up, scatter the onion around it, and cook for another 15 minutes.

4. Remove the pheasant from the pan and keep it warm. Deglaze the roasting pan with the wine and reduce the sauce over medium-high heat by half.

5. Remove the bay leaf and thyme from inside the pheasant and add them to the sauce while reducing.

6. Add the cream to the sauce and reduce over medium heat. Add the lemon juice and reduce the sauce to ³/₄ cup. Strain. Adjust the seasoning and pour over the pheasant.

    Yield: 3 to 4 servings.

❖ ❖ ❖

Broiled Quails with Herb-Sausage Stuffing

Today quails, like most game, are rarely wild. They are grown mainly on game farms and come cleaned, partly boned, and ready to cook. Quails can be delectable, faintly gamey, and moist. They are also among the quickest of birds to cook. One of the fastest techniques—and my favorite—is broiling.

I like to broil quails (or grill when weather permits) and make a stuffing of sausage, chopped shallots, parsley, and a dash of cognac. As part of the basting flavor, I throw in a little finely chopped rosemary.

The birds cook in less than a quarter of an hour, including the time spent cooking the sausage.

> 8 quails (about 1½ pounds), boned except for the thigh and leg portions
> ½ pound bulk sausage meat
> 1 tablespoon finely chopped shallots
> 1 tablespoon finely chopped parsley
> 1 tablespoon brandy or cognac
> Salt to taste if desired
> Freshly ground pepper to taste
> ¼ cup olive oil
> 1 tablespoon finely chopped fresh rosemary or 2 teaspoons dry

1. Preheat the broiler.

2. Place the quails on a flat surface.

3. Combine the sausage meat, shallots, parsley, and brandy. Blend well. Divide the mixture into 8 portions.

4. Salt and pepper the cavity of each quail, then add stuffing. With your hands, press down gently to flatten the quails so that they cook evenly.

5. Pour the oil into a baking dish large enough to hold the quails in one layer. Add the quails and sprinkle with half the rosemary. Turn the quails in the oil and sprinkle with the remaining rosemary. Arrange them, breast side down. Place them under the broiler about 6 inches from the heat. Leave the door partly open. Cook 5 minutes and turn the quails, breast side up. Return to the broiler and cook, basting occasionally, 5 minutes longer.

6. Transfer the quails to the bottom rack of the oven. Set the oven heat at 400 degrees. Continue cooking 5 minutes.

   Yield: 4 servings.

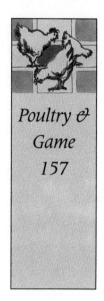

Braised Quails with Grapes

8 quails, cleaned and ready to cook
  Salt and freshly ground pepper to taste
3 tablespoons butter
2 tablespoons finely chopped shallots
2 sprigs fresh thyme or ¼ teaspoon dry
1 bay leaf
¼ cup cognac
½ cup fresh or canned chicken broth
1 teaspoon tomato paste
40 green seedless grapes

1. Sprinkle the quails with salt and pepper.

2. Heat 2 tablespoons butter in a saucepan over high heat. Brown the quails on all sides for about 5 minutes over medium-high heat. Pour off the fat.

3. Add the shallots, thyme, and bay leaf. Stir well. Add the cognac, tilt the pan slightly, and ignite. When the flames die down add the broth and tomato paste. Stir well. Add the grapes, bring to a boil, and simmer for 8 minutes, covered.

4. Remove the quails to a serving platter; keep warm. Swirl the remaining 1 tablespoon butter into the sauce. Pour the sauce over the quails.

   Yield: 8 servings.

❖ ❖ ❖

Cornish Game Hens with Cranberry Sauce

Rock Cornish game hens are extremely versatile for quick cooking. There has been talk for some time of dropping the word ''game'' from the name; certainly they do not taste at all gamey.

Originally, I have been told, they were produced in this country by breeding native American Plymouth Rock fowl with English Cornish game hens. Considering their size— each weighs about one and a quarter pounds—they have a great deal of meat. One bird is sufficient for a single serving.

I like to roast the hens (they could be referred to as pullets) and prepare a sauce for them. Fresh cranberries are particularly good.

4 Cornish game hens with giblets, each about 1¼ pounds
2 tablespoons corn, peanut, or vegetable oil
  Salt to taste if desired
  Freshly ground pepper to taste
1 onion, peeled
¼ cup dry white wine
1 tablespoon honey
1 cup fresh or canned chicken broth
1 tablespoon tomato paste
2 cups fresh cranberries
1 tablespoon butter

1. Preheat the oven to 450 degrees.

2. Put the game hens in a shallow flameproof baking dish without crowding. Rub the hens all over with the oil and sprinkle with salt and pepper. Cut the onion in half and place the halves, cut side down, around the hens. Arrange the gizzards and livers around the hens.

3. Place the baking dish on top of the stove over low heat. Turn the hens around in the dish to coat them with the oil. Arrange the hens on their sides. Place in the oven and bake 15 minutes, basting often.

4. Turn the hens on the other side and continue baking 15 minutes, basting often.

5. Turn the hens, breast side up, and continue baking about 10 minutes, basting often.

6. Transfer the hens to a heated serving platter and cover with foil to keep warm.

7. Skim the fat from the pan liquid. Put the baking dish on top of the stove and bring the pan liquid to a boil. Add the wine and stir to dissolve any brown particles that may cling to the bottom of the pan. Strain the sauce into a saucepan and bring to a boil. Cook down by half and add the honey, broth, and tomato paste. Stir. Add any liquid that has accumulated inside or around the hens. Add the cranberries and bring to a boil.

8. Cook until the cranberries pop, about 3 minutes, stirring often. Swirl in the butter. Add salt and pepper. Pour the sauce over the hens.

   Yield: 4 servings.

◆ ◆ ◆

Cornish Game Hen Fricassee

One of my fondest memories of Sunday dinner as a boy growing up in Burgundy is fricassee of chicken made with freshly killed poultry from our backyard. The fricassee always included fresh mushrooms gathered from the countryside. It was usually made with Chablis bottled in nearby vineyards.

I prepare this fricassee with Cornish game hens, which, because of their size, lend themselves to this type of cooking. The hens should be cut into pieces before cooking. This can be done by a butcher.

  4 Cornish game hens (about 1 pound each) with giblets
    Salt to taste if desired
    Freshly ground pepper to taste
 12 small white onions, about ½ pound
 ¾ pound baby carrots, about 20
  2 tablespoons butter
 ½ pound mushrooms, left whole if small or quartered or sliced if
    larger (about 2 cups)
  1 bay leaf
  2 sprigs fresh thyme or ½ teaspoon dry
  2 whole cloves
  2 tablespoons flour
 ½ cup dry white wine or champagne
  2 cups fresh or canned chicken broth
 1½ cups fresh or frozen peas
  1 cup light or heavy cream
    Rice Pilaf with Livers (recipe follows)

1. Split the hens in half, cutting along both sides of the backbone. Reserve the backbones. Cut each piece in half crosswise to separate the breast and legs. Sprinkle the pieces with salt and pepper.

2. Peel the onions. There should be about 2 cups.

3. Trim away the stem ends of the carrots and scrape them. There should be about 2 cups.

4. Heat the butter in a large casserole or skillet and add the hen pieces, including backs and necks. (Reserve the livers for the rice pilaf.) Cook briefly, turning the pieces until they start to take on color but do not let them brown.

Add the onions and mushrooms and stir to blend. Add the bay leaf, thyme, and cloves and stir. Cook about 5 minutes without browning.

5. Sprinkle with the flour and stir to coat the pieces. Add the wine and broth and stir. Bring to a boil.

6. Add the carrots and stir. Cover tightly and cook 20 minutes or until the pieces are tender.

7. Transfer the hen pieces to a warm platter. Discard the necks, backs, and bay leaf. Let the sauce with the onions, mushrooms, and carrots cook down, stirring, about 5 minutes or until reduced to about 5 cups.

8. Add the peas. (If frozen peas are used, thaw them under warm water before adding to the sauce.) Add the cream, salt, and pepper and bring to a boil. Return the hen pieces to the sauce. Stir to blend and serve hot with the pilaf.

Yield: 4 servings.

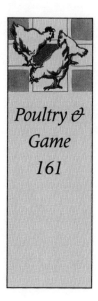

Rice Pilaf with Livers

    1 tablespoon butter
    ½ cup finely chopped onion
    4 livers from Cornish game hens, cut in half
    1 cup converted rice
    1½ cups fresh or canned chicken broth
    1 bay leaf
    2 sprigs fresh thyme or ½ teaspoon dry
    Salt to taste if desired
    Freshly ground pepper to taste
    ¼ cup finely chopped parsley

1. Heat the butter in a saucepan and add the onion. Cook, stirring, until wilted. Add the livers and stir briefly. Add the rice and stir.

2. Add the broth, bay leaf, thyme, salt, and pepper and bring to a boil. Cover and cook exactly 17 minutes. Fluff the rice with a fork and stir in the parsley.

Yield: 4 servings.

Game Hens Bonne Femme

Game hens, which resemble the baby chickens in France called poussin, *are a convenient and versatile staple. The method I use to prepare the game hens, referred to as* bonne femme, *appeared frequently on our family table in Burgundy because chickens were so widely available and inexpensive.*

The name means literally ''good woman'' or ''good wife.'' The cooking method for this homespun dish involves browning the hens on all sides and letting them simmer, tightly covered, with potatoes, mushrooms, small white onions, a little white wine, and seasonings. Once the dish is in the pot, there is no further to-do, leaving ample time to prepare a green salad and a dish of simply cooked rice—the ideal accompaniments.

4 Cornish game hens, about 1 pound each
  Salt to taste if desired
  Freshly ground pepper to taste
8 small red waxy potatoes, about ³/₄ pound
2 tablespoons vegetable oil
1 tablespoon butter
8 small white onions (about ³/₄ pound), peeled
¹/₂ pound mushrooms, thinly sliced
1 bay leaf
4 sprigs fresh thyme or 1 teaspoon dry
¹/₂ cup dry white wine
¹/₂ cup fresh or canned chicken broth
2 tablespoons finely chopped parsley

1. Sprinkle the hens inside and out with salt and pepper. Ideally you should truss them with string, but it is not essential.

2. Trim the ends off the potatoes and cut them lengthwise into quarters. Place them in a saucepan with cold water to cover and salt to taste. Simmer about 3 minutes and drain.

3. Heat the oil in a heavy casserole large enough to hold the hens comfortably in one layer. Add the hens and cook, turning often, until nicely browned all over, about 5 to 7 minutes. Remove the hens and pour off the fat from the pan.

4. Add the butter to the pan. Sauté the onions, potatoes, and mushrooms, stirring, for about 3 minutes. Return the hens to the pan. Add the bay leaf and thyme and cook, stirring, for 3 minutes.

5. Add the wine and broth. Stir well to remove any particles clinging to the bottom of the pan. Simmer for 30 minutes. Remove the bay leaf. Serve the chicken and vegetables sprinkled with the parsley.

Yield: 4 servings.

Duck Braised in Red Wine and Thyme

Duck should not be an intimidating meat to cook. It is really no more difficult than chicken. I like duck cut into serving pieces and sautéed in a skillet in a red-wine sauce.

When serving duck, count on one bird for two people. To prepare them I cut each duck into four pieces—two breast halves and two leg and thigh portions—which is simple to do with a little practice. Before cooking poultry you should turn the leg parts skin side down and cut partway through the joints. This will help insure that the heat penetrates that area.

The pieces are browned well on the skin side for about ten minutes and for about five minutes on the other side. The fat, which will be considerable, should be poured from the skillet. Other ingredients, including the red wine and seasonings, are added, and the duck is left to simmer for half an hour.

    2 ducks (4 pounds each) with the gizzards
      Salt to taste if desired
      Freshly ground pepper to taste
    2 tablespoons corn, peanut, or vegetable oil
    1/2 pound mushrooms
    1/2 cup finely chopped onion
    1 teaspoon finely minced garlic
    2 cups dry red wine
    1 tablespoon tomato paste
    1 bay leaf
    4 sprigs fresh thyme or 1/2 teaspoon dry
    3 sprigs parsley
    2 teaspoons cornstarch or arrowroot
    1/2 cup cold fresh or canned chicken broth

1. Cut off the duck legs. Cut away the breast meat. Cut off the wings and discard the tips. Separate the wings at the center joint. Discard the peripheral fat (the butcher will remove it if you wish). Turn the leg portions, skin side down, and cut partway through the center joint so the leg lies flat and cooks more evenly. (Use the carcass for another purpose such as soup.)

2. Sprinkle the pieces with salt and pepper.

3. Heat the oil in a heavy skillet large enough to hold the pieces in one layer. Add the pieces, skin side down. Cut the gizzards in half and add them. Cook over high heat 10 minutes or until browned and rendered of fat. Turn and cook over medium-high heat for 5 minutes. Transfer the pieces to a platter.

4. Pour off the fat from the pan and return the pieces to the skillet. Add the mushrooms, onion, and garlic. Cook, stirring and turning the pieces occasionally, 3 minutes. Add the wine, tomato paste, bay leaf, thyme, parsley, salt, and pepper. Cover and cook over medium-low heat 30 minutes.

5. Remove the pieces and carefully skim as much fat as possible from the surface of the sauce. Bring to a boil. Blend the cornstarch and broth and stir into the sauce. Return the duck pieces to the sauce. Bring to a boil and simmer for 5 minutes. Discard the bay leaf. Turn to coat and serve.

Yield: 4 servings.

Roast Mallard Duck with Juniper Berries and Apples

    12 juniper berries
     2 mallard ducks, 2½ pounds each
       Salt and freshly ground pepper to taste
     1 tablespoon vegetable oil
     1 onion, peeled and halved
     2 Granny Smith apples, peeled and each cut into 8 wedges

3 tablespoons butter
1 tablespoon brown sugar
1 tablespoon red-wine vinegar
1 cup fresh or canned chicken broth
2 tablespoons gin

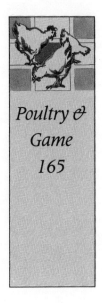
1. Preheat the oven to 475 degrees.

2. Put 2 juniper berries in the cavity of each duck.

3. Sprinkle salt and pepper in the cavities. Truss the ducks. Season well with salt and pepper and rub with the oil.

4. Place the ducks in a roasting pan. Add the onion and roast on one side for 10 minutes. Turn on the other side and cook another 10 minutes. Turn, breast side up, and cook 10 minutes for rare; cook 5 to 10 minutes more for medium.

5. While the ducks are roasting, sauté the apple slices in a nonstick pan with 1 tablespoon butter over medium heat until lightly browned, about 8 minutes.

6. Remove the ducks from the oven and keep them warm. Skim the fat from the roasting pan. Place the pan over high heat and add the sugar, vinegar, and broth. Add the remaining 8 juniper berries. Simmer for 5 minutes. Scrape the bottom of the pan to remove any clinging particles.

7. Pour the mixture into a small saucepan and reduce it over medium-high heat to about $\frac{1}{2}$ cup. Strain. Return the sauce to the saucepan.

8. Stir in the gin. Bring to a boil and cook for 1 minute. Stir in the remaining 2 tablespoons butter. Add the apples and keep the sauce warm.

9. Cut the ducks into serving pieces, remove the skin, and cover the ducks with the sauce.

   Yield: 4 to 6 servings.

◆ ◆ ◆

Venison Stew

6 pounds venison stew meat, cut into 2-inch cubes and marinated
  (recipe follows)
6 tablespoons vegetable oil
¼ cup flour
¼ cup cognac
1 cup water
24 pearl onions, peeled
½ pound salt pork, cut into ¼-inch strips
12 ounces mushrooms, halved
  Freshly ground pepper to taste
3 tablespoons red currant jelly

1. Remove the venison from the marinade and place it in a colander to drain. Strain the marinade into a bowl. Reserve the herbs and vegetables and tie them in cheesecloth.

2. Brown the venison over high heat in four batches, using 1 tablespoon oil for each batch. Transfer the meat as it is cooked with a slotted spoon to a cast-iron Dutch oven.

3. Preheat the oven to 350 degrees.

4. When all the venison is in the Dutch oven, sprinkle the flour over the meat and stir well over high heat. Add the cognac, 7 cups marinade, and the water. Stir well and place the cheesecloth bundle in the pot.

5. Bring to a boil, scraping the bottom of the Dutch oven. Cover and place in the oven. Cook for 1 hour and 45 minutes or until the meat is tender. Remove the cheesecloth bundle. Squeeze the bundle to return the juice to the pot. Discard the bundle.

6. Meanwhile, place the onions in a saucepan and cover with cold water. Bring to a boil and blanch for 5 minutes. Drain.

7. Put the salt pork in a saucepan and cover with water. Bring to a boil and blanch for 1 minute. Drain.

8. Add the remaining 2 tablespoons vegetable oil to a sauté pan over medium-high heat and cook the salt pork for 1 minute. Add the mushrooms and

onions. Season with pepper. Sauté for 2 to 3 minutes or until the onions are lightly browned. Drain.

9. When the stew is cooked, add the salt-pork mixture.

10. Put ³/₄ cup of the cooking liquid in a small saucepan. Add the jelly and cook over medium heat until it is melted. Add the mixture to the stew. Simmer for several minutes, stirring well. Taste for seasoning and serve.

Yield: 10 servings.

Marinade

    2 cups onion chunks
    1¹/₂ cups leek green chunks
    1¹/₂ cups celery chunks
    1¹/₂ cups carrot chunks
    3 cloves garlic, peeled and halved
    2 bay leaves
    4 sprigs fresh thyme or 1 teaspoon dry
    4 whole cloves
    1 tablespoon chopped fresh rosemary or 2 teaspoons dry
    1 tablespoon chopped fresh sage or 1 teaspoon dry
    1 teaspoon coriander seeds
    8 juniper berries
    1 tablespoon chopped fresh marjoram or 2 teaspoons dry
    6 whole allspice
    1 teaspoon black peppercorns
    6 parsley sprigs
    1 cup red-wine vinegar
    6 cups dry red wine
    Salt to taste

1. Combine all the ingredients in a large bowl or pot and stir well. Use it to marinate venison in a cool spot, covered, for 4 to 5 days.

Yield: 10 to 12 cups.

◆ ◆ ◆

Venison Steaks in Red-Wine Sauce

1½ pounds loin of venison, sliced diagonally into 8 medallions, each
   about 1½ inches thick, and marinated (see Note)
   Salt and freshly ground pepper to taste
2 tablespoons vegetable oil
2 tablespoons finely chopped shallots
1 tablespoon cognac
¾ cup Marinade (see preceding recipe) or red wine
2 tablespoons butter

1. Drain the medallions and sprinkle them with a little salt and a lot of pepper on both sides.

2. Heat the oil in a large nonstick sauté pan over high heat. Sauté the venison for about 2 minutes on each side for rare. Transfer to a warm serving platter.

3. Pour off the fat from the pan and add the shallots. Cook, stirring, over medium-high heat for about 1 minute. Add the cognac, tilt the pan, and flambé. When the flame dies down add the marinade and any juices that have accumulated on the venison platter. Reduce the sauce over high heat by half. Add the butter and whisk the sauce until smooth. Pour the sauce over the meat and serve immediately.

   Yield: 4 servings.

   NOTE: Half of the above recipe for Marinade is sufficient.

◆ ◆ ◆

Beef

Boeuf Bourguignon

Boeuf bourguignon is one of those old French dishes that has been adapted and interpreted in this country for so many years that it is really half American. The authentic recipe, though, is worth setting forth here for those who enjoy the earthy pleasure of a long-simmered stew with winy nuances. It goes without saying—especially for a native Burgundian—that the only cooking wine allowed comes from the area between Lyons and Chablis.

> ½ pound salt pork, cut into ¼-inch cubes and blanched in water
> 4 pounds lean, boneless chuck or brisket of beef, cut into 1½-inch cubes
> Salt and freshly ground pepper to taste
> 1 tablespoon chopped garlic
> 24 white pearl onions (about ¾ pound), peeled
> 1 pound small button mushrooms
> 5 tablespoons flour
> 5 cups dry red Burgundy wine
> 2 whole cloves
> 2 whole allspice
> 1 bay leaf
> ½ teaspoon dry thyme
> 4 parsley sprigs

1. Cook the salt pork in a large heavy skillet over medium heat, stirring with a slotted spoon, until it is crisp. Remove the salt pork and set aside. Leave the rendered fat in the skillet.

2. Add the beef to the skillet. Sprinkle with salt and pepper and brown over high heat, stirring and turning the pieces often, for about 10 minutes.

3. Add the garlic, onions, and mushrooms, stirring often. Sprinkle with the flour and stir to coat evenly.

4. Add the wine and stir. Add the salt pork, cloves, allspice, bay leaf, thyme, parsley, and salt and pepper to taste. Bring to a boil. Cover and simmer for 1½ hours or until the meat is tender.

5. Remove the bay leaf, parsley sprigs, and any fat on top.

   Yield: 10 servings.

Boeuf Braisé au Beaujolais

(BEEF BRAISED IN BEAUJOLAIS)

4 pounds brisket of beef, well trimmed and cut into 1¹/₂-inch cubes
   Salt and freshly ground pepper to taste
1 tablespoon vegetable oil
2 cups chopped onions
1 tablespoon chopped garlic
1 pound mushrooms, trimmed
4 sprigs fresh thyme or 1 teaspoon dry
¹/₄ cup all-purpose flour
4 cups Beaujolais wine
1 cup fresh or canned beef or chicken broth
1 bay leaf
2 whole cloves
2 whole allspice

1. Sprinkle the beef with salt and pepper. Heat the oil in a nonstick skillet large enough to hold the meat in one layer. Add the beef and cook over medium heat, stirring until well browned on all sides, about 10 minutes.

2. Transfer the meat to a heavy cast-iron kettle and add the onions, garlic, mushrooms, and thyme. Cook and stir for about 5 minutes. Add the flour. Blend well and stir for 1 minute. Add the wine, broth, bay leaf, cloves, and allspice. Blend well and bring to a simmer. Cook, covered, over low heat for 3¹/₂ to 4 hours or until the meat is tender. Remove the bay leaf. Serve with mashed potatoes, noodles, or rice.

   Yield: 8 servings.

◆ ◆ ◆

Beer-Braised Beef with Onions

    1 4-pound piece of beef top chuck
      Salt and freshly ground pepper to taste
    2 tablespoons vegetable oil
1½ pounds onions, quartered and sliced (about 6 cups)
    1 tablespoon minced garlic
    2 tablespoons flour
  24 ounces beer
  ½ teaspoon loosely packed saffron
  ⅛ teaspoon ground cinnamon
    4 whole cloves
    1 tablespoon tomato paste
    1 bay leaf
  ½ teaspoon dry thyme
    1 cup fresh or canned chicken broth

1. Preheat the oven to 350 degrees.

2. Sprinkle the meat with salt and pepper. Heat the oil in a Dutch oven over high heat and brown the meat on all sides. Remove the meat from the pot. Add the onions and garlic to the pot and stir periodically until the onions are brown. Season with salt and pepper to taste.

3. Stir in the flour and beer. Add the saffron, cinnamon, and cloves. Bring to a boil. Add the tomato paste, bay leaf, thyme, and broth. Put the meat back in the pot, bring to a boil, and braise, covered, in the oven for about 2 hours and 15 minutes or until done. To test the meat, pierce it with a carving fork. If the fork comes out clean without effort, the meat is done. Slice the beef and serve in a deep dish with the cooking liquid.

   Yield: 6 to 8 servings.

❖ ❖ ❖

Roast Fillet of Beef

*Cuisine
Rapide
174*

1 9-inch fillet of beef (about 1¾ pounds), well trimmed and tied
 Salt and freshly ground pepper to taste
1 tablespoon vegetable oil
2 tablespoons butter

1. Preheat the oven to 450 degrees.

2. Sprinkle the meat on all sides with salt and pepper. Rub with the oil.

3. Place the beef in a small shallow roasting pan and put it in the oven. Bake 20 minutes, turning once or twice as it roasts.

4. Pour off the fat from the pan and add the butter to the pan. Continue baking 3 to 5 minutes.

5. Remove the roast from the oven and remove the strings. Cover with foil and let stand in a warm place about 10 minutes. Serve sliced with the pan liquid.

   Yield: 4 to 6 servings.

Filet de Boeuf à la Ficelle

(BEEF FILLET TIED WITH STRING)

One of my favorite dishes is called in French boeuf à la ficelle, *or beef tied with string. Few people seem to have heard of it, and no one I know can pinpoint its origin. You will not find it in Escoffier nor in most books on traditional or modern French cooking. Yet it is simple to make and always a big hit.*

 Basically, the preparation is no more complicated than poaching beef in broth along with vegetables. A sauce is not necessary, but you could serve a horseradish sauce, a tomato sauce with herbs, or perhaps some pickled onions or cornichons.

1¼ pounds center-cut fillet of beef
1 6-inch length center part of a leek
1 6-inch length center part of a parsnip
2 carrots, trimmed and scraped
1 small white onion, trimmed and peeled
4 cups fresh or canned beef broth
1 bay leaf
2 sprigs parsley
3 sprigs fresh thyme or ½ teaspoon dry
2 whole cloves
⅛ teaspoon cayenne pepper
   Salt to taste if desired
   Freshly ground pepper to taste
   Horseradish Sauce (see page 290)

1. Neatly trim off each end of the fillet. Carefully tie the piece lengthwise and crosswise with string. Leave a piece of string overhanging to facilitate removal from the cooking liquid.

2. Trim off the bottom end of the leek. Discard any blemished leaves. Cut the leek into 1½-inch lengths. Cut each piece lengthwise in half. Cut each half lengthwise into very thin strips (julienne). There should be about 2 cups.

3. Cut the parsnip crosswise into 1½-inch lengths. Cut each piece lengthwise into very thin slices. Stack the pieces and cut into very thin strips. There should be about 2 cups.

4. Cut the carrots crosswise into 1½-inch lengths. Cut the pieces into slices and then into very thin strips as above. There should be about 2 cups.

5. Cut the onion in half. Cut each half into very thin slices. There should be about ¾ cup.

6. Pour the broth into a small kettle large enough to hold the meat in one layer. Add the bay leaf, parsley, thyme, cloves, cayenne, salt, and pepper. Add the beef, leaving a length of string outside the kettle.

7. Bring the broth to a simmer and cook exactly 5 minutes.

8. Immediately add the leek, parsnip, carrots, and onion and stir to distribute. Cover tightly and simmer exactly 7 minutes longer. Remove from the heat and let rest, covered, for 5 minutes.

9. Cut the beef into thin slices, each ½ inch thick or slightly less, and place on a warm platter. Spoon the vegetables on the side and spoon a little of the broth over all. Serve with the horseradish sauce on the side.

Yield: 4 servings.

Chateaubriand with Chateau Sauce

A chateaubriand is the center cut of a fillet of beef, about 6 or 7 inches long, which is wrapped in a piece of cheesecloth or a clean kitchen towel and pressed down to flatten or ''telescope'' it. The top of the meat is pounded with a flat mallet until it is round like a very large hamburger, about 1½ inches thick and about 5 or 6 inches in diameter. It is then grilled or cooked in a skillet and served with a sauce, perhaps a béarnaise. The classic sauce, though, is Chateau Sauce, which is made with finely chopped shallots, a little white wine, and beef broth.

Many people are put off by a chateaubriand, assuming that it is an exorbitantly priced extravagance. Yet you get full value from this cut of beef. Boneless and with minimal external fat, there is little waste; 1¼ pounds easily serve four.

> 1 center-cut fillet of beef, about 1¼ pounds and about 7 inches long
> Salt to taste if desired
> Freshly ground pepper to taste
> 1 tablespoon corn, peanut, or vegetable oil
> ¼ cup finely chopped shallots
> ⅓ cup dry white wine
> ⅓ cup fresh or canned beef broth
> ¼ teaspoon dry tarragon
> 2 tablespoons butter

1. Lay a length of cheesecloth or a clean kitchen towel on a flat surface. Stand the piece of meat vertically—like a pole—in the center. Press the top down with your hands to partly flatten it. Cover it completely with the cloth.

Using a meat pounder or a heavy skillet, pound the meat until it is the shape of a large patty about 1½ inches thick and 5 to 6 inches in diameter. Sprinkle with salt and pepper.

2. Heat the oil in a heavy skillet and add the meat. Cook over medium-high heat about 5 minutes or until browned and slightly charred on one side. Turn the meat and cook 5 minutes.

3. Turn the meat once more and cook 3 minutes.

4. Transfer the meat to a warm platter and cover it loosely with foil to keep it warm.

5. Pour off the fat from the skillet and add the shallots. Cook briefly, stirring, and add the wine. Cook about 1 minute and add the broth and tarragon. Add any juices that have accumulated around the beef. Cook about 3 minutes or until the sauce is reduced to about ½ cup. Swirl in the butter.

6. Transfer the meat to a clean skillet and heat it. Strain the sauce over the meat and serve it sliced on the bias with some sauce spooned over each serving.

   Yield: 4 servings.

◆ ◆ ◆

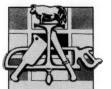

Filet Mignon with Mushrooms and Madeira Sauce

4 slices filet mignon (about ½ pound), each 1 to 1½ inches thick
Salt and freshly gound pepper to taste
½ pound mushrooms
1 tablespoon vegetable oil
2 tablespoons butter
2 tablespoons finely chopped shallots
¼ cup Madeira
½ cup fresh or canned beef broth
1 teaspoon tomato paste

1. Sprinkle the meat on both sides with salt and pepper.

2. Cut the mushrooms into thin slices. There should be about 3 cups.

3. Heat the oil in a heavy skillet large enough to hold the meat without crowding. Add the filets and cook until well browned on one side, about 5 minutes. Turn and continue cooking about 15 minutes or slightly longer. Turn the slices every 5 minutes as they cook.

4. Remove the filets to a warm serving platter. Add 1 tablespoon butter to the skillet and when it melts add the mushrooms. Cook, stirring, over medium-high heat until the mushrooms are browned. Add the shallots and stir.

5. Cook briefly, stirring, and pour in the Madeira.

6. Blend the broth with the tomato paste and add the mixture to the skillet. Add any liquid that has accumulated around the pieces of meat.

7. Cook over medium-high heat about 5 minutes or until the mixture has acquired a sauce-like consistency. There should be about 1 cup or slightly more. Add salt and pepper to taste.

8. Swirl in the remaining tablespoon butter and serve the sauce with the meat.

   Yield: 4 servings.

Broiled Skirt Steak Cajun Style

Skirt steak goes by many names, including hanger steak, oyster steak, and butcher steak. The last arose because butchers traditionally kept these sinewy yet exceptionally juicy and flavorful cuts for themselves.

I remember going to Les Halles, the old central food market in Paris, where at 4 A.M. butchers feasted on skirt steaks and red wine in bistros before starting the workday. If you know how to cook a skirt steak it can be delicious, and it is far less expensive than sirloin or fillet.

The skirt steak comes from the pad of muscle that runs from the rib cage toward the loin. It is usually sold in sections of about twelve ounces each and has a thin, silvery membrane that should be removed by the butcher. Because skirt steak contains a lot of moisture, it should be cooked very fast over high heat to sear. Let the steak reach room temperature before broiling or grilling.

Let the cooked steak sit for several minutes before carving, so the juices can settle. Cut the steak on a bias across the fibrous muscle, over a cutting board that can catch the runoff. Pour the juices back over the steak when serving or use them in a sauce.

> 4 skirt steaks, ½ pound each
> Salt to taste
> 2 tablespoons olive oil
> 1 teaspoon chili powder
> ½ teaspoon ground cumin
> ¼ teaspoon cayenne pepper
> ¼ teaspoon freshly ground black pepper
> 1 teaspoon minced garlic
> ½ teaspoon dry thyme
> 2 tablespoons butter
> 2 tablespoons finely chopped parsley

1. Thirty minutes before broiling or grilling, sprinkle the steaks with salt. Blend well the oil, chili powder, cumin, cayenne, black pepper, garlic, and thyme in a bowl. Brush this mixture on all sides of the steaks. Cover the steaks with plastic wrap but do not refrigerate.

2. Preheat the broiler or a charcoal grill.

3. If broiling, arrange the steaks on a rack and place them under the broiler about 6 inches from the heat. Broil for 2 minutes with the door partly open.

Turn the steaks and continue broiling, leaving the door partly open. Broil about 3 minutes more or to the desired degree of doneness.

4. If grilling, put the steaks on a very hot grill and cover. Cook 2 minutes. Turn the steaks, cover, and cook about 3 minutes more or to the desired degree of doneness.

5. Transfer the steaks to a hot platter and dot with the butter. Let them stand in a warm place 5 mintues to redistribute the internal juices. Sprinkle with the parsley and serve with the accumulated juices.

Yield: 4 servings.

Rib Steak with Marrow and Red-Wine Sauce

1/4 pound marrow from beef bones
2 rib steaks, about 1 1/2 pounds
  Salt to taste if desired
  Freshly ground pepper to taste
1 tablespoon corn, peanut, or vegetable oil
4 tablespoons butter
3 tablespoons finely chopped shallots
1 1/2 cups dry red wine
1 tablespoon red-wine vinegar
1/4 teaspoon honey
1/2 cup fresh or canned chicken broth
1 teaspoon tomato paste

1. Cut the marrow crosswise into slices 1/2 inch thick. Put the pieces in a bowl and add cold water to cover. Set aside for 10 minutes or longer.

2. Sprinkle the meat on both sides with salt and pepper.

3. Heat the oil in a heavy skillet large enough to hold both steaks. Add the steaks and cook about 10 minutes or until thoroughly browned and seared on one side. Turn and continue cooking until thoroughly browned and seared, about 5 minutes. Cook about 5 minutes longer, turning the meat occasionally.

4. Transfer the steaks to a warm platter and pour off the fat from the skillet.

5. Add 1 tablespoon butter to the skillet and when it melts add the shallots, wine, vinegar, and honey. Cook over high heat until the liquid is almost completely reduced, about 12 minutes.

6. Add the broth and any juices that may have accumulated around the steaks. Cook about 3 minutes and swirl in the remaining 3 tablespoons butter.

7. Meanwhile, drain the pieces of marrow and put them in a saucepan. Add cold water to cover and salt to taste. Bring to a simmer but do not boil. Cook as briefly as possible, only until the marrow is barely heated. If the marrow cooks longer it will turn into liquid fat. Using a slotted spoon, transfer the marrow pieces to the sauce. Slice the steaks and serve them with the marrow sauce.

   Yield: 4 servings.

Rib Steak with Red-Wine and Shallot Sauce

> 4 rib steaks, about ¹/₂ pound each
>   **Salt and freshly ground pepper to taste**
> ¹/₄ finely chopped shallots
> ³/₄ cup red Burgundy wine
> ¹/₂ cup fresh or canned beef broth
> 4 tablespoons butter
> 2 tablespoons chopped parsley

1. Sprinkle the meat on both sides with salt and pepper.

2. Heat a cast-iron skillet large enough to hold 2 steaks at a time over high heat. Add the steaks and brown them for 3 minutes for medium-rare meat.

3. Turn and continue cooking until they are thoroughly browned, about 3 minutes. Remove to a platter and keep warm.

4. Pour off all fat from the skillet and reduce the heat to medium. Add the shallots and cook, stirring, for 30 seconds. Add the wine over high heat and reduce it for 45 seconds. Add the broth and bring to a boil. Stir to dissolve the brown particles that cling to the bottom of the skillet. Add any juices from the platter.

5. Reduce the sauce by half and stir in the butter. Add salt and pepper if necessary. Pour the sauce over the steaks. Garnish with the parsley.

NOTE: This dish goes wonderfully with French fries (see page 318).

Yield: 4 servings.

Shell Steaks with Mustard Butter

In my youth, when I was apprenticing in a Burgundy kitchen, one of the first foods I was allowed to prepare without supervision was maître d'hôtel butter. This is a dish of softened butter blended with salt and pepper plus a small amount of lemon juice. It can be made well in advance and applied to a hot slice of beef just before serving.

A little later in my career, while thumbing through Escoffier, I learned that maître d'hôtel butter is only one of dozens of compound butters flavored with such ingredients as garlic, anchovy, tarragon, and truffles. If sealed properly, these butters may be refrigerated for several weeks or frozen indefinitely.

One that I have enjoyed many times is an herb butter for shell steaks. The steaks are seared on both sides in a very hot black iron skillet—the best utensil for such cookery—and served with a softened butter blended with a Dijon-style mustard along with chopped shallot, parsley, and a dash of Worcestershire.

> 4 boneless shell steaks, each about ½ inch thick
> Salt and freshly ground pepper to taste
> 4 tablespoons butter at room temperature
> 2 teaspoons Dijon-style mustard
> ½ teaspoon Worcestershire sauce
> 2 teaspoons finely minced garlic
> 1 tablespoon finely chopped shallots
> 2 tablespoons finely chopped parsley
> 1 tablespoon lemon juice

1. Trim off all peripheral fat from the steaks. Sprinkle the steaks on both sides with salt and a generous grinding of pepper.

2. Put the butter in a food processor or blender and add the mustard, Worcestershire sauce, garlic, shallots, parsley, lemon juice, salt, and pepper. Blend thoroughly.

3. Heat a heavy skillet (preferably cast iron) until it is almost smoking. Cook the steaks, 1 at a time, until almost blackened on one side, about 2 to 3 minutes. Turn and cook on the other side about 2 to 3 minutes. If your stove has a ventilating fan, it is best to turn it on because the steaks will smoke. When each steak is done, transfer it to a warm serving dish and spread the butter mixture over the top.

   Yield: 4 servings.

❖ ❖ ❖

Steak au Poivre

2 tablespoons black peppercorns

2 tablespoons white peppercorns

2 trimmed boneless strip steaks, each about 1½ inches thick and
    1½ pounds

2 tablespoons minced shallots

2 tablespoons minced onion

4 tablespoons butter

2 tablespoons brandy

¾ cup dry red wine

¼ cup fresh or canned beef or chicken broth

1 teaspoon tomato paste

2 tablespoons brandy, optional

1. Place the white and black peppercorns on a hard surface and crush them with the bottom of a heavy skillet. Make sure all are crushed. This should be done shortly before cooking to get the most flavor from the peppercorns.

2. Lay the steaks over the peppercorns to coat them on all sides. Pat in the pepper with your hands.

3. Lightly oil a heavy skillet (preferably cast-iron) and heat it over high heat until it is smoking hot. Lay the steaks in the pan and cook for about 20 minutes, flipping several times to cook evenly. (This will yield medium-rare steaks.)

4. Remove the steaks from the pan and set aside in a clean skillet. Discard all the burned particles in the first skillet (do not rinse it out). Let it cool slightly. Return the skillet to medium heat and add the shallots, onion, and 1 tablespoon butter. Cook for about 1 minute. Add the brandy and red wine. Reduce to half volume. Add the broth and tomato paste. Reduce the liquid to about ½ cup.

5. Add the remaining 3 tablespoons butter and stir constantly until it melts to bind the sauce. If desired, pour 1 more tablespoon brandy over the steaks and flambé them. When the flame dies out pour the sauce over them and serve.

    Yield: 6 to 8 servings.

Hamburger au Poivre
with Red-Wine Sauce

Being French-born, I can't resist taking an American national dish and giving it a Gallic twist. The recipe here can be prepared on a grill, under the broiler, or even in a skillet. Whether you grill or broil, cook the patties about six inches from the heat for about three minutes on each side or until done as desired.

If you are cooking on the stove top, use a heavy cast-iron skillet. Cast iron sears extremely well when hot, but it has to be smoking hot before the meat is put in. Be sure the ventilation fan is on.

The sauce is similar to that for steak au poivre.

1½ pounds ground lean chuck
2 teaspoons vegetable oil
1 cup finely chopped onions
2 teaspoons finely chopped garlic
2 tablespoons chili powder
1 teaspoon freshly ground pepper
⅛ teaspoon red pepper flakes
  Salt to taste
3 tablespoons butter
2 tablespoons finely chopped shallots
½ cup dry red wine
¼ cup fresh or canned beef or chicken broth

1. Put the meat in a mixing bowl and set aside.

2. Heat the oil in a small skillet and add the onions. Cook, stirring, until wilted. Add the garlic and cook briefly, stirring. Cool.

3. Combine the meat lightly with the onion mixture, chili powder, ground pepper, pepper flakes, and salt. Divide the mixture into 4 patties.

4. Heat a heavy cast-iron skillet large enough to hold the patties in one layer. (Do not add fat of any kind.) When the skillet is quite hot, add the patties. Cook until well browned on one side, about 3 minutes. Turn and cook 3 minutes on the second side. Transfer to a warm platter.

5. Heat 1 tablespoon butter in a small skillet. Add the shallots and cook, stir-

ring, for 1 minute. Add the wine and broth and cook until reduced to about
¼ cup. Swirl in the remaining 2 tablespoons butter. Pour over the patties
and serve the dish immediately.

Yield: 4 servings.

Hamburgers with Garlic and Shallot Butter

1½ pounds ground beef, preferably sirloin
    Salt to taste if desired
½ teaspoon freshly ground pepper
1 teaspoon Worcestershire sauce
2 tablespoons Dijon-style mustard
3 tablespoons finely chopped shallots
¼ cup dry white wine
1 tablespoon finely minced garlic
4 tablespoons butter at room temperature
2 tablespoons finely chopped parsley

1. Put the meat in a mixing bowl and add the salt, pepper, Worcestershire
   sauce, and mustard. Blend well, using your fingers. Divide the mixture into
   4 patties.

2. Combine the shallots and wine in a small saucepan. Cook over medium-
   high heat about 3 minutes or until the wine is almost evaporated. Cool
   briefly. Add the garlic, butter, and parsley and blend well.

3. The burgers may be broiled or cooked in a hot skillet. If they are to be
   broiled, preheat the broiler. Put the burgers on a rack and place them under
   the broiler about 2 or 3 inches from the heat. Cook about 5 minutes, turning
   occasionally. If the burgers are to be cooked in a skillet, heat the skillet (preferably cast-iron) until it is very hot. Brush it lightly with oil. Add the burgers
   and cook about 2 minutes on one side. Turn and cook about 3 minutes
   longer, turning occasionally.

4. Smear the top of each burger with herb butter and serve.

   Yield: 4 servings.

Bitoks of Beef and Veal

Bitok, *a quick and simple entrée, is one of the most interesting distortions of an English word. It was first borrowed by the French and further misappropriated by the Russians, who introduced the dish to France around 1920.*

   Russian chefs mispronounced and misspelled the French coinage bifteck, *meaning beefsteak (as doubtless pronounced by the English). The Russians took* bifteck haché, *or ground beef, and shaped it into patties (their version of the American hamburger) to be deep-fried and served with a sauce of sour cream or heavy cream and paprika. Alternately the patties were simply fried in butter and later simmered briefly in sour cream.*

   Larousse Gastronomique *states that* bitoks *may be made with ground veal, chicken, or rabbit. Traditionally, the meat is mixed with milk-soaked bread and raw or cooked onions and then put through the grinder once or twice until smoothly textured. I save time by blending fine fresh bread crumbs with lightly cooked finely chopped onions and milk and add this to the ground beef.*

      1 **pound lean ground beef**
   ¹/₂ **pound ground veal**
      2 **tablespoons butter**
      1 **cup finely chopped onions**
   1¹/₂ **cups fine fresh bread crumbs**
      1 **egg**
   ¹/₂ **cup milk**
       Salt to taste if desired
       Freshly ground pepper to taste
      2 **tablespoons corn, peanut, or vegetable oil**
   ¹/₄ **teaspoon paprika**
      1 **tablespoon red-wine vinegar**
   ¹/₄ **cup fresh or canned beef broth**
   ¹/₄ **cup heavy cream**
   ¹/₄ **cup sour cream**
      4 **teaspoons finely chopped parsley**

1. Put the beef and veal in a mixing bowl.

2. Heat 1 tablespoon butter in a small saucepan and add ¾ cup onions. Cook, stirring often, about 3 minutes without browning. Cool.

3. Combine the cooked onions, 1 cup bread crumbs, the egg, and milk and add to the beef and veal. Add salt and pepper and blend well with your hands.

4. Divide the mixture into 8 portions of more or less equal weight. Shape each portion into a ball. Flatten each ball into a patty and coat them with the remaining ½ cup bread crumbs.

5. Heat the oil in a heavy skillet large enough to hold the patties in one layer. Cook until well browned on one side, about 3 minutes. Turn and cook about 3 minutes on the second side. Transfer the patties to a warm platter.

6. Heat a smaller skillet and add the remaining 1 tablespoon butter. Add the remaining ¼ cup chopped onion and cook until wilted. Add the paprika and stir. Add the vinegar and beef broth. Bring to a boil. Add the heavy cream and sour cream, stirring. Cook about 1 minute or less. There should be about ¾ cup sauce. Pour over the patties and dot the center of each with ½ teaspoon parsley. Serve immediately.

   Yield: 4 servings.

Hamburgers with
Fried Eggs and Anchovies

This unusual combination of ingredients is a particular favorite of mine—the salty anchovies and rich eggs give the lean beef a wonderful extra dimension of flavor.

    1/2 **pound lean ground sirloin**
        Salt and freshly ground pepper to taste
     1 **tablespoon vegetable oil**
     3 **tablespoons butter**
     4 **eggs**
   12 **flat anchovy fillets**
     2 **tablespoons drained capers**
     2 **tablespoons finely chopped parsley**

1. Divide the beef into 4 patties, each about 1 inch thick. Sprinkle with salt and pepper.

2. Heat the oil in a heavy cast-iron skillet over high heat. Cook the hamburgers about 2 minutes per side for rare. Transfer the patties to serving plates.

3. Heat 1 tablespoon butter in a nonstick skillet over medium heat. Cook the eggs until they reach desired doneness. Season with salt and pepper. Slip 1 egg, yoke side up, onto each hamburger.

4. Place 3 anchovies around each yolk in a triangular fashion.

5. Heat the remaining 2 tablespoons butter until foamy and add the capers and parsley. Cook until the butter begins to brown. Pour the sauce over the hamburgers.

    Yield: 4 servings.

◆ ◆ ◆

Hamburgers with Goat Cheese

1½ pounds very lean ground beef, preferably top round
   Salt to taste if desired
   Freshly ground pepper to taste
¼ pound goat cheese
 2 tablespoons chopped fresh tarragon or 1 tablespoon dry,
   optional

1. Preheat the broiler.

2. Divide the beef into 4 patties, each about 1 inch thick. Sprinkle with salt and pepper. Place a wire rack on a baking dish and arrange the patties on it. Put the meat under the broiler 1 or 2 inches from the heat, leaving the door slightly ajar. Cook about 3 minutes on one side for rare. If you prefer it more well done, cook up to 6 minutes on one side, then turn and continue cooking 2 to 4 minutes.

3. Meanwhile, crumble the cheese and top each portion of meat with some cheese, pressing to keep the mounds of cheese intact. Return the cheese-topped patties to the broiler and broil about 2 minutes or until the cheese is browned on top and partly melted.

4. Sprinkle each patty with tarragon.

   Yield: 4 servings.

◆ ◆ ◆

German-Style Hamburgers with Onions and Vinegar

1½ pounds ground round steak
2 teaspoons plus 1 tablespoon vegetable oil
½ cup finely chopped onions
¼ cup fine fresh bread crumbs
½ cup finely chopped dill pickles
½ teaspoon finely minced garlic
Salt to taste
2 tablespoons butter
1 tablespoon red-wine vinegar
1 teaspoon paprika
½ cup sour cream
2 tablespoons finely chopped parsley

1. Put the meat in a mixing bowl.

2. Heat 2 teaspoons oil in a small saucepan or skillet and add ¼ cup onions. Cook, stirring, until wilted. Cool briefly.

3. Add the cooked onions to the meat. Add the bread crumbs, pickles, garlic, salt, and pepper and blend thoroughly with your hands.

4. Divide the mixture into 4 patties, each 1 inch thick.

5. Heat the remaining 1 tablespoon oil in a skillet and when it is very hot add the patties. Cook over medium heat about 5 minutes or until browned on one side. Turn the patties and cook 2 minutes or to the desired degree of doneness on the other side. Transfer the patties to a warm platter.

6. Pour off the fat from the skillet and add the butter. When it is hot and melted, add the remaining ¼ cup onions. Cook, stirring, until wilted and add the vinegar and paprika, stirring. Cook about 45 seconds and stir in the sour cream. Stir and heat without bringing to a boil. Pour the sauce over the patties. Sprinkle with the parsley and serve.

Yield: 4 servings.

Chili à la Franey

1 pound coarsely ground very lean pork
1 pound coarsely ground very lean beef
1 tablespoon olive oil
2 cups finely chopped onions
1 cup finely chopped green sweet pepper
1 cup finely chopped celery
1 tablespoon finely chopped garlic
1 tablespoon crumbled dry oregano
2 bay leaves
2 teaspoons ground cumin
3 tablespoons chili powder
3 cups tomatoes with tomato paste
1 cup fresh or canned beef broth
1 cup water
  Salt to taste if desired
  Freshly ground pepper to taste
½ teaspoon red pepper flakes
2 cups drained kidney beans
  Sour cream as garnish, optional
  Lime wedges as garnish, optional

1. If possible, grind the pork and beef together.

2. Heat the oil in large heavy kettle and add the meat. Cook, stirring with a heavy metal kitchen spoon to break up lumps.

3. Add the onions, green pepper, celery, garlic, oregano, bay leaves, cumin, and chili powder. Stir to blend well.

4. Add the tomatoes, broth, water, salt, and pepper. Add the pepper flakes. Bring to a boil and cook, stirring often, about 20 minutes. Add the beans and cook 10 minutes longer. Serve in hot bowls with a dollop of sour cream and lime wedges if desired.

   Yield: **8 or more servings.**

Pot-au-feu à la Minute

A pot-au-feu, or pot on the fire, is one of the most basic peasant foods in the French repertory, a dish I have known and dined on since my childhood. Originally the dish was cooked almost exclusively in glazed earthenware pots, and the ingredients were usually beef and chicken. As it became more elaborate, veal and pork were used. In the classic pot-au-feu the beef rib or brisket demands several hours of slow cooking to tenderize the meat; I have shortened the cooking time by using beef fillet, which is served rare.

You can make a fine pot-au-feu within an hour by using beef fillet along with chicken legs and Chinese cabbage.

The ideal partner is a well-seasoned tomato sauce. I recommend a sauce that is flavored with horseradish, a standard accompaniment for the dish in France. It is best to use freshly grated horseradish, but the bottled version is acceptable. If the bottled type is used, the liquid in which the horseradish is packed should be pressed out and discarded.

            1 head Chinese cabbage, about 3½ pounds
          ¼ pound lean bacon, cut into ½ inch pieces
            4 whole chicken legs (about 2 pounds), separated into legs and
                thighs
              Salt to taste if desired
              Freshly ground pepper to taste
        1½ pound fillet of beef, trimmed
            1 cup finely chopped onion
            1 tablespoon finely minced garlic
          ½ cup dry white wine
        1½ cups fresh or canned chicken broth
            8 red waxy potatoes, about 1 pound
          12 baby carrots (about 1 pound), trimmed and scraped
            2 whole cloves
            2 whole allspice
            1 bay leaf
          ½ teaspoon dry thyme
              Tomato and Horseradish Sauce (recipe follows)

1. Slice off and discard the bottom end of the cabbage. Cut it in half lengthwise and cut each half crosswise into 2-inch pieces. Put the pieces in a kettle and add cold water to cover. Bring to a boil. When the water reaches a rolling boil, drain the cabbage. Rinse under cold running water until well chilled. Drain well.

2. Put the bacon in a casserole or kettle and cook it, stirring often, until it is rendered of fat. Add the chicken legs and thighs, skin side down, and sprinkle with salt and pepper. Cook about 2 minutes.

3. Coat the fillet of beef with salt and pepper. Add the beef to the casserole. Sprinkle with the onion and garlic. Cook briefly, stirring, and add the wine and broth. Bring to a simmer and add the cabbage, potatoes, carrots, cloves, allspice, bay leaf, and thyme. Cover tightly and cook 20 minutes. Uncover and continue cooking 5 minutes. Remove the bay leaf.

4. Serve the meats and vegetables with a little of the broth and the sauce.

Yield: 4 servings.

Tomato and Horseradish Sauce

1 tablespoon olive oil
1 tablespoon butter
½ cup finely chopped onion
½ teaspoon finely minced garlic
1 tablespoon red-wine vinegar
3 cups cubed tomatoes
Salt to taste if desired
Freshly ground pepper to taste
2 tablespoons freshly grated or bottled horseradish

1. Heat the oil and butter in a saucepan and add the onion and garlic. Cook, stirring, until the onion is wilted but not browned.

2. Add the vinegar and stir. Add the tomatoes, salt, and pepper. Bring to a boil and simmer about 5 minutes. If freshly grated horseradish is used, add it. If bottled horseradish is used, press it in a fine sieve and discard the liquid. Add the horseradish to the sauce and stir.

Yield: 4 servings.

Ham &
Pork

Charcuterie

Ham Steaks with Madeira and Mustard Sauce

Ham steaks are exceptionally handy for the busy home cook, for they are purchased already cooked and need only be heated. This quick Madeira and Mustard Sauce brings out the best of the sweet-edged meat.

> 2 ham steaks, about 1³/₄ pounds
> 2 apples, preferably McIntosh (about 1 pound)
> 3 tablespoons butter
> 2 tablespoons finely chopped shallots
> 4 tablespoons Madeira wine
> 1 teaspoon tomato paste
> 1 teaspoon Dijon-style mustard

1. Remove any excess fat from each ham steak.

2. Cut the apples into quarters. Cut away and discard the cores. Peel the quarters.

3. Use 2 skillets, preferably nonstick, large enough to hold the ham pieces. Heat 1 tablespoon butter in each skillet. Add 1 tablespoon shallots to each skillet. Cook briefly, stirring, and add 1 ham steak to each.

4. Arrange one quartered apple around each steak. Spoon half the Madeira over the apples in each skillet. Cover closely and cook 5 minutes. Transfer the ham steaks to a hot platter and arrange the partly cooked apples around or over the pieces of meat.

5. Pour the cooking liquid from one skillet into the other skillet. Add the remaining 2 tablespoons wine, tomato paste, and mustard, and stir to blend. Bring to a simmer. Swirl in the remaining tablespoon butter and pour the sauce over the ham and apples.

   Yield: 4 servings.

◆ ◆ ◆

Asperges et Jambon Mornay

(ASPARAGUS AND HAM WITH CHEESE SAUCE)

24 asparagus spears, about 2 pounds
Salt to taste
3 tablespoons butter
3 tablespoons flour
1½ cups milk
¾ cup grated cheese, preferably Gruyère or Swiss
1 egg yolk
Freshly ground pepper to taste
⅛ teaspoon freshly grated nutmeg
Pinch of cayenne pepper
2 tablespoons freshly grated Parmesan cheese
24 thin slices cooked ham or prosciutto

1. Place the asparagus spears on a flat surface. Cut off the bottoms so that all the spears are the same length, about 7 inches long.

2. Bring enough water to a boil in a skillet to cover the asparagus. Add salt to taste. Add the asparagus spears and cook about 1 minute or longer. The cooking time depends on individual tastes. After 1 minute the asparagus will still be al dente. If you like it softer, cook 3 to 4 minutes. Drain well.

3. Meanwhile, heat the butter in a saucepan and add the flour, stirring with a wire whisk. Add the milk, stirring rapidly with the whisk. Cook, stirring, about 5 minutes or until thickened and smooth. Remove from the heat.

4. Add the Gruyère, stirring rapidly with the whisk. Add the egg yolk, pepper, nutmeg, and cayenne and beat to blend.

5. Preheat the broiler.

6. Select a baking dish large enough to hold the asparagus spears in one layer slightly overlapping. Wrap 1 slice of ham compactly around each asparagus spear. Arrange the asparagus spears slightly overlapping in the dish.

7. Spoon the sauce over all and sprinkle with the Parmesan.

8. Run the dish under the broiler about 5 inches from the heat. Broil until bubbling and golden brown on top. Serve immediately.

Yield: 4 servings.

Brochettes of Honey-Marinated Pork

¹/₄ cup soy sauce
¹/₂ cup water
¹/₄ cup honey
2 tablespoons red-wine vinegar
1 tablespoon finely chopped garlic
1 tablespoon chopped fresh sage or 1 teaspoon dry
1 tablespoon freshly grated ginger
Salt to taste if desired
1 teaspoon paprika
2¹/₂ pounds boneless pork loin
Oil for brushing the pork
1 tablespoon lemon juice
4 tablespoons butter
1 tablespoon chopped fresh coriander (optional)

1. In a mixing bowl combine the soy sauce, water, honey, vinegar, garlic, sage, ginger, salt, and paprika. If wooden skewers are to be used, soak them in water.

2. Cut the pork into 1¹/₂-inch cubes and put them in the soy sauce mixture. Cover. Let stand briefly or until ready to cook.

3. Preheat a charcoal grill or broiler.

4. Drain the pork, reserving the marinade. Arrange the cubes on 8 skewers. Brush the meat with oil. Place the skewers on the grill or under the broiler. Cook, brushing with the reserved marinade and turning often so the meat cooks evenly, about 15 minutes or until thoroughly cooked.

5. In a small saucepan combine ¹/₄ cup of the marinade, the lemon juice, butter, and coriander. Heat thoroughly. Spoon onto the meat and serve hot.

Yield: 8 servings.

Cold Pork with Tuna Sauce

This pork recipe is a variation on the classic Italian dish, vitello tonnato, *or veal with tuna sauce. It also works very well with turkey breast.*

2¼ pounds well-trimmed pork loin (the loin should be about 12 inches long)
1 cup dry white wine
1 cup coarsely chopped carrots
1 cup coarsely chopped onions
½ cup coarsely chopped celery
1 bay leaf
1 sprig fresh thyme
2 cloves garlic, peeled
2 sprigs parsley
6 black peppercorns
2 whole cloves
Salt to taste
1 cup fresh or canned chicken broth
Tuna Sauce (recipe follows)
20 cornichons
5 cherry tomatoes, quartered
1 tablespoon drained capers

1. Put all the ingredients except the cornichons, tomatoes, and capers in a soup pot. Cover and bring to a boil. Reduce to a simmer and cook for about 1½ hours. Remove from the heat, drain (reserving the liquid for the tuna sauce) and cool. Chill the liquid; when it is cool, skim the fat from the surface.

2. When the pork is cool, slice it into serving pieces about ¼ inch thick and arrange on a platter. Pour some of the tuna sauce over it. Reserve the rest of the sauce and serve it on the side. Garnish the meat with the cornichons, cherry tomatoes, and capers.

Yield: 8 servings.

Tuna Sauce

7 ounces Italian-style tuna packed in olive oil (available in most supermarkets)

½ cup cooking liquid from the pork
1 cup mayonnaise, preferably homemade (see page 289)
White pepper to taste

1. Place the tuna and packing oil in a food processor or blender. Add the cooking liquid and purée well. Mix the purée with the mayonnaise. Taste for seasoning. Chill until ready to serve.

   Yield: about 1½ cups.

Pork Cutlets with Vinegar and Herbs

Vinegar is not often thought of as a principal ingredient in cooking. Most people probably view it as something to put in a salad. Yet there are many dishes in which vinegar—red, white, or flavored—plays an important role: sweet-and-sour dishes from Germany to China, steamed mussels, chicken sautés.

Today, with so many flavored versions available (raspberry, pear, green peppercorn, tarragon) the range of dishes employing vinegar is expanding.

I have had great success with a center cut of pork loin cut into thin slices. I cook it with a few mushrooms, using a quarter of a cup of red-wine vinegar to deglaze the pan and adding tomatoes and chopped basil.

 1 boneless center-cut pork loin, trimmed of fat (1¼ pounds trimmed weight)
  Salt and freshly ground pepper to taste
 2 tablespoons corn, peanut, or vegetable oil
 ¼ cup finely chopped onion
 1 teaspoon finely minced garlic
 ¼ pound mushrooms, sliced thin
 ¼ cup red-wine vinegar
 1 cup peeled, seeded, and finely chopped tomatoes
 ¼ cup fresh or canned chicken broth
 2 tablespoons chopped fresh basil
 2 tablespoons finely chopped parsley

1. Cut the loin into 12 slices of approximately the same thickness.

2. Sprinkle the meat on both sides with salt and pepper.

3. Heat the oil in a skillet until almost smoking and add the pork. Cook over high heat 2 minutes and turn. Continue cooking 2 minutes.

4. Transfer the meat to a serving dish.

5. Add the onion and garlic to the skillet and cook, stirring, until wilted. Add the mushrooms and cook until wilted. Add the vinegar and cook over high heat 15 seconds. Add the tomatoes and broth and cook down to about 1¾ cups. Add the liquid accumulated around the meat. Add the basil. Spoon the sauce over pork, sprinkle with the parsley, and serve.

Yield: 4 servings.

Sautéed Medallions of Pork with Port

    8 boneless pork loin slices (about 3 ounces each), trimmed of
        excess fat
      Salt and freshly ground pepper to taste
    2 teaspoons ground cumin
    1 teaspoon paprika
    2 tablespoons vegetable oil
    3 sprigs fresh rosemary or ½ teaspoon dry
  ½ cup finely chopped onion
    1 teaspoon finely chopped garlic
  ¼ cup port
    1 tablespoon red-wine vinegar
  ¼ cup water or chicken broth
    2 tablespoons butter
    2 tablespoons coarsely chopped fresh coriander

1. Place the pork slices in a flat dish. Sprinkle with the salt, pepper, cumin, and paprika.

2. Heat the oil in a nonstick skillet large enough to hold the slices in one layer. When the oil is very hot, add the meat and rosemary and cook over medium-high heat about 5 minutes or until brown.

3. Turn the slices and cook for about 5 minutes. Reduce the heat and continue cooking about 2 minutes longer, turning occasionally.

4. Transfer the meat to a warm serving dish.

5. Pour off most of the fat from the skillet. Add the onion and garlic and cook, stirring, until the onion is wilted and lightly browned. Add the port, vinegar, and water. Stir to dissolve the brown particles that cling to the bottom of the pan. Cook until reduced to about ½ cup. Add the butter and blend well.

6. Spoon the sauce over the pork and sprinkle with the coriander. Serve immediately.

   Yield: 4 servings.

Pork Tenderloin with Potatoes and Apples

> 3 whole boneless pork tenderloins, about 1¾ pounds
> Salt and freshly ground pepper to taste
> 2 tablespoons vegetable oil
> 1 teaspoon dry or chopped fresh rosemary
> 1 onion (about ¼ pound), peeled and cut in half crosswise
> 8 waxy red potatoes, about 1 pound
> 2 Golden Delicious apples
> ¼ cup fresh or canned chicken broth
> 2 tablespoons finely chopped parsley

1. Preheat the oven to 450 degrees.

2. Sprinkle the tenderloins with salt and pepper. Put the oil in a pan large enough to hold the tenderloins in one layer. Sprinkle with the rosemary and turn the pork in the mixture to coat it all over. Place on top of the stove. Arrange the onion, cut side down, around the pork. Heat the pork, turning to make certain the pieces do not stick. Cook until the pieces are lightly browned all over. Place the pan in the oven.

3. Meanwhile, peel the potatoes and put them in a saucepan with water to cover and salt to taste. Bring to a boil and cook 5 minutes.

4. Peel, core, and quarter the apples as the potatoes cook.

5. Drain the potatoes and arrange them around the meat. Turn the pork and continue baking for a total of 30 minutes.

6. At the end of that time, scatter the apple quarters around the meat and return the pan to the oven. Continue baking 15 minutes.

7. Remove the meat to a warm serving platter. Add the broth to the pan. Stir and boil about 5 minutes. Remove from the heat. Cut the pork crosswise into pieces and serve it with the potatoes, apples, and sauce. Sprinkle with the parsley.

Yield: 4 to 6 servings.

Roast Pork Tenderloin with Sweet Peppers and Paprika Sauce

  2 boneless pork tenderloins, about 1³/₄ pounds
    Salt and freshly ground pepper to taste
¹/₂ teaspoon paprika
  2 tablespoons corn, peanut, or vegetable oil
¹/₂ cup finely chopped onion
  1 tablespoon finely chopped garlic
¹/₄ cup dry white wine
  1 bay leaf
¹/₂ cup fresh or canned chicken broth
¹/₄ teaspoon dry thyme
  2 teaspoons chopped fresh marjoram or ¹/₂ teaspoon dry
  2 large red sweet peppers, cored, seeded, and deveined
  2 tablespoons sour cream
  2 tablespoons heavy cream
  2 tablespoons chopped parsley

1. Sprinkle the tenderloins with salt, pepper, and paprika.

2. Heat the oil in a heavy skillet until hot and add the tenderloins. Cook, turning the pieces so they brown evenly on all sides, about 5 minutes.

3. Pour off the fat from the pan and scatter the onion and garlic around the meat. Cook about 3 minutes and add the wine, bay leaf, broth, thyme, and marjoram. Bring to a boil, stirring, and cover tightly. Cook 15 minutes.

4. Meanwhile, cut the peppers into thin strips, about ¼ inch thick. Scatter the pepper strips over the meat and cook about 5 minutes.

5. Transfer the meat to a serving plate and add the sour cream and heavy cream to the skillet. Stir to blend. Remove the bay leaf and pour the sauce over the meat. Sprinkle with the parsley.

Yield: 4 servings.

Pork Chops with Apples and Sweet-and-Sour Sauce

8 loin rib pork chops (about 2¾ pounds), each ½ inch thick (see Note)
   Salt to taste if desired
   Freshly ground pepper to taste
2 cooking apples such as Granny Smiths, about 1 pound
¼ cup flour
1 teaspoon ground cumin
2 tablespoons corn, peanut, or vegetable oil
2 tablespoons finely chopped shallots
2 tablespoons red-wine vinegar
¾ cup fresh or canned chicken broth
1 tablespoon honey
1 tablespoon tomato paste

1. Sprinkle the chops with salt and pepper to taste.

2. Cut each apple into quarters. Peel the quarters and core them.

3. Dredge the chops in the flour blended with the cumin. Heat the oil in a large heavy skillet and add the chops. Cook until well browned on one side, about 5 minutes. Turn the chops and continue cooking about 5 minutes.

4. Remove the chops and add the quartered apples. Cook about 2 minutes, turning the apples often. Remove the apples and pour off the fat from the skillet.

5. Add the shallots and vinegar to the skillet and cook briefly, stirring with a wooden spoon. Add the broth and honey. Cook about 1 minute and stir in the tomato paste.

6. Return the chops and apples to the skillet. Bring the sauce to a boil, spoon it over the chops, and cover tightly. Cook 10 minutes. Transfer the chops and apples to a serving dish and pour the sauce over them.

Yield: 4 servings.

NOTE: You should hack away (or have the butcher do it) the backbone of each chop, leaving the rib bone intact. The ready-to-cook chops will weigh about 2¼ pounds.

Pork Chops with Lentils

Among the many foods that have a natural affinity are pork and such legumes as dried peas and beans. This pairing is perhaps most notably celebrated in cassoulets.

There are certain seasonings that marry particularly well with pork, and these include mustard—which I used in this recipe. It is the accompaniment, however, that gives the dish its special caliber: The lentils are blended with a light and quick-cooking tomato sauce made with onions, garlic, and leeks.

Contrary to popular opinion, lentils do not require a lengthy period of cooking. Although the recipe for lentil soup outlined on the package of the brand I used called for a two-hour time, I found half an hour sufficient.

8 lean pork loin chops (about 2 pounds), each about ½ inch thick
Salt to taste if desired
Freshly ground pepper to taste

   ¼ cup flour
   1 teaspoon paprika
   2 tablespoons vegetable oil
   ½ cup finely chopped onion
   ½ cup dry white wine
   ½ cup fresh or canned chicken broth
   2 teaspoons hot mustard
   2 teaspoons finely chopped parsley
   Lentils with Tomato Sauce (recipe follows)

1. Sprinkle the chops on both sides with salt and pepper.

2. Blend the flour with the paprika in a shallow dish. Dredge the chops on both sides in the mixture and shake off the excess.

3. Heat the oil in a very heavy skillet and add the chops. Cook over medium-high heat until well browned on one side, about 8 minutes. Turn the chops and continue cooking about 8 minutes or until done.

4. Remove the chops to a warm platter.

5. Pour off most of the fat from the pan and add the onion. Cook, stirring, until wilted. Add the wine, broth, and mustard, stirring. Cook over high heat about 2 minutes. Stir in the parsley.

6. Pour the sauce over the chops. Serve with the lentils.

   Yield: 4 servings.

Lentils with Tomato Sauce

   ½ pound dried lentils, about 2 cups
   3 cups water
   Salt to taste if desired
   1 small onion, peeled
   2 whole cloves
   2 tablespoons butter
   ¾ cup finely chopped leeks
   1 cup finely chopped onions
   1 teaspoon finely minced garlic
   1½ cups crushed or chopped tomatoes
   Freshly ground pepper to taste

1. Pick over the lentils and discard any foreign particles. Rinse the lentils well and drain.

2. Put the lentils in a saucepan and add the water and salt. Bring to a boil. Stick the whole onion with the cloves and add it to the saucepan. Cover and simmer 25 to 30 minutes or until tender.

3. Meanwhile, heat the butter in a skillet and add the leeks, chopped onions, and garlic. Cook, stirring, about 5 minutes. Do not brown.

4. Add the tomatoes, salt, and pepper to the skillet. Stir and bring to a boil. Cover and simmer about 10 minutes.

5. When the lentils are tender, drain them. Add them to the tomato sauce and bring to a boil.

   Yield: 4 servings.

Pork Chops Basque Style

    4 pork loin chops, about 2 pounds
      Salt and freshly ground pepper to taste
    2 tablespoons flour
    1 tablespoon vegetable oil
    1 tablespoon olive oil
    ½ teaspoon finely minced garlic
    1 cup coarsely chopped onion
    1 cup cored, seeded, and thinly sliced green sweet pepper
    1 cup cored, seeded, and thinly sliced red sweet pepper
    ¼ cup dry white wine
    1 cup cubed plum tomatoes
    ½ cup fresh or canned chicken broth
    1 bay leaf
    3 sprigs fresh thyme or ½ teaspoon dry

1. Sprinkle the chops on both sides with salt and pepper. Dredge in the flour and shake off the excess.

2. Heat the vegetable oil in a heavy skillet over medium-high heat and add the chops. Cook 5 minutes or until well browned on one side. Turn and cook until well browned on the other side, about 5 minutes. Transfer the chops to a platter.

3. Drain the fat from the skillet and add the olive oil. Add the garlic, onion, and peppers and cook, stirring, about 1 minute. Add the wine. Cook about 1 minute and add the tomatoes, broth, bay leaf, thyme, salt, and pepper. Bring to a boil and top with the pork chops. Cover tightly and simmer 25 minutes or until tender.

4. Transfer the chops to a warm platter and bring the sauce to a boil. Cook about 3 minutes or until reduced to about 2¼ cups. Remove the bay leaf. Pour the sauce over the chops and serve.

   Yield: 4 servings.

Pork Chops and Sausage with Sauerkraut

  2 pounds sauerkraut
  1 tart apple, about ½ pound
  4 pork loin chops, about ½ pound each
    Salt to taste if desired
    Freshly ground pepper to taste
  4 Italian sausage links (or any good-quality fresh sausage), about ¼ pound each
  2 tablespoons lard or peanut, vegetable, or corn oil
  ¾ cup finely chopped onion
  1 teaspoon finely minced garlic
  2 cups dry white wine
  1 bay leaf
  3 sprigs fresh thyme or ½ teaspoon dry
  1½ cups fresh or canned chicken broth
  6 juniper berries
  ½ teaspoon caraway seeds
  2 whole cloves

1. If you want a less salty sauerkraut, put the sauerkraut in a sieve and run cold water over it. Press to extract most of the liquid. If you want a more salty dish, do not rinse the sauerkraut but press to extract most of the packaged liquid.

2. Peel the apple, remove the stem, and cut the apple into quarters. Cut away and discard the core. Cut the flesh into ½-inch cubes.

3. Sprinkle the chops with salt and pepper.

4. Heat the lard in a casserole and add the pork chops and sausage. Cook until brown on one side, about 4 minutes.

5. Turn the chops and sausage and cook about 4 minutes longer or until browned on the second side.

6. Pour off the fat from the casserole and add the onion and garlic. Stir and cook briefly. Add the apple cubes, wine, bay leaf, and thyme. Add the sauerkraut and stir to distribute evenly. Pour the broth over all. Add the juniper berries, caraway seeds, and cloves and stir. Cover tightly and cook 45 minutes. Remove the bay leaf and serve.

   Yield: 4 servings.

Pork Chops with Fresh Cranberry Sauce

> 4 lean pork loin chops, about 1½ pounds
>   Salt and freshly ground pepper to taste
> 1 navel orange, about ½ pound
> 1½ cups fresh cranberries
> 2 tablespoons flour
> 2 tablespoons vegetable oil
> 2 tablespoons butter
> ½ cup finely chopped onion
> 2 tablespoons honey
> 2 tablespoons red-wine vinegar
> 1 tablespoon tomato paste

½ cup fresh or canned chicken broth
1 tablespoon finely chopped parsley

1. Sprinkle the chops on both sides with salt and pepper.

2. Peel the orange and cut it crosswise into 4 slices of equal thickness. Cut each slice into 8 equal-size pieces. Put the cranberries and orange pieces in a food processor or blender and blend coarsely. There should be about 1½ cups.

3. Dredge the chops on both sides in the flour and shake off the excess.

4. Heat the oil in a heavy skillet large enough to hold the chops in one layer. When the oil is quite hot, add the chops and cook until browned on one side, about 8 minutes. Turn the chops and cook until browned on the other side, about 5 minutes. Reduce the heat. Cover and simmer 12 minutes.

5. Transfer the chops to a warm serving platter and pour off the fat from the skillet.

6. Add 1 tablespoon butter to the skillet and when it is melted add the onion. Cook, stirring, until wilted. Add the honey and stir to dissolve. Add the vinegar and tomato paste and stir until blended. Add the cranberry and orange mixture and broth. Stir to blend. Add any liquid that has accumulated around the chops. Simmer about 1 minute. Stir in the remaining 1 tablespoon butter. Pour the sauce over the chops and sprinkle with the parsley.

Yield: 4 servings.

Pork Chops Milanese

8 thin slices boneless pork loin, about 1½ pounds (see Note)
  Salt to taste if desired
  Freshly ground pepper to taste
1 egg, lightly beaten
3 tablespoons water
1 teaspoon ground cumin
1 cup fine fresh bread crumbs
¼ cup freshly grated Parmesan cheese
¼ cup vegetable oil
  Tomato Sauce with Peppers (recipe follows)

1. Pound each slice of pork lightly on a flat surface with a flat mallet. Sprinkle on both sides with salt and pepper.

2. Put the egg, water, cumin, salt, and pepper in mixing bowl. Beat well.

3. Combine the bread crumbs and cheese in a flat dish. Blend well.

4. Dip the pork slices in the egg mixture to coat. Dredge the slices on both sides in the crumb and cheese mixture. Pat lightly with the flat side of a kitchen knife to help the crumbs adhere.

5. Heat 2 tablespoons oil in a heavy skillet and add as much meat as possible in one layer. When the slices are golden brown on one side, about 3 minutes, cook on the other side 2 to 3 minutes. As the pieces are done, transfer them to a heated platter.

6. Add 1 tablespoon oil to the skillet and more slices in one layer. Continue cooking, adding a little oil as necessary. Serve the slices with a little tomato sauce spooned over them.

Yield: 4 servings

NOTE: Properly sliced pork will look like veal scaloppine.

Tomato Sauce with Peppers

> 2 cups canned tomatoes, preferably imported
> 1 tablespoon olive oil
> 1 tablespoon finely minced garlic
> 1/8 teaspoon red pepper flakes
> 3/4 cup chopped green sweet peppers, preferably long Italian
> 1/4 teaspoon crumbled dry oregano
> Salt and freshly ground pepper to taste

1. Blend the tomatoes thoroughly in a food processor or blender.

2. Heat the oil in a saucepan and add the garlic, pepper flakes, and peppers. Cook, stirring occasionally, about 3 minutes. Do not brown.

3. Add the tomatoes, oregano, salt, and pepper. Simmer, uncovered, about 7 minutes.

Yield: about 2 1/4 cups.

Smoked Pork Shoulder with Cider and Sauerkraut

    1 porkette (cooked smoked shoulder butt), 1¹/₂ pounds
    2 green apples, about ³/₄ pound
    3 Idaho potatoes, about 1¹/₄ pounds
  ¹/₄ cup lard or solid white shortening
1¹/₂ cups coarsely chopped onions
    1 teaspoon finely minced garlic
    1 teaspoon caraway seeds
    2 whole cloves
    2 pounds sauerkraut
    6 juniper berries
    1 bay leaf
    2 sprigs fresh thyme or ¹/₂ teaspoon dry
  ³/₄ cup apple cider
  ³/₄ cup fresh or canned chicken broth
    6 to 8 Boulettes of Pork with Cumin and Coriander (recipe follows)
    1 link kielbasa or Polish sausage, about 1¹/₄ pounds

1. Cut and pull away the cloth covering of the pork butt.

2. Remove the stems from the apples. Peel and core the apples and cut them into quarters. Cut the quarters crosswise into thin pieces. There should be about 2¹/₂ cups.

3. Peel the potatoes and cut each in half crosswise. Let the potatoes stand in water to cover until ready to use.

4. Heat the lard in a large heavy casserole and add the onions and garlic. Cook, stirring, until the onions are wilted.

5. Add the caraway seeds and cloves and cook briefly. Add the apples, stirring.

6. Rinse and drain the sauerkraut. Squeeze it to extract the excess liquid. Add the sauerkraut and juniper berries to the casserole.

7. Place the pork butt in the center of the sauerkraut. Add the bay leaf, thyme, cider, and broth. Cover tightly. Bring to a boil and cook 15 minutes.

8. Arrange the boulettes of pork and kielbasa over the sauerkraut. Drain the potatoes and add them. Cover tightly and continue cooking 20 minutes. Remove the bay leaf.

9. Slice the meats and serve with the boulettes, potatoes, apples, and sauerkraut.

   Yield: 6 to 8 servings.

Boulettes of Pork with Cumin and Coriander

The French term boulette *is roughly equivalent to the American meatball.*

   1 **pound lean ground pork**
   1 **slice white bread, broken into pieces**
   ¼ **cup milk**
   ½ **cup finely chopped onion**
   ½ **teaspoon finely minced garlic**
   ¼ **cup finely chopped parsley**
   ½ **teaspoon ground cumin**
   ½ **teaspoon ground coriander**
   Salt to taste if desired
   Freshly ground pepper to taste

1. Put the pork in a mixing bowl and set aside.

2. In another bowl combine the bread and milk. Blend thoroughly with your fingers and add to the pork with the onion, garlic, parsley, cumin, coriander, salt, and pepper. Blend thoroughly with your fingers.

3. Shape the mixture into 6 to 8 meatballs of about the same size.

   Yield: 6 to 8 meatballs.

Choucroute Garnie

(GARNISHED SAUERKRAUT)

Sauerkraut is one of the simplest of foods to cook. It is mainly a question of rinsing and pressing the sauerkraut (I know some cooks who prefer to cook it in its pure, strong state) and putting it in a pot with seasonings and meats—many of which need only be heated through.

My own favorite recipe for choucroute garnie, *as it is known in French, is different. I enjoy the dish most when it is served with small pork balls made with ground pork and a touch of chopped caraway. These add an admirable contrast in both flavor and texture.*

3	pounds sauerkraut
2	tablespoons lard or solid white shortening
1½	cups finely chopped onions
1	teaspoon finely minced garlic
6	smoked pork hocks, about 2½ pounds
½	cup dry white wine
1½	cups fresh or canned chicken broth
4	sprigs parsley
1	bay leaf
3	sprigs fresh thyme or ½ teaspoon dry
2	whole cloves
6	juniper berries (optional)
1	tablespoon butter
1	pound finely ground pork
1	teaspoon finely crushed caraway seeds
¼	cup finely chopped parsley
	Salt to taste if desired
	Freshly ground pepper to taste
1½	pounds porkette (cooked smoked pork butt)
1	pound kielbasa (Polish sausage)

1. Put the sauerkraut in a colander and rinse well. Press with your hands to extract the excess liquid.

2. Heat the lard in a large heavy casserole or Dutch oven. Add 1 cup chopped onions and the garlic. Cook, stirring, until wilted and add the pork hocks. Scatter the sauerkraut over all. Add the wine and chicken broth.

3. Tie the parsley sprigs, bay leaf, and thyme in a small bundle and add it. Add the cloves and juniper berries. Cover tightly and bring to a boil.

4. Meanwhile, heat the butter in a saucepan and add the remaining 1/2 cup chopped onion. Cook, stirring, until wilted.

5. Put the ground pork in a mixing bowl and add the cooked onion, caraway seeds, and chopped parsley. Add salt and pepper to taste.

6. Blend the pork mixture well. Shape it into 12 balls of approximately the same size. Arrange them on top of the sauerkraut. Add the smoked pork butt and continue cooking.

7. When the sauerkraut and meats have cooked for 30 minutes after the first boil, add the kielbasa. Cover and cook 15 minutes longer. Serve the sauerkraut with the sliced meats.

Yield: 6 or more servings.

Cassoulet à la Minute

Making a true cassoulet *(the most famous of them are those of Castelnaudary, Toulouse, and Carcassonne, each slightly different from the other) is an elaborate and time-consuming process. It requires some ingredients that are a bit exotic, such as preserved goose and mutton, but it is a dish I enjoy preparing from scratch—even down to preserving my own goose, which takes days.*

To satisfy a friend, I came up with what I would call cassoulet à la minute. *As a substitute for the traditional* haricot blanc *beans, which must be soaked for several hours, I used canned white kidney beans, some of the best of which are the Italian cannellini. For the garlic sausages, which require fairly long simmering, I resorted to kielbasa or Polish sausages purchased from my local supermarket and for the meats I used one whole fresh duck, boned and cut into small cubes, lean pork, and lean lamb.*

It takes somewhat less than an hour for me to prepare the dish, and I think it quite possible for the skilled home cook to make it in about the same amount of time.

1 duck, 4½ to 5 pounds
½ pound lean pork, preferably loin
½ pound lean loin of lamb
1 pound kielbasa (Polish sausage)
2 cups finely chopped onions, about 1 pound
1 tablespoon finely minced garlic
4 cups crushed and chopped canned imported tomatoes
6 sprigs fresh thyme or 1 teaspoon dry
2 bay leaves
  Salt to taste if desired
  Freshly ground pepper to taste
6 cups canned white kidney beans (cannellini), drained
½ cup dry white wine
3 tablespoons fine fresh bread crumbs
2 tablespoons melted butter

1. Preheat the oven to 425 degrees.

2. Cut the duck into serving pieces. Prepare it further by cutting away the meat from the breastbone. Cut away the peripheral fat surrounding the thighs, legs, and breast. Reserve enough of the fat to produce 2 tablespoons when finely chopped and discard the rest. Cut the boneless breast meat into 1½-inch pieces. Cut the thighs into 4 pieces. Cut the legs crosswise into 1½-inch lengths.

3. Cut the pork and lamb into 1-inch cubes.

4. Add the chopped fat to a large heavy skillet and cook until rendered.

5. Meanwhile, cut half of the kielbasa on the diagonal into slices measuring about ⅓ inch thick. Cut the remaining kielbasa into round slices of about the same thickness.

6. Add the duck, pork, and lamb to the skillet. Cook over high heat, stirring from the bottom, until the fat is rendered from the duck pieces. Cover and cook about 15 minutes.

7. Spoon 2 tablespoons of the rendered fat into a separate skillet and add the onions and 2 teaspoons garlic. Cook, stirring, until wilted. Cook about 5 minutes and add the tomatoes, half the thyme, 1 bay leaf, salt, and pepper. Continue cooking about 10 minutes and add the beans. Add the round slices of kielbasa and continue cooking 15 minutes.

8. Meanwhile, when the meats have cooked for about 12 minutes, reduce the heat and add the remaining 1 teaspoon garlic, thyme, and bay leaf; stir. Add the wine and stir to dissolve the brown particles that cling to the pan. Reduce the heat, cover tightly, and continue cooking 20 minutes.

9. Add the bean mixture to the meat mixture and stir to blend.

10. Pour the cassoulet into a heatproof baking dish, about 15 by 10 by 3 inches. Cover the cassoulet with a layer of diagonal kielbasa slices. Sprinkle with the bread crumbs and melted butter.

11. Place in the oven and bake 10 minutes or until ready to serve.

   Yield: 10 to 12 servings.

Pork Burgers with Garlic and Cumin

I enjoy the challenge of turning ground beef, pork, veal, or chicken into a spectacular dish. One of my family's favorite recipes is a fantasy that I created one winter's day from the foods I found at hand after I had purchased a pound or so of lean ground pork. I chopped up a few cornichons—those small tarragon-flavored sour gherkins—and added them. I used an ample amount of Dijon-style mustard, chopped onion, and garlic. Once the mixture was cooked (about twelve minutes to make certain the pork was well done), I made a skillet sauce of reduced chicken broth and added a bit of tomato paste for color and taste.

   1½ pounds lean ground pork
   2 tablespoons vegetable oil
   1 cup finely chopped onions
   ½ teaspoon finely minced garlic
   ½ cup finely chopped sour pickles, preferably cornichons

¼ teaspoon ground cumin
2 tablespoons Dijon-style mustard
1 egg, lightly beaten
1 cup fine fresh bread crumbs
1 cup fresh or canned chicken broth
Salt to taste if desired
Freshly ground pepper to taste
2 tablespoons red-wine vinegar
1 teaspoon tomato paste
1 tablespoon butter

1. Put the pork in a bowl and set aside.

2. Heat 1 tablespoon oil over medium-high heat in a small skillet and add the onions and garlic. Cook, stirring, until wilted. Cool briefly and add to the pork. Add the chopped pickles.

3. Add the cumin, mustard, egg, ½ cup bread crumbs, ¼ cup broth, salt, and pepper. Blend well with your fingers.

4. Shape the mixture into 8 patties, each about 4 inches in diameter and ½ inch thick. Put the remaining ½ cup bread crumbs on a flat surface and coat patties all over with them.

5. Heat the remaining tablespoon oil over medium heat in a skillet large enough to hold the patties in one layer. Cook on one side 4 to 5 minutes and carefully turn the patties with a pancake turner or spatula. Continue cooking 8 minutes. Transfer the patties to a warm platter.

6. Pour off the fat from the skillet and add the vinegar. Cook briefly, stirring, and add the remaining ¾ cup chicken broth and the tomato paste. Cook, stirring, about 5 minutes or until reduced to about ½ cup. Swirl in the butter and strain the sauce through a sieve. Pour the sauce over the patties and serve.

Yield: 4 servings.

◆ ◆ ◆

Lamb & Veal

Parsleyed Rack of Lamb

One of the most elegant and festive dishes for entertaining is rack of lamb with parsley. There are many ways to vary this preparation. You may alter the herbs by using a bit of dried rosemary. You could, if you wish, vary this by using crumbled dried oregano or chopped fresh tarragon. You could also, before adding the bread crumbs, smear the rack all over with a good imported mustard.

> 2 racks of lamb, about 2½ pounds
> Salt and freshly ground pepper to taste
> 2 tablespoons olive oil
> ½ cup fine fresh bread crumbs
> 3 tablespoons chopped parsley
> 1 clove garlic, minced fine
> 1 shallot, minced fine
> 2 tablespoons butter, melted

1. Have the butcher hack or saw off the chine bone (the flat, continuous bone at the top of the ribs), leaving the meat exposed.

2. Preheat the broiler to high. If the oven is heated separately, preheat it to 500 degrees.

3. Using your fingers and a sharp knife, pull and slice off the top thick layer of fat from the racks of lamb. The loins and ribs should be almost clean of fat. Hack off the ends of the ribs, leaving about 1½ inches of the ribs intact and extending from the loin meat. Sprinkle the racks with salt and pepper.

4. The baking dish should be large enough to hold the racks of lamb in one layer. Place the racks, meat side down, in the dish and brush the meat with 1 tablespoon olive oil.

5. Meanwhile, combine the bread crumbs, parsley, garlic, shallot, and 1 table-spoon olive oil in a bowl.

6. Place the racks of lamb under the broiler and cook 3 minutes. Turn and cook 3 minutes more.

7. Sprinkle the meaty side of the ribs with the bread crumb mixture. Pour the butter over the ribs. Place in the oven and bake 8 to 10 minutes, depending on the doneness desired.

   Yield: 4 to 6 servings.

Roast Leg of Lamb with Rosemary

1 leg of lamb, 6 to 7 pounds
3 cloves garlic, cut into 12 slivers
1 tablespoon vegetable oil
4 sprigs fresh thyme or 2 teaspoons dry
1 tablespoon chopped fresh rosemary or 2 teaspoons dry
  Salt and freshly ground pepper to taste
1 medium onion, peeled and cut in half crosswise
¾ cup water

1. Preheat the oven to 425 degrees.

2. Prepare the leg of lamb for roasting. (Follow steps 1 through 4 of instructions on page 226.) Set the hipbone aside.

3. With a paring knife, make 12 small incisions in the meat and insert a sliver of garlic in each.

4. Rub the lamb with the oil and place it in a roasting pan. Rub with the thyme and rosemary and sprinkle with salt and pepper. Put an onion half on each side.

5. Roast the lamb on the bottom rack of the oven, basting every 15 to 20 minutes. After 1 hour, remove all the fat from the pan and add the water.

6. Continue roasting for 15 minutes or until the internal temperature reaches 140 degrees for medium-rare.

7. Remove from the oven and place the bone under the roast to serve as a rack in the pan. Keep warm for 15 minutes. Carve and serve with the pan gravy.

   Yield: 8 servings.

Charcoal-Grilled Butterflied Leg of Lamb Provençal Style

    1 leg of lamb with bone in (8 pounds), or a 5½-pound boned leg of
        lamb, butterflied and trimmed
      Freshly ground pepper to taste
  ¼ cup olive oil
    3 tablespoons whole white mustard seeds
    3 tablespoons finely chopped fresh tarragon
    1 tablespoon minced garlic
    4 sprigs fresh thyme or 1 teaspoon dry
    2 tablespoons chopped fresh rosemary or 1 teaspoon dry
    1 teaspoon fennel seeds
    1 bay leaf, crumbled
  ¼ cup tarragon vinegar
      Salt to taste
    4 tablespoons butter

1. Preheat a charcoal grill or the broiler.

2. Prepare the lamb for grilling (see pages 226–27). Lay the lamb out flat and
   sprinkle it generously with pepper on all sides.

3. Put the oil in a baking dish large enough to hold the lamb. Add the lamb and
   sprinkle it on both sides with the mustard seeds, tarragon, garlic, thyme,
   rosemary, fennel seeds, bay leaf, vinegar, and salt. Turn and rub the lamb so
   it is evenly coated with the ingredients. It is by no means essential that the
   lamb be refrigerated before cooking. If it is, however, let it return to room
   temperature before cooking.

4. If a grill is used, put the lamb flat on the grill. Heat the marinade briefly and
   set it aside. If the broiler is used, place the lamb under the broiler 4 or 5
   inches from the heat. Cook the lamb, uncovered, on the grill or under the
   broiler about 10 minutes. Turn and cook 10 minutes on the second side.

5. Transfer the lamb to the dish of marinade. Dot with the butter.

6. Let the meat rest 10 or 20 minutes before carving. Slice the meat thinly. Serve
   it with the pan gravy. Serve rare or well done according to the desires of each
   guest.

   Yield: 6 or more servings.

*Cuisine
Rapide
226*

PREPARING A LEG OF LAMB FOR GRILLING

1. Remove most but not all of the outer fat.

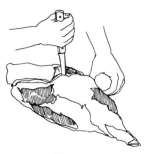

2. Find the hipbone with the tip of a boning knife—it runs roughly at a 45-degree angle from the leg bone. Run the knife along the hipbone on all sides to sever the meat.

3. You will see the ball joint and socket that connect the leg to the hip. Cut through the tendons that join the ball joint and socket.

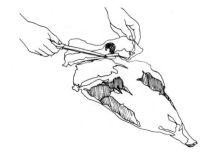

4. Remove the hipbone.

5. Turn the lamb on the other side. Cut from the socket to the end of the leg.

6. Continue cutting all around the leg bone to sever the meat.

PREPARING A LEG OF LAMB FOR GRILLING

7. Remove the leg bone and all the sinew and fat inside.

8. Split the meat as shown to form a butterfly-like pattern.

Haricots d'Agneau

(BRAISED LAMB WITH BEANS)

THE BEANS:

1 pound dried lima beans or any small white beans
7 cups water
4 sprigs fresh thyme or 1 teaspoon dry
1 bay leaf
1 medium onion stuck with 2 cloves
4 large carrots, trimmed and scraped
Salt to taste

THE LAMB:

3 pounds lean lamb shoulder, cut into 2-inch cubes including the bones
Salt and freshly ground pepper to taste
1 cup chopped onion
1 tablespoon chopped garlic
1 cup dry white wine
1 cup water
1 28-ounce can crushed tomatoes
4 sprigs fresh thyme or 1 teaspoon dry
1 bay leaf

1. To prepare the beans, soak them overnight in cold water.

2. Drain the beans, transfer them to a saucepan, and add the water, thyme, bay leaf, onion, carrots, and salt. Bring to a boil and simmer for 45 minutes or until the beans are tender, skimming the foam that collects on the surface.

3. To prepare the lamb, sprinkle the meat with salt and pepper. Heat a nonstick skillet large enough to hold the meat in one layer. Do not add fat. Add the cubed meat and cook, stirring, until well browned on all sides, about 10 to 15 minutes.

4. Transfer the meat to a heavy cast-iron skillet. Add the onion and garlic. Cook and stir over medium heat for 3 minutes. Add the wine, water, tomatoes, thyme, bay leaf, and salt and pepper to taste. Stir well, cover, and simmer for about 1½ hours or until done.

5. When the lamb is cooked, drain the beans, reserving 1 cup liquid. Remove the bay leaf, onion with cloves, and carrots. Remove the cloves from the onion. Cut the onion and carrots into ½-inch cubes. Add the beans, carrots, and onion to the lamb. Simmer 5 minutes. If desired, transfer to an oven-proof serving dish and place under the broiler until lightly browned on top.

Yield: 8 servings.

NOTE: If the final dish seems too thick, add some of the reserved bean liquid.

Lamb and White Beans with Vegetables

    1 tablespoon vegetable oil
    4 pounds lean lamb stew meat from the leg or shoulder, cut into
        ¾-inch cubes
      Salt and freshly ground pepper to taste

2 cups coarsely chopped carrots
2 cups coarsely chopped onions
1 tablespoon chopped garlic
2 bay leaves
1 teaspoon dry thyme
1 cup white wine
1 cup canned crushed tomatoes
1 tablespoon tomato paste
3 cups fresh or canned chicken broth
9 cups water
1 pound white beans, soaked in water overnight
1 carrot, peeled
1 whole onion stuck with 1 clove
1 clove garlic, peeled
½ cup chopped parsley

1. Preheat the oven to 350 degrees.

2. Heat the oil in a heavy cast-iron skillet over high heat, add half the meat, and brown it on all sides. Season with salt and pepper. Remove the meat from the pot, set aside, and brown the remaining meat. When that is browned, add the already cooked meat with the chopped carrots, onions, and garlic. Add 1 bay leaf and the thyme and cover with the white wine, tomatoes, tomato paste, broth, and 8 cups water. Bring to a boil, cover, and simmer in the oven for 1 hour.

3. Meanwhile, place the beans in a large pot, add the peeled carrot, the onion stuck with the clove, remaining bay leaf, and the peeled garlic clove. Cover with the remaining 1 cup water and season with salt. Bring to a boil, cover, and simmer for about 1 hour or until soft.

4. Drain the beans and reserve 1 cup cooking liquid, the carrot, and the onion. Remove the clove from the onion. Chop the carrot and onion into ½-inch cubes. Add the beans, carrot, and onion to the lamb with the reserved cooking liquid. Stir well. Return the pot to the oven and cook 15 minutes longer or until tender. Remove the pot from the oven and check for salt and pepper. Sprinkle with the parsley and serve.

Yield: 8 to 10 servings.

Lamb Shanks with Lentils

1 pound dried lentils
2 cloves garlic, minced
2 sprigs fresh rosemary, chopped, or 1 tablespoon dry
6 lamb shanks (about 7 pounds), trimmed of excess fat
  Salt and freshly ground pepper to taste
1 tablespoon olive oil
9 cups water
1 bay leaf
2 tablespoons butter
1 cup chopped onions
1 tablespoon chopped garlic mixed with ½ teaspoon dry thyme
1½ cups chopped leeks
2 cups canned crushed tomatoes
  Chopped parsley for garnish

1. Preheat the oven to 425 degrees. Inspect the lentils for small stones or spoiled beans. Rinse thoroughly in cold water.

2. Combine the minced garlic and rosemary and rub the mixture over the lamb shanks. Sprinkle with salt and pepper. Rub the olive oil over the shanks. Place in a roasting pan and cook for 1 hour.

3. Meanwhile, place the lentils in a deep pot with 7 cups water, the bay leaf, and salt to taste. Bring to a boil and simmer about 30 minutes or until the lentils are soft.

4. Melt the butter in a frying pan over medium heat and sauté the onions and garlic-thyme mixture for 5 minutes or until they wilt. Add the leeks and salt and pepper to taste. Add the tomatoes, stir well, and cook over medium-low heat for 2 minutes.

5. Drain the lentils, remove the bay leaf, and add the lentils to the tomato mixture. Simmer for 15 to 20 minutes.

6. After the shanks are cooked, remove the pan from the oven and pour off the fat. Add the remaining 2 cups water to the pan and cover the shanks loosely with foil. Reduce the oven to 350 degrees and cook 30 minutes more or until tender.

7. Serve shanks with the pan gravy, lentils, and a sprinkling of chopped parsley.

   Yield: 6 servings.

Medallions of Lamb with Tomatoes and Basil

       2 skinless, boneless loins of lamb, about 1½ pounds
       4 ripe plum tomatoes, about ¾ pound
       3 tablespoons olive oil
       1 teaspoon finely chopped garlic
      12 fresh basil leaves, chopped
          Salt and freshly ground pepper to taste
       1 teaspoon ground cumin
       3 tablespoons butter
       4 peeled garlic cloves
       4 sprigs fresh thyme or ½ teaspoon dry
       2 tablespoons chopped shallots
      ½ cup water

1. Cut the lamb into 12 pieces of equal size.

2. Remove the skin and seeds of the tomatoes and cut them into ¼-inch chunks. There should be about 1½ cups.

3. Heat 2 tablespoons of the olive oil in a small saucepan and add the chopped garlic. Cook briefly but do not brown. Add the tomatoes, basil leaves, salt, and pepper. Stir and simmer 5 minutes. Keep warm.

4. Sprinkle the lamb with cumin, salt, and pepper.

5. Heat the remaining tablespoon olive oil with 1 tablespoon butter in a non-stick skillet large enough to hold the lamb in one layer. Add the lamb, garlic

cloves, and thyme. Brown the lamb quickly on all sides and cook over relatively high heat about 4 minutes for rare. Remove the lamb pieces to a warm platter.

6. Add the shallots to the pan and cook briefly, stirring, until wilted. Add the water. Bring to a boil and cook 1 minute. Swirl in the remaining 2 tablespoons butter and any juices that have accumulated around the lamb. Blend well. Taste for seasoning. Remove garlic cloves if desired. Keep warm.

7. Divide the tomato sauce equally on 4 plates. Place 3 pieces of lamb over the sauce. Spread some shallot sauce over the lamb pieces.

   Yield: 4 servings.

Lamb Curry

I have carried with me a recipe for homemade curry for decades—ever since my days as a chef's apprentice in Paris. It consists of diced apples and bananas cooked with onion, celery, garlic, and curry powder. The degree of hotness depends on how much curry powder is added.

My version is what might be called an all-purpose curry sauce, for it can be blended with sautéed shrimp, chicken, or meat. On one occasion, I used a very good and tender loin of lamb.

The important thing about preparing the lamb, which is cut into thin slices, is that it must be cooked quickly in order to assure the best flavor and texture. If the lamb is cooked too long before it is added to the sauce, it is apt to become dry and less tasty. And once it is added to the still-simmering sauce, it should be removed from the heat to prevent further cooking.

      1 loin of lamb (2½ pounds), boned and with the fat removed
    ½ cup raisins
      3 tablespoons butter
    ½ cup finely chopped onion

$^1/_4$ cup finely chopped celery
$^3/_4$ cup finely diced apple
$^1/_2$ cup finely diced banana
 1 teaspoon finely minced garlic
2 to 3 tablespoons curry powder, preferably homemade
    (see page 293)
$^1/_2$ cup crushed Italian tomatoes
 1 cup fresh or canned chicken broth
 1 bay leaf
    Turmeric Rice (see page 282)

1. Place the loin on a flat surface and cut it diagonally into $^1/_4$-inch slices.

2. Soak the raisins in warm water to cover for about 30 minutes.

3. Heat 2 tablespoons butter in a saucepan and add the onion. Cook, stirring, until wilted. Add the celery, apple, banana, garlic, and curry powder. Cook briefly and add the tomatoes. Add the broth and bay leaf. Bring to a boil and simmer for 10 minutes. Remove the bay leaf. Pour and scrape the mixture into a food processor. Blend until smooth. There should be about 2 cups.

4. Return the sauce to the saucepan and heat. Drain the raisins and add them.

5. Heat the remaining tablespoon butter in a skillet and, when it is quite hot and starting to brown, add the meat. Cook over high heat, stirring constantly to separate the pieces and cook them evenly. Cook about 1 or 2 minutes, no longer. Add the meat to the simmering sauce and remove from the heat. Do not let the meat cook in the sauce but serve it immediately. Serve with the rice.

    Yield: 2 or 3 servings.

◆ ◆ ◆

Country-Style Lamb Loaf

2 pounds ground lean lamb
1 tablespoon vegetable oil
1 cup finely chopped onion
1 cup finely diced celery
1 cup finely chopped green peppers
½ cup coarsely chopped mushrooms, about ¼ pound
1 teaspoon minced garlic
Salt and freshly ground pepper to taste
⅛ teaspoon freshly grated nutmeg
1 teaspoon ground cumin
2 teaspoons Worcestershire sauce
⅛ teaspoon Tabasco sauce
1 tablespoon Dijon-style mustard
½ cup fine fresh bread crumbs
1 egg, lightly beaten

1. Preheat the oven to 400 degrees.

2. Put the meat in a mixing bowl and set aside.

3. Heat the oil in a saucepan and add the onion, celery, green peppers, mushrooms, and garlic. Cook, stirring, over medium-high heat until the vegetables are wilted and the moisture is evaporated. Cool briefly.

4. Add the cooked vegetables to the meat. Add the salt, pepper, nutmeg, cumin, Worcestershire sauce, Tabasco sauce, mustard, bread crumbs, and egg. Blend well with your fingers.

5. Pack the mixture in a 6-cup loaf pan. Smooth the top.

6. Place the pan in the oven and bake 50 minutes. Remove from the oven and let stand 10 minutes. Slice and serve.

   Yield: 6 or more servings.

◆ ◆ ◆

Curried Lamb Meatballs

This dish begins with ground lamb, although beef or pork could also be used. I season the meat with cumin and coriander, two spices commonly used in Indian food. I prepare a sauce separately using chopped apples and bananas to give a nice balance to the spiciness of the meatballs. Incidentally, this dish could be made hours in advance and reheated; leftovers are also good when reheated a day or so later with a bit of broth to dilute the sauce. Rice and chutney are traditional accompaniments for curried food.

$1^1/_4$ pounds ground lean lamb

2 tablespoons butter

$1^1/_4$ cups finely chopped onions

2 teaspoons finely minced garlic

1 teaspoon ground cumin

1 teaspoon ground coriander

$^1/_2$ cup finely chopped fresh coriander or parsley

$^1/_2$ cup fine fresh bread crumbs

1 egg, lightly beaten

  Salt to taste if desired

  Freshly ground pepper to taste

1 tablespoon curry powder, preferably homemade (see page 293)

1 cup finely diced apple

$^1/_2$ cup finely diced banana

$^1/_4$ cup canned crushed tomatoes

$1^1/_2$ cups fresh or canned chicken broth

1 bay leaf

1 tablespoon vegetable oil

  Rice with Mushrooms and Pistachios (see page 283)

1. Put the lamb in a mixing bowl.

2. Heat 1 tablespoon butter in a small skillet and add $^1/_2$ cup onion and 1 teaspoon garlic. Cook briefly, stirring, until wilted. Sprinkle with the cumin and ground coriander and stir. Cool briefly.

3. Scrape the onion mixture onto the lamb. Add the fresh coriander, bread crumbs, egg, salt, and pepper. Blend well with your fingers. Shape the mixture into 20 balls.

4. Heat the remaining tablespoon butter in a saucepan and add the remaining $^3/_4$ cup onions, 1 teaspoon garlic, and the curry. Cook, stirring, until the onions are wilted. Add the apple and banana and stir to blend.

5. Add the tomatoes, broth, and bay leaf and bring to a boil. Simmer 15 minutes. Remove the bay leaf and pour the mixture into a food processor or blender. Blend thoroughly. Return the mixture to a saucepan. Bring to a simmer.

6. Meanwhile, heat the oil in a heavy nonstick skillet and add the meatballs. It may be necessary to use 2 skillets or brown the meatballs in 2 batches. Turn the meatballs so that they brown evenly, about 5 minutes.

7. Add the meatballs to the sauce, cover, and simmer about 15 minutes.

Yield: 4 to 6 servings.

NOTE: Leftover meatballs are good when reheated.

Lamb Burgers with Feta Cheese

There is no reason hamburgers have to be made only with ground beef. All sorts of interesting textures and flavors can be achieved by mixing ground meats of other types, such as turkey, pork, veal, and lamb.

One of my favorite combinations is ground lamb and cumin, which has a distinctly Middle Eastern taste. I sprinkle the lamb patties with a small amount of the ground spice and then cook them in a skillet or on the grill. Then I top the patties with crumbled feta cheese and run them under the broiler.

$1\frac{1}{2}$ pounds ground lean lamb
Salt to taste if desired
Freshly ground pepper to taste
$\frac{1}{4}$ teaspoon ground cumin
$\frac{1}{4}$ teaspoon red pepper flakes
2 teaspoons finely chopped fresh rosemary or 1 teaspoon dry
$\frac{3}{4}$ cup crumbled feta cheese
4 teaspoons finely chopped parsley

1. Divide the lamb into 8 portions of equal size. Shape each into a patty and sprinkle on both sides with salt and pepper.

2. Sprinkle the top of each patty with an equal amount of cumin, pepper flakes, and rosemary. Pat to help the herb and spices adhere.

3. The patties may be broiled or cooked in a skillet. If broiled, preheat the broiler. Place the patties on a baking sheet and place about 3 inches from the heat. Broil 2 minutes for rare, 4 minutes for well done. Turn the patties and cook 1 minute for rare, 2 minutes for well done.

4. If the patties are cooked in a skillet, select one large enough to hold them in one layer. Brush the skillet with a little oil and heat thoroughly. Cook the patties over medium-high heat for 2 minutes for rare, 4 minutes for well done. Turn the patties and continue cooking 1 minute for rare, 2 minutes for well done.

5. Top each patty with a portion of feta cheese. Place under the broiler about 3 inches from the heat. Broil about 1 minute. Dot the center of each patty with ½ teaspoon parsley.

   Yield: 4 servings.

Moussaka with Feta Cheese

Moussaka is among my favorite Greek dishes. While moussaka is traditionally made with eggplant, it may be also made with such vegetables as green beans, potatoes, or artichokes. The only invariable ingredient seems to be ground meat.

I once created a version that I particularly like. It is made with eggplant slices sautéed in olive oil, then layered with a meat sauce, a tomato-flavored white sauce, and a topping of crumbled feta cheese. (Although the cheese most often called for is kefalotyri, this was not available in my local markets so I used feta instead.)

This moussaka, excellent in small or large quantities, is fine for entertaining. The components could be assembled a day or so in advance and the dish placed in the oven shortly before serving.

1 eggplant, about 1½ pounds
1 tablespoon olive oil
1 cup finely chopped onion
2 teaspoons finely minced garlic
1½ pounds ground lean meat, preferably lamb although beef is acceptable
Salt to taste if desired
Freshly ground pepper to taste
½ teaspoon cayenne pepper
¼ teaspoon ground cinnamon
¼ cup dry red wine
½ cup fresh or canned beef broth
2 tablespoons tomato paste
1¼ cups canned crushed tomatoes
1 tablespoon butter
2 tablespoons flour
1 cup milk
1 egg yolk
5 or more tablespoons corn or olive oil
½ pound feta cheese, crumbled (about 1½ cups)

1. Preheat the oven to 500 degrees.

2. Trim off the ends of the eggplant. Cut the eggplant into 12 slices of equal width.

3. Heat the olive oil in a skillet and add the onion and garlic. Cook, stirring, until the onion is wilted. Add the meat and cook, chopping down with the edge of a heavy metal spoon to break up any lumps. Add the salt, pepper, cayenne, and cinnamon. Cook, stirring, until the meat loses its raw look.

4. Add the wine, broth, tomato paste, and 1 cup tomatoes and stir. Bring to a boil and cover. Simmer for 10 minutes.

5. Meanwhile, melt the butter in a saucepan and add the flour, stirring with a wire whisk. Add the milk, stirring rapidly with the whisk. Season with salt and pepper. Stir in the remaining ¼ cup tomatoes. Bring to a simmer and cook for 5 minutes. Stir in the egg yolk and remove from the heat.

6. Sprinkle the eggplant slices with salt and pepper. Heat 1 tablespoon corn oil in a large nonstick skillet and add enough eggplant slices to cover the bot-

tom. Cook about 45 seconds on one side; turn the slices and continue cooking for about 45 seconds. Remove the slices and drain. Continue cooking the remaining eggplant in the same manner, adding a little more oil as necessary for each batch.

7. Arrange about a third of the eggplant slices in one layer in the bottom of a 2 1/2 quart baking dish. Spoon a third of the meat sauce over the eggplant slices. Continue making the layers in the same manner, ending with a layer of meat sauce. Spoon the tomato white sauce over all.

8. Sprinkle the cheese over all and place the dish in the oven. Bake 15 minutes. If desired, run the dish briefly under the broiler until the cheese is lightly browned.

   Yield: 6 servings.

Individual Meat Loaves

When I was a youngster in Burgundy, individual meat loaves—some round, some rectangular—were a specialty of most meat shops in the small towns. I suspect that they are still commonplace in most charcuteries in France, where they are sometimes called gâteaux de viande *(meat cakes) or* pains de viande *(meat breads).*

These small individual loaves, made from a mixture of meats, bake in thirty minutes. I use individual soufflé dishes that hold about one and a half cups each.

To my taste, pork provides a certain silkiness, beef a desirable texture, and veal lightness. In combination they provide a superior loaf, although any one meat might be used for the recipe. The meat should be quite lean, although a small percentage of fat is necessary for texture. A quickly made tomato and mushroom sauce is ideal as an accompaniment.

½ pound finely ground lean beef
½ pound finely ground veal
½ pound finely ground lean pork
1 tablespoon butter
1 cup finely chopped onion
½ teaspoon finely minced garlic
1 cup fine fresh bread crumbs
1 egg, lightly beaten
½ cup finely chopped parsley
¼ cup milk
Salt to taste if desired
Freshly ground pepper to taste
⅛ teaspoon freshly ground nutmeg
⅛ teaspoon ground allspice
⅛ teaspoon ground cumin
3 tablespoons freshly grated Parmesan cheese
Tomato Sauce with Mushrooms (recipe follows)

1. Preheat the oven to 425 degrees.

2. Put the meats in a mixing bowl.

3. Melt the butter in a saucepan and add the onion and garlic. Cook, stirring, until they are wilted. Add to the meats with the bread crumbs, egg, parsley, milk, salt, pepper, nutmeg, allspice, and cumin. Blend well.

4. Divide the mixture into 4 equal portions. Pack each portion into a 1½-cup mold, such as an individual soufflé dish. Sprinkle the tops with the cheese.

5. Place in the oven and bake 30 minutes. Run briefly under the broiler until browned and glazed. Let the loaves cool about 5 minutes before unmolding. Spoon the tomato sauce over the loaves and serve. These loaves are excellent when cold and may be used sliced in sandwiches.

    Yield: 4 servings.

Tomato Sauce with Mushrooms

2 tablespoons butter
½ teaspoon finely minced garlic
½ pound mushrooms, thinly sliced (about 4 cups)

3 cups imported canned tomatoes
1 bay leaf
¼ teaspoon dry thyme
  Salt to taste if desired
  Freshly ground pepper to taste

1. Heat the butter in a skillet and add the garlic. Cook briefly, stirring, without browning and add the mushrooms. Cook, stirring, until the mushrooms give up their liquid.

2. Blend the mushrooms to a purée with a food mill or food processor. Heat the purée in a saucepan over medium heat.

3. Add the tomatoes, bay leaf, thyme, salt, and pepper. Simmer, stirring occasionally, about 15 minutes. Remove the bay leaf.

    Yield: about 4 cups.

Veal Chops with Fresh Corn

4 veal loin chops (3 pounds), each about 1 inch thick
  Salt and freshly ground pepper to taste
2 to 4 ears corn on the cob
¼ cup white vinegar
¼ cup flour
2 tablespoons vegetable oil
2 tablespoons butter
3 tablespoons finely chopped shallots
¼ cup dry white wine
½ cup fresh or canned chicken broth
¼ cup heavy cream
1 teaspoon Dijon-style mustard

1. Sprinkle the chops on both sides with salt and pepper.

2. Cut the kernels of corn from the cobs. There should be about 1 cup. Put in a bowl and add the vinegar. Set aside until ready to use. Stir occasionally.

3. Coat the chops on both sides with the flour and shake off the excess.

4. Heat the oil and butter in a heavy skillet large enough to hold the chops in one layer. When it is quite hot, add the chops and cook 10 minutes or until browned on one side. Turn the chops and cook about 12 minutes longer. Transfer to a warm platter.

5. Meanwhile, drain the corn.

6. Drain the oil from the skillet in which the chops cooked. Add the shallots to the skillet. Cook briefly, stirring, and add the corn and wine, stirring. Add any liquid that may have accumulated around the chops. Add the chicken broth and bring to a boil. Cook about 30 seconds.

7. Add the cream and mustard and stir to blend. Add salt and pepper. Cook about 30 seconds and pour the sauce over the chops.

   Yield: 4 servings.

Veal Scaloppine Milanese

  8 large veal scaloppine, about 1½ pounds
    Salt and freshly ground pepper to taste
  1 egg, beaten
  3 tablespoons water
  ¼ to ½ cup plus 1 teaspoon vegetable oil
  ⅓ cup flour
  2 cups fine fresh bread crumbs, sifted
  ½ cup freshly grated Parmesan cheese
  4 tablespoons butter
  1 pound spaghetti, cooked
    Fresh Tomato Sauce (see page 291)

1. Pound the scaloppine lightly without breaking the flesh. Sprinkle on both sides with salt and pepper.

2. Blend the egg, water, 1 teaspoon oil, salt, and pepper in a flat dish.

3. Put the flour in a flat dish.

4. Combine the bread crumbs and Parmesan cheese in another flat dish.

5. Dip the veal, 1 piece at a time, in the flour, shaking off the excess. Dip in the egg mixture to coat well and then dip in the crumbs until well coated. Pat with the flat side of a heavy kitchen knife to make the crumbs adhere.

6. Heat ¼ cup oil in a skillet and cook as many scaloppine as the pan will hold without crowding. Cook about 2 minutes on one side or until golden brown. Cook about 2 minutes on the second side. As the pieces are cooked, transfer them to a warm platter. Continue adding oil to the skillet and cooking the scaloppine until all are cooked.

7. Heat the butter in a clean skillet until it almost browns. Pour this over the veal. Serve with the spaghetti and Fresh Tomato Sauce.

   Yield: 4 servings.

Veal Rolls with Basil

  8 thin veal scaloppine of uniform size, about 1½ pounds
    Salt to taste if desired
    Freshly ground pepper to taste
16 fresh basil leaves, or 2 tablespoons chopped fresh rosemary or 1
     tablespoon dry
½ pound bulk sausage meat (see Note)
¼ cup chopped parsley
¼ pound mushrooms
 3 tablespoons butter
½ cup finely chopped onion
¼ cup dry white wine
½ cup fresh or canned chicken broth

1. Place the veal slices on a flat surface and pound lightly with a flat mallet, taking care not to make holes in the meat.

2. Sprinkle the veal with salt and pepper.

3. Place 2 basil leaves in the center of each piece of veal.

4. Put the sausage meat in a bowl and add 2 tablespoons parsley. Blend well. Divide the mixture into 8 equal portions and place 1 portion in the center of each piece of veal.

5. Fold the sides of each piece of veal toward the center. Fold over the top and bottom of each piece to enclose the filling. Tie each bundle with string.

6. Slice the mushrooms thinly. There should be about 2½ to 3 cups.

7. Heat 2 tablespoons butter in a skillet and add the meat rolls. Cook about 15 minutes, turning often so that they brown evenly all over. Transfer the meat rolls to a platter. Cut off and discard the strings.

8. Pour off the fat from the skillet and add the onion. Cook, stirring, until wilted. Add the mushrooms and cook, stirring, until wilted and lightly browned.

9. Add the wine and cook until reduced by half. Add the broth and cook, stirring, about 3 minutes. Add the remaining 1 tablespoon butter and stir until melted. Add the meat rolls and spoon the sauce over all. Heat briefly and sprinkle with the remaining 2 tablespoons parsley.

Yield: 4 servings.

NOTE: If bulk sausage is not available, you may remove and use the meat from the casings of ½ pound of sausage links.

Julienne of Veal with Mustard Sauce

   1 pound thin veal slices, preferably from the leg
   2 tablespoons butter
     Salt to taste if desired
     Freshly ground pepper to taste
   ½ pound mushrooms, thinly sliced (about 3 cups)
   3 tablespoons finely chopped shallots
   ¼ cup dry white wine
   1 cup heavy cream
   2 tablespoons imported mustard, preferably moutarde de Meaux

1. Cut the veal into julienne strips.

2. Melt the butter in a heavy skillet and, when it bubbles and starts to brown, add the veal. Sprinkle with the salt and pepper. Cook, stirring, over high heat about 1½ minutes. Do not overcook.

3. Using a slotted spoon, transfer the veal to a saucepan.

4. Add the mushrooms and shallots to the skillet in which the veal was cooked. Cook, stirring, about 3 minutes and add the wine. Cook, stirring, about 3 minutes longer or until the mixture is thickened and sauce-like. Add salt and pepper.

5. Add the cream and cook about 1 minute. Stir in the mustard and cook about 2 minutes. There should be about 1¾ cups sauce. Taste the sauce and, if desired, add more mustard. Pour over the veal. Cook only until the veal is heated through.

   Yield: 4 servings.

   NOTE: This dish also works well with turkey or chicken breasts.

◆ ◆ ◆

Julienne of Veal with Paprika and Sour Cream

1 pound thin veal slices, preferably from the leg
Salt and freshly ground pepper to taste
2 tablespoons butter
¼ cup finely chopped onion
2 teaspoons imported paprika
¼ cup dry white wine
¼ cup heavy cream
½ cup sour cream

1. Cut the veal into julienne strips. Sprinkle with salt and pepper.

2. Heat the butter in a skillet and, when it bubbles and starts to brown, add the veal. Cook, stirring, over high heat about 30 seconds.

3. Add the onion and cook, stirring, about 1 minute. Do not overcook. Sprinkle with the paprika and stir.

4. Using a slotted spoon, transfer the veal to a saucepan. Add the wine to the skillet. Cook over high heat about 3 minutes and add the cream. Cook about 1 minute.

5. Add the sour cream and cook about 1 minute. There should be about 1¼ cups sauce. It is not essential to strain this sauce, but it is preferable to put it through a fine sieve. Reheat the sauce and pour over the veal. Heat briefly until the veal is piping hot.

Yield: 4 servings.

NOTE: This recipe works equally well with chicken or turkey meat.

Tendrons de Veau Braisés

(BRAISED BREAST OF VEAL)

  1 7-pound breast of veal, cut across the breast
      to make 6 strips of equal width
 ½ cup flour
    Salt and freshly ground pepper to taste
 ¼ cup vegetable oil
 ½ cup chopped onion
  1 tablespoon chopped celery
  1 tablespoon chopped garlic
  1 cup diced carrots
  1 cup dry white wine
  1 bay leaf
  4 sprigs fresh thyme or 1 teaspoon dry
  3 cups fresh or canned chicken broth
 ½ cup canned crushed tomatoes

1. Halve each of the 6 strips of veal crosswise.

2. Dredge the breast sections in flour seasoned with salt and pepper.

3. Heat the oil in a large cast-iron skillet over medium heat. Add the veal pieces, turning often to brown all over, about 10 minutes.

4. Drain the fat from the skillet and add the onion, celery, garlic, and carrots. Cook, stirring, for 2 minutes. Add the wine, bay leaf, thyme, broth, and tomatoes. Bring to a boil, cover, and simmer for 2 hours or until the meat is well cooked.

5. Remove the excess fat if necessary, then remove the bay leaf.

    Yield: 6 to 10 servings.

◆ ◆ ◆

Veal Shanks with Oriental Vegetables

1 veal shank, about 3 pounds
4 cloves garlic, each cut lengthwise into 3 strips
Freshly ground pepper to taste
2 tablespoons butter
3 cups fresh or canned chicken broth
2 cups water
2 tablespoons light soy sauce
2 whole cloves
1 cup white wine
1½ cups scallions, cut into 1-inch pieces
5 cups kale, coarsely chopped (about 5 cups)
½ head Chinese cabbage, coarsely chopped (about 5 cups)
3 parsnips, cut lengthwise into 3 or 4 strips
½ cup chopped fresh coriander
½ pound snow peas
1½ cups bean sprouts

1. Make small incisions all over the veal shank and insert the strips of garlic. Sprinkle the pepper over the meat.

2. Melt the butter in a large kettle over medium-high heat. Sear the veal on all sides but do not brown it. Add the broth, water, soy sauce, cloves, and wine. Bring to a boil, cover, and simmer for 1 hour and 15 minutes or until tender. Add the scallions, kale, Chinese cabbage, and parsnips. Cook for 15 minutes. Add the coriander, snow peas, and bean sprouts and cook for 5 minutes. Taste for seasoning. Add salt if necessary.

   Yield: 6 servings.

Veal Meatballs Avgolemono

I have always been interested in how different cultures come up with their own repertoire of seasonings. One of the most fascinating regional flavors is the Greek blend of eggs and lemon juice called avgolemono. *I have occasionally dined in the homes of Greek friends and been regaled with* avgolemono *soup and stuffed vine leaves filled with meat and served with the sauce on top. The sauce is easily made with either a whole egg or an egg yolk plus a generous amount of lemon juice. Unless you are an experienced cook, it would be best to use a small amount of cornstarch in the preparation of an* avgolemono *sauce.*

The avgolemono *offered here is made by poaching the meatballs in a broth, which is then converted into the sauce. The meatballs, which are simple to make and easy to cook, are delicate in flavor. Although I use veal in my preparation, you could substitute ground lamb or pork.*

1¼	pounds ground veal
3	tablespoons butter
1	cup finely chopped onion
2	teaspoons minced fresh garlic
½	cup fine fresh bread crumbs
2	tablespoons finely chopped dill
⅛	teaspoon freshly grated nutmeg
	Salt to taste if desired
	Freshly ground pepper to taste
1½	cups fresh or canned chicken broth
2	eggs
1	tablespoon cornstarch
⅓	cup fresh lemon juice

1. Put the veal in a mixing bowl.

2. Heat 1 tablespoon butter in a skillet and add ½ cup onion and the garlic. Cook over medium-high heat, stirring, until wilted. Cool. Add to the veal.

3. Add the bread crumbs, 1 tablespoon dill, the nutmeg, salt, and pepper. Blend well. Shape the mixture into 28 balls of equal size, each about 2 inches in diameter.

4. Heat the remaining 2 tablespoons butter in a casserole and add the remaining ½ cup onion. Cook briefly until wilted. Add the veal balls and cook,

turning gently to brown lightly. Add the broth and bring to a boil. Cover and simmer 10 minutes.

5. Meanwhile, beat the eggs with a wire whisk in a bowl until well blended. Add the cornstarch and continue beating until thoroughly smooth and blended. Beat in the lemon juice.

6. Pour 1 cup liquid from the meatballs into the egg mixture. Beat to blend.

7. Pour this mixture into the meatballs with their liquid and stir. Cook over low heat until thickened. Sprinkle with the remaining 1 tablespoon dill and serve.

   Yield: 4 servings.

Ginger-Flavored Veal Loaf

Fresh ginger, chopped or shredded, lends an intriguing Oriental zest to many dishes that used to be considered wholly Western. A basic meat loaf made of veal displays a whole new personality after a tablespoon of chopped fresh ginger is added.

The veal and ginger combination here can be made in only forty minutes. You may choose to add a fresh tomato sauce lightly flavored with rosemary.

> 2 pounds ground lean veal
>   Salt to taste if desired
>   Freshly ground pepper to taste
> 1 tablespoon butter
> 3/4 cup finely chopped onion
> 3/4 cup finely diced celery
> 1 teaspoon finely minced garlic
> 2 cups bread cubes
> 1/2 cup milk
> 1 egg, lightly beaten
> 1/2 teaspoon ground cumin
> 1/4 teaspoon freshly grated nutmeg
> 1 tablespoon finely minced fresh ginger
>   Fresh Tomato Sauce (see page 291)

1. Preheat the oven to 425 degrees.

2. Put the veal in a mixing bowl and add salt and pepper.

3. Heat the butter in a saucepan and add the onion, celery, and garlic. Cook, stirring occasionally, until wilted. Do not brown. Cool.

4. Combine the bread cubes, milk, egg, cumin, nutmeg, and ginger and blend until the bread is softened.

5. Add the bread mixture and onion mixture to the meat. Blend thoroughly with your hands.

6. Pack the mixture into a 6-cup loaf pan, smoothing the top. Bake 40 minutes or until the internal temperature on a meat thermometer is 150 degrees. The meat loaf may be served at this point. If time permits it is best to let it stand 20 minutes before slicing. Serve with the tomato sauce.

Yield: 4 to 6 servings.

Foie de Veau Lyonnaise aux Câpres

(SAUTÉED CALF'S LIVER WITH ONIONS AND CAPERS)

Foie de veau Lyonnaise *is thinly sliced calf's liver cooked quickly in very hot oil and then blended with browned onions and a dash of red-wine vinegar. When I glanced at the bottle of capers in my refrigerator one day, it occurred to me that they might be a natural complement to the liver in the same way as the touch of vinegar. The salty capers add a lovely counterpoint to the sweet onions.*

6 thin slices calf's liver, about 1½ pounds
Salt to taste if desired
Freshly ground pepper to taste
2 tablespoons olive oil
2 cups thinly sliced onions
2 whole cloves
¼ cup corn oil
3 tablespoons butter
⅓ cup drained capers
1 tablespoon red-wine vinegar
2 tablespoons finely chopped parsley

1. Trim away and discard any tough membranes in the liver slices. Cut the slices into thin strips about ¼-inch wide. Sprinkle with salt and pepper.

2. Heat the olive oil in a small heavy skillet and add the onions and cloves. Cook, stirring often, over medium-high heat about 10 minutes or until the onions are golden brown. Reduce the heat as necessary. Do not allow the onions to burn or they will be bitter.

3. When the onions are almost ready, heat a wide heavy skillet and add 2 tablespoons corn oil. When hot and almost smoking, add half the liver strips. Cook over high heat, turning the liver pieces so that they cook evenly. Cook about 3 minutes. Transfer the pieces to a dish.

4. Heat the remaining 2 tablespoons corn oil. When it is very hot, add remaining liver strips. Cook as before. Remove the liver and add to the dish.

5. Pour off the fat from the skillet and wipe it out thoroughly. Return the skillet to the heat and add the butter and capers. Cook, shaking the skillet and stirring, about 1 minute. Add the liver and onions. Stir to blend well.

6. Cook until hot. Sprinkle with the vinegar and toss about 15 seconds. Add salt and pepper to taste. Sprinkle with the parsley and serve.

Yield: 4 servings.

Calf's Liver with Caramelized Apples

4 thin slices calf's liver, about 1¼ pounds
Salt to taste if desired
Freshly ground pepper to taste
2 tablespoons flour
4 Golden Delicious apples, about 1½ pounds
3 tablespoons butter
2 tablespoons brown sugar
2 tablespoons corn, peanut, or vegetable oil
2 tablespoons finely chopped shallots
1 tablespoon vinegar, preferably balsamic
1 tablespoon finely chopped parsley

1. Sprinkle the liver with salt and pepper. Dredge the slices in the flour and shake off the excess.

2. Cut each apple into quarters. Cut away and discard the core and skin of each quarter. Cut the quarters into thin slices. There should be about 5 cups.

3. Heat 1 tablespoon butter in a skillet and add the apple slices. Cook over high heat, shaking the skillet and stirring, about 5 minutes. Sprinkle with the brown sugar and continue cooking, redistributing the apple pieces, about 5 minutes. The apples should be lightly browned.

4. Heat the oil in a nonstick skillet large enough to hold the liver pieces in one layer.

5. Add the liver and cook over high heat about 1½ minutes on each side or until browned all over. Transfer the pieces to a hot serving dish and surround with the apples.

6. Add the remaining 2 tablespoons butter and the shallots to the skillet in which the apples were cooked. Cook briefly, stirring, and add the vinegar. Bring to a boil and pour the sauce over the liver. Sprinkle with the parsley and serve.

Yield: 4 servings.

Pasta
& Rice

Spaghetti with Clams and Green Beans

One evening some friends dropped in unexpectedly, presenting me with the challenge of extending a casual dinner to make enough for company. I had planned to make pasta with clam sauce and needed a way to stretch it. I decided to add the last of my green bean crop to the sauce to add color as well as texture. I cooked the beans al dente, then drained them, reserving the liquid to cook the pasta. Whenever possible I cook pasta in water that has been used to cook vegetables to give it extra flavor.

I drained the pasta when it was just short of al dente, a technique I learned from an Italian chef years ago. I usually finish cooking pasta in the same pan with the sauce, which allows it to absorb both the flavors and the sauce better.

I made the sauce by sautéing garlic in olive oil, then adding tomatoes, red pepper flakes, and clam juice. I also added ¹/₃ cup lemon-flavored vodka. Vodka-spiked pasta sauces have become popular in recent years, a phenomenon that has perplexed me. I have never found that vodka adds much to a sauce except a pleasing alcohol-induced warmth, but the idea of lemon along with it appealed to me. The result was delicious. Of course, the vodka is optional. You could also try fresh lemon juice and vermouth or white wine.

- 18 cherrystone clams, shucked, with clam juice reserved (about 2 cups)
- 1 pound green beans
- 12 cups water
  Salt to taste
- 1 pound imported spaghetti
- 2 tablespoons olive oil
- 1 tablespoon finely chopped garlic
- 5 ripe plum tomatoes, about 1 pound, cut into ¹/₂-inch cubes
- ¹/₈ teaspoon red pepper flakes
- ¹/₃ cup Absolut lemon vodka or regular vodka flavored with the juice of ¹/₂ lemon, optional
- ¹/₃ cup heavy cream
  Freshly ground pepper to taste
- ¹/₂ cup coarsely chopped fresh basil leaves or ¹/₂ cup chopped Italian parsley
  Freshly grated pecorino or Parmesan cheese, optional

1. Chop the clams coarsely; there should be about 1 cup.

2. Trim or break off the ends of the beans and remove the strings. Cut the beans into 2-inch lengths.

3. Bring the water, salted to taste, to a boil in a kettle and add the grean beans. Bring to a simmer and cook for 6 to 7 minutes. Do not overcook; the beans should remain crisp. Drain and reserve the cooking liquid.

4. Bring the reserved cooking liquid to a boil. Add the spaghetti, stir, and cook for about 6 minutes. Drain.

5. Meanwhile, heat the oil in a large skillet. Add the garlic and cook briefly, stirring, without browning. Add the tomatoes, pepper flakes, and reserved clam juice. Cook, stirring, over medium heat until the liquid has been reduced to about 2 cups.

6. Add the drained spaghetti, beans, vodka if desired, cream, and freshly ground pepper. Bring to a simmer. Cook until the spaghetti is al dente, stirring, and add the clams and basil. Toss and cook 1 minute. Serve immediately with pecorino or Parmesan cheese, if desired.

Yield: 4 servings.

Spaghettini with Vegetables and Pepper-Vodka Sauce

  1 bunch broccoli, about 1¼ pounds
  ¼ pound snow peas
  5 plum tomatoes, about 1 pound
    Salt to taste
  ¾ pound spaghettini
  2 tablespoons olive oil
  1 tablespoon finely chopped garlic
  ¼ pound sliced prosciutto, cut into ¼-inch strips
  ⅛ teaspoon red pepper flakes
  ¼ cup pepper vodka
  ½ cup heavy cream

Freshly ground pepper to taste
½ cup grated pecorino Romano cheese
12 basil leaves, coarsely chopped
¼ cup chopped chives

1. Cut the broccoli florets off the stem and cut them into bite-size pieces. Cut away the stem's outer skin. Cut the stem into 1¼-inch lengths, then into ½-inch slices. There should be about 6 cups stems and florets.

2. Trim the snow peas. Core the tomatoes. Drop the tomatoes into boiling water for about 10 to 12 seconds. Drain immediately and peel. The skin should come off easily if you use a paring knife. Cut the tomatoes into ½-inch cubes. There should be about 2½ cups.

3. Bring a saucepan of salted water to a boil and add the broccoli. Bring to a simmer and cook for 1 minute. Add the snow peas and bring to a boil. Cook for 2 minutes. Do not overcook. The vegetables must remain crisp. Drain and reserve the cooking liquid.

4. Bring the reserved cooking liquid to a boil and add the spaghettini. Cook according to package directions. The pasta should be al dente. Drain and reserve ½ cup of the cooking liquid.

5. Heat the oil in a large skillet. Add the garlic and prosciutto. Cook and stir briefly without browning. Add the tomatoes and red pepper flakes and cook, stirring, 1 minute. Add the vodka, cream, salt, and pepper to taste. Bring to a simmer and cook for 1 minute.

6. Transfer the pasta and vegetables to the skillet with the tomato mixture. Add the cheese, basil, chives, and reserved cooking liquid. Bring to a simmer and toss well for 1 minute. Serve immediately.

Yield: 4 servings.

◆ ◆ ◆

Macaroni and Cheese

Salt to taste if desired
1½ cups uncooked elbow macaroni
1 cup milk
½ cup heavy cream
Pinch cayenne pepper
⅛ teaspoon freshly grated nutmeg
¼ cup freshly grated Parmesan cheese

1. Bring 3 quarts water to a boil and add the salt and macaroni. Stir frequently and cook until tender, about 12 minutes. Drain thoroughly.

2. Return the macaroni to the kettle and add the milk, cream, cayenne, and nutmeg. Bring to a boil and cook about 4 minutes or until the liquid thickens. Pour the macaroni into a flat baking dish.

3. Preheat the broiler to high.

4. Sprinkle the top of the macaroni evenly with the cheese. Place the dish under the broiler and broil until the top is lightly browned.

Yield: 4 servings.

Fettuccine with Shrimp and Vegetables

1 zucchini, about ½ pound
1 summer squash, about ½ pound
1¼ pounds unshelled raw shrimp
Salt to taste if desired
½ pound green beans, trimmed and cut into 2-inch lengths
10 ounces fresh or dry fettuccine
2 tablespoons olive oil
1 tablespoon finely minced garlic

  1½ cups cubed ripe tomatoes
   1 cup heavy cream
    Freshly ground pepper to taste
   2 tablespoons butter
   2 tablespoons finely chopped fresh basil

1. Trim the ends of the zucchini and squash. Cut each lengthwise into quarters. Cut each quarter crosswise into thin slices about ¼ inch thick.

2. Peel and devein the shrimp.

3. Bring enough salted water to a boil to cover the beans. Add the beans and simmer 7 minutes. Add the zucchini and squash. Bring to a boil and simmer 2 minutes more.

4. Have a saucepan ready and line it with a sieve. Pour the vegetables into the sieve and reserve both the cooking liquid and vegetables.

5. Put the cooking liquid in a saucepan and add enough water to measure 8 cups. Add salt to taste. Bring to a boil. Add the pasta and return to a boil. If the pasta is fresh, cook it about 5 minutes; if it is dry, cook about 4 minutes longer or to the desired degree of doneness. Drain the pasta and return it to the saucepan.

6. Meanwhile, heat the oil in a nonstick skillet over medium-high heat and add the garlic. Cook, stirring, briefly. Do not allow the garlic to brown. Add the tomatoes and stir for 1 minute over high heat. Add the cooked vegetables and shrimp. Cook, stirring occasionally, about 1½ minutes. Pour in the cream. Add salt and pepper to taste. Bring to a boil and cook about 1 minute. Remove from the heat.

7. Pour and scrape the vegetable mixture over the pasta. Add the butter and basil. Toss and serve.

  Yield: 4 servings.

     ◆ ◆ ◆

Fettuccine with Asparagus

6 asparagus spears, about ¹/₂ pound
Salt to taste if desired
10 ounces fresh fettuccine or ³/₄ pound dry
2 tablespoons butter
Freshly ground pepper to taste
¹/₈ teaspoon freshly grated nutmeg
2 tablespoons finely chopped fresh basil or parsley
¹/₂ cup freshly grated Parmesan cheese

1. Cut off the tough stem ends of each asparagus spear.

2. Cut each spear diagonally into 1-inch lengths. There should be about 1¹/₂ cups. Rinse well and drain.

3. Bring 3 cups water to a boil and add the salt. Add the asparagus and, when the water returns to a boil, cook about 2 minutes. Drain, reserving 2 tablespoons cooking liquid.

4. Drop the fettuccine into boiling salted water. Cook 2 to 2¹/₂ minutes or to desired degree of doneness. Cooking time will range from about 2¹/₂ minutes for fresh pasta to 9 minutes or more for dry. Drain.

5. Heat the butter in the pot in which the pasta was cooked. Add the asparagus and fettuccine. Add salt, pepper, and nutmeg. Add the reserved 2 tablespoons cooking liquid and basil. Toss to blend. Serve hot with Parmesan cheese on the side.

   Yield: 4 servings.

◆ ◆ ◆

Fettuccine with Pecans

    ³/₄ pound fresh or dry fettuccine or other flat noodle
        Salt to taste if desired
     2 tablespoons butter
    ¹/₄ cup finely chopped pecans
    ¹/₈ teaspoon Tabasco sauce
    ¹/₈ teaspoon freshly grated nutmeg
    ¹/₄ cup heavy cream
    ¹/₂ cup finely chopped fresh basil, optional
    ¹/₂ cup freshly grated Parmesan cheese

1. Cook the fettuccine in boiling salted water 9 minutes if dry or 5 minutes if fresh, or to the desired degree of doneness. Drain, reserving ¹/₄ cup cooking liquid.

2. Return the noodles to the kettle and add the butter. Toss and add the reserved cooking liquid, pecans, Tabasco, nutmeg, cream, and basil. Toss to blend.

3. Serve the grated cheese on the side.

    Yield: 4 servings.

Green Pasta with Shrimp and Clams

The fresh-pasta craze in recent years has obscured the fact that almost any dish calling for pasta can be made equally well with many of the excellent dried packaged versions. The differences in flavor and texture are a matter of personal preference. I find that fresh pasta is more delicate and works best with light seafood and vegetable-based sauces; dried pastas have more texture and, depending on the composition, different flavors that marry well with more gutsy sauces.

Either kind would work with the shrimp and clam sauce offered here. I happen to use a good dried spinach pasta, which gives the dish an interesting visual twist. The shrimp

are left whole. The clams are shucked, and, when opening them, it is important to use a sharp clam knife, taking care not to injure yourself in the process.

18 cherrystone clams
   Salt to taste if desired
1/4 cup olive oil
 1 tablespoon finely minced garlic
1/2 teaspoon red pepper flakes
 1 pound medium shrimp (about 32), shelled and deveined
   Freshly ground pepper to taste
24 basil leaves, rinsed and patted dry
 3 tablespoons finely chopped parsley
 1 pound fresh or dry green pasta
 2 tablespoons butter

1. Shuck the clams and reserve the juice. There should be about 3/4 cup raw clams and about 1 cup juice.

2. Chop the clams coarsely.

3. Bring 4 quarts water to a boil and add salt to taste.

4. Heat the oil in a heavy nonstick skillet and add the garlic. Cook briefly without browning. Add the pepper flakes, shrimp, salt, and pepper. Cook, stirring and shaking the skillet, about 1 minute. Add the clams, cook about 15 seconds, and add the basil leaves and parsley. Stir to blend and remove from the heat.

5. Meanwhile, add the pasta to the boiling water and cook about 2 minutes when it returns to a boil. Drain, reserving 1/2 cup cooking liquid. Pour the pasta into a kettle and add the reserved 1 cup clam juice. Heat thoroughly and add the reserved 1/2 cup cooking liquid and butter.

6. Pour and scrape the clam and shrimp mixture onto the pasta. Toss to blend and serve immediately.

   Yield: 4 servings.

◆ ◆ ◆

Paglia e Fieno with Salmon

  1½ pounds skinless, boneless salmon fillets
      Salt to taste
  ½ pound dry green noodle "nests" (see Note)
  ½ pound dry yellow noodle "nests" (see Note)
  4 tablespoons butter
  ⅓ cup finely chopped shallots
  1 small dried red hot pepper, or ⅛ teaspoon red pepper flakes
  ¼ cup dry white wine
      Freshly ground pepper to taste
  1 cup heavy cream
  ⅛ teaspoon freshly grated nutmeg
  2 ounces imported red lumpfish caviar, preferably Danish
  ¼ cup finely chopped fresh basil
  ¼ cup finely chopped chives

1. Cut the salmon lengthwise into 1½-inch widths. Cut each piece diagonally into 1½-inch lengths.

2. Bring 4 quarts water to a boil in a kettle and add salt to taste. Add the green and yellow noodles and bring to a boil, stirring. Cook until al dente.

3. As the pasta cooks, heat 2 tablespoons butter in a nonstick skillet and add the shallots and hot pepper. Cook about 30 seconds, stirring.

4. Add the salmon pieces and cook about 45 seconds, stirring. Add the wine and cook about 45 seconds longer. Add salt and pepper to taste.

5. Add the cream and, when the sauce returns to a boil, cook over high heat about 3 to 4 minutes. Add the nutmeg. Remove the hot pepper.

6. Drain the pasta and return it to the kettle. Add the remaining 2 tablespoons butter and toss. Put the pasta on a platter.

7. Pour the salmon sauce over the pasta. Add the caviar and toss gently. Sprinkle with the basil and chives and serve.

Yield: 4 to 6 servings.

NOTE: Noodle "nests" are sold at most stores carrying imported pasta.

Ziti with Shrimp and Green Beans

½ pound green beans
1¼ pounds shrimp, about 36
¼ cup olive oil
2 teaspoons minced garlic
28-ounce can crushed tomatoes
3 tablespoons tomato paste
Salt to taste if desired
Freshly ground pepper to taste
¾ pound dry ziti No. 2
1 red hot pepper, or ⅛ teaspoon dried red pepper flakes
¼ cup heavy cream

1. Trim the ends of the green beans and cut them into 1-inch lengths. Drop them into boiling salted water to cover and simmer 8 to 10 minutes, depending on size, or until crisp-tender. Drain immediately.

2. Peel and devein the shrimp.

3. Heat 2 tablespoons oil in a saucepan and add 1 teaspoon garlic. Cook briefly and add the tomatoes and tomato paste. Add salt and pepper. Cook, stirring, about 15 minutes or until reduced to about 2½ cups. Remove the hot pepper.

4. Drop the ziti into boiling water and cook about 12 minutes.

5. As the ziti cooks, heat the remaining 2 tablespoons oil in a large heavy skillet and add the shrimp, hot pepper, and remaining 1 teaspoon garlic. Cook, stirring, about 1 minute. Add the green beans and tomato mixture. Bring to a boil and simmer about 1 minute.

6. Drain the ziti and add it to the shrimp mixture. Add the cream. Bring to a boil and serve.

   Yield: 4 servings.

◆ ◆ ◆

Ziti with Prosciutto and Tomato Sauce

5 plum tomatoes (about 1 pound), cored
24 asparagus spears, about 1½ pounds
¼ pound very thinly sliced prosciutto
Salt to taste if desired
¾ pound dry ziti
¼ cup olive oil
1 tablespoon finely minced garlic
Freshly ground pepper to taste
1 cup heavy cream
½ cup coarsely chopped fresh basil
¼ cup freshly grated Parmesan cheese

1. Bring 4 quarts water to a boil for cooking the ziti and vegetables.

2. Cut the tomatoes into ½-inch cubes. There should be about 2½ cups.

3. Scrape the ends of the asparagus spears and cut off and discard about 2 inches of the tough bottoms. Cut off and reserve the asparagus tips, each about 2 inches long. Cut the center portions of the asparagus diagonally into 1-inch pieces. There should be about 4 cups of asparagus including the tips.

4. Stack the prosciutto slices and cut them into ¼-inch-wide strips. There should be about 1¼ cups.

5. Drop the asparagus pieces into the boiling water and cook 2 minutes. Scoop out the asparagus. Let the water continue to boil.

6. Add the salt and ziti. When the water returns to a boil, cook the ziti to the desired degree of doneness, about 12 minutes or longer. Drain the ziti, reserving ½ cup cooking liquid.

7. Meanwhile, heat the oil in a large skillet and add the garlic. Cook briefly, stirring, and add the prosciutto. Add the tomatoes, salt, and pepper and cook, stirring occasionally, about 3 minutes. Add the cream and bring to a boil. Add the ziti and stir. Add the asparagus pieces, basil, and reserved ½ cup cooking liquid. Stir to blend and sprinkle with the cheese. Toss and serve.

Yield: 4 or more servings.

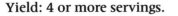

Farfalle and Mussels with Ginger-Mustard Vinaigrette

Here is a quick dish that can be served cool or at room temperature. It combines mussels, zucchini, and tomatoes with a piquant mustard-based sauce and pasta. Notice that I save the steaming juices from the mussels and add them to the pasta's cooking water for extra flavor. This recipe calls for farfalle, the bow-tie-shaped pasta, although many pastas will work.

  3 pounds mussels, well scrubbed and with beards and barnacles
        removed (see page 40)
  2 bay leaves
  6 whole cloves
  4 cups water
  2 zucchini (about ³/₄ pound), cut into ¹/₂-inch chunks
¹/₂ pound imported farfalle pasta (bow ties)
  1 egg yolk
  1 tablespoon Dijon-style mustard
  2 tablespoons red- or white-wine vinegar
     Salt and freshly ground pepper to taste
  1 cup olive or corn oil
     Pinch cayenne pepper
¹/₄ cup finely chopped shallots or scallions
  1 tablespoon finely chopped garlic
  1 tablespoon grated fresh ginger
  2 ripe tomatoes (about ³/₄ pound), peeled and cut into ¹/₂-inch
        cubes
¹/₂ cup coarsely chopped fresh basil or Italian parsley

1. Place the mussels in a saucepan with the bay leaves and cloves. Cover tightly and cook over high heat, shaking the pan occasionally to redistribute the mussels, about 4 minutes or until all the mussels are opened.

2. Remove the mussels with a slotted spoon and set them aside to cool. Strain the broth. There should be about 2¹/₂ cups. Reserve the broth. When the mussels are cool enough to handle, remove the meat and discard the shells.

3. Add the reserved broth and water to a large saucepan or kettle. Bring to a boil and add the zucchini. Cook 3 minutes and remove the zucchini with a slotted spoon. Cool.

4. Add the pasta to the saucepan, stir, and bring to a boil. Cook 15 to 20 minutes or according to package instructions. It should be al dente. Drain well and cool.

5. Meanwhile, put the egg yolk, mustard, vinegar, salt, and pepper in a mixing bowl. Beat the mixture with a wire whisk while slowly adding the oil a few drops at a time at first, then in a slow drizzle. When all the oil is incorporated, add the cayenne, shallots, garlic, and ginger. Blend the sauce well.

6. Place the zucchini, tomatoes, pasta, and mussels in a large bowl. Add the sauce and basil. Toss well. Check the seasoning and serve.

   Yield: 4 servings.

Linguine with Scallops and Broccoli

1 bunch broccoli, about ³/₄ pound
2 tomatoes (about 1 pound), peeled
1 pound mushrooms
2 tablespoons olive oil
¹/₄ cup finely chopped shallots
¹/₄ to ¹/₂ teaspoon red pepper flakes
  Salt to taste if desired
  Freshly ground pepper to taste
³/₄ cup heavy cream
1¹/₂ pounds fresh bay or sea scallops (see Note)
9 ounces linguine, preferably fresh
2 tablespoons butter
¹/₄ cup coarsely chopped basil or finely chopped parsley

1. Cut the broccoli into florets. Peel the stems and cut each lengthwise into quarters. There should be about 4 cups of florets and stems. Drop the broccoli in boiling salted water and, when the water returns to a boil, cook exactly 1 minute. Drain.

2. Cut away the outer thick portion of the tomatoes and cut the pieces into lengthwise strips, each about $1/4$ inch thick. There should be about 2 cups. Chop the inner portion of the tomatoes with their seeds. There should about $3/4$ cup.

3. Cut the mushrooms into thin slices. There should be about 3 cups.

4. Heat the olive oil in a skillet and add the mushrooms. Cook, stirring, about 3 minutes. Add the shallots and stir.

5. Add the chopped inner portion of the tomatoes, the pepper flakes, salt, and pepper. Cook, stirring, about 1 minute and add the cream. Bring to a boil and add the scallops. Cook 30 seconds and add the broccoli. Add the tomato strips and stir.

6. Meanwhile, add the pasta to boiling water. If fresh pasta is used, it will require about 1 to $1 1/2$ minutes of cooking time. If dried pasta is used, cook it to the desired degree of doneness, about 7 to 9 minutes. Drain the pasta and return it to the kettle in which it was cooked. Pour the scallop and broccoli sauce over the pasta. Add the butter and basil and blend gently but thoroughly. Serve immediately.

Yield: 4 or more servings.

NOTE: If bay scallops are used, leave them whole. If sea scallops are used, cut them into quarters.

◆ ◆ ◆

Pasta with Chicken and Asparagus

1 skinless, boneless chicken breast, about 1 pound
1 pound asparagus spears
¾ pound fresh or dry linguine or fettucine
2 tablespoons butter
   Salt and freshly ground pepper to taste
3 tablespoons finely chopped shallots
1 cup heavy cream
1 dried red hot pepper, or ⅛ teaspoon red pepper flakes
⅛ teaspoon freshly grated nutmeg
¼ pound Gorgonzola cheese
2 tablespoons chopped fresh tarragon or 1 teaspoon dry
½ cup freshly grated Parmesan cheese

1. Remove all the sinews and soft cartilage from the chicken breast. Cut the breast into small strips about 1½ inches long and ½ inch wide. There should be about 1½ cups.

2. Scrape and trim the asparagus. Cut off and discard any tough ends. Cut the asparagus diagonally into 1½-inch lengths. Drop the pieces into boiling water and drain.

3. Add the pasta to boiling water and cook it until it is al dente.

4. Meanwhile, heat the butter in a deep skillet. Add the chicken strips and cook, stirring to separate the pieces, quickly. Add salt and pepper to taste. Cook about 30 seconds or just until the chicken changes color.

5. Add the asparagus and stir. Add salt, pepper, and the shallots and cook briefly, about 30 seconds. Add the cream, red hot pepper, and nutmeg and stir.

6. Break the cheese into small lumps and add it. Cook just until the cheese melts. Add a generous grinding of pepper and the tarragon. Remove the hot pepper. Stir. Drain the pasta and add to the sauce. Toss well. Serve with grated Parmesan on the side.

   Yield: 4 to 6 servings.

Egg Noodles with Carrots and Lemon

2 carrots (about ¼ pound), trimmed and scraped
1 tablespoon butter
1 teaspoon grated lemon rind
¼ cup dry white wine
2 tablespoons lemon juice
½ cup heavy cream
⅛ teaspoon freshly grated nutmeg
   Salt to taste if desired
½ pound very thin dry egg noodles
¼ cup freshly grated Parmesan cheese

1. Cut the carrots crosswise into 1-inch lengths. Cut the pieces lengthwise into very thin slices. Stack the slices and cut them into very thin strips. There should be about 1 loosely packed cup.

2. Heat the butter in a saucepan and add the carrot strips and lemon rind. Cook, stirring, about 2 minutes. Add the wine and cook about 1 minute.

3. Add the lemon juice and cook about 3 minutes, stirring occasionally. Add the cream and nutmeg and bring to a boil.

4. Meanwhile, bring 4 quarts water to a boil in a kettle and add salt to taste. Add the noodles and cook 3 minutes or until the noodles achieve the desired degree of tenderness.

5. Drain the noodles and return them to the hot kettle. Add the carrots, lemon sauce, and cheese. Stir to blend and serve immediately.

   Yield: 4 servings.

◆ ◆ ◆

Chicken Livers and Mushroom Ravioli

THE FILLING:

- 1 tablespoon butter
- 2 tablespoons minced shallots
- ½ pound mushrooms, trimmed and minced (about 2 cups)
- ½ pound chicken livers, trimmed and diced (about ¾ cup)
- 1 tablespoon brandy or cognac
- 2 tablespoons heavy cream
- Salt and freshly ground pepper to taste
- 72 wonton skins
- 1 quart fresh or canned chicken broth (or lightly salted water) for poaching
- Leek Sauce (recipe follows)

1. Melt the butter in a saucepan over medium heat. Add the shallots and sauté lightly, about 2 minutes. Add the mushrooms and cook 3 to 5 minutes, stirring often to evaporate the water.

FILLING WONTON SKINS TO MAKE RAVIOLI

Rolling out ravioli dough can be a time-consuming and tricky task. Several years ago I learned of a shortcut that many chefs now use when they want to serve light, thin-skinned ravioli. They use Chinese wonton skins, which are available fresh in Oriental groceries or frozen in many supermarkets.

There are a few tricks to working with fragile wonton wrappers. If fresh, they must be stored in the refrigerator and wrapped in an airtight container. The thinnest ones last only several days before they begin to dry out, so if you are keeping them longer place them, well wrapped, in the freezer. When working with them, always keep unused wrappers covered with a damp cloth or towel to keep them from drying out and cracking. As you make the ravioli, place them on paper towels or a dry cloth and cover them with plastic wrap.

The potential fillings are as varied as your imagination.

FILLING WONTON SKINS TO MAKE RAVIOLI

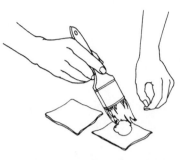

1. Lay 1 wonton skin on a counter and place a small amount of filling in the center. Brush egg wash (a beaten egg) around the perimeter.

3. Use the blunt side of a small cookie cutter to seal the ravioli dough around the filling and give it a circular shape.

2. Place a second skin on top.

4. Trim the excess dough with a larger cookie cutter or a sharp knife. Cover the finished ravioli with a moist towel as you make them to prevent dryness.

2. Add the chicken livers and stir constantly for 1 minute. Add the brandy, stir well, and add the cream. Cook for 2 to 3 minutes, stirring well, or until there is very little moisture left in the pan. Add salt and pepper to taste. Cool to room temperature before using with the wonton skins to make ravioli (see instructions above).

3. Poach the ravioli in the simmering chicken broth, 5 or 6 at a time, for about 1 minute or until they rise to the surface. Drain well on paper towels and keep warm. Serve with the sauce.

Yield: about 36 ravioli.

Leek Sauce

1 tablespoon butter
½ cup chopped onion
¼ cup minced shallots
3 leeks, trimmed, leaving some of the green section, washed, and chopped (about 3 cups)
Salt and freshly ground pepper to taste
Freshly grated nutmeg to taste
1½ cups fresh or canned chicken broth
½ cup heavy cream

1. Heat the butter in a saucepan over medium-high heat and sauté the onion and shallots until wilted, about 2 minutes. Add the leeks and cook several minutes more or until they are soft. Add salt, pepper, and nutmeg to taste.

2. Pour in the broth and bring to a boil. Cover and simmer for 10 minutes. Add the cream, bring to a boil, and remove from the heat. Pour the mixture into a blender and purée well. Keep the sauce warm until serving.

Yield: about 2½ cups.

NOTE: This sauce, and the others that follow, can be made in advance and reheated before serving.

◆ ◆ ◆

Pork and Ginger Ravioli

  2 tablespoons sesame oil
  4 medium pork chops, trimmed well and chopped fine with a large
      knife or heavy cleaver
  1 teaspoon minced garlic
  3 tablespoons minced fresh ginger
  ½ cup fresh or canned water chestnuts
  ⅛ teaspoon red pepper flakes
  2 tablespoons soy sauce
  1 tablespoon dry sherry
  6 tablespoons minced scallions
  1 tablespoon cornstarch mixed with 2 tablespoons dry sherry
  72 wonton skins
  1 quart fresh or canned chicken broth (or lightly salted water) for
      poaching
      Hoisin-Ginger Sauce (recipe follows)

1. Heat the sesame oil in a saucepan over medium heat. Add the pork and stir constantly until it turns white, about 3 to 5 minutes.

2. Add the garlic, ginger, and water chestnuts and stir for 2 minutes. Add the pepper flakes, soy sauce, sherry, and scallions. Stir for 1 minute and add the cornstarch-sherry mixture. Stir well for 30 seconds and remove from the heat. Cool to room temperature before using with the wonton skins to make ravioli (see pages 273–74).

3. Poach the ravioli in the simmering chicken broth, 5 or 6 at a time, for about 1 minute or until they rise to the surface. Drain well on paper towels and keep warm. Serve with the sauce.

   Yield: about 36 ravioli.

   NOTE: You may use a food processor to chop the pork, but do not purée it to a paste. Leave it slightly chunky.

Hoisin-Ginger Sauce

  ½ cup dry white wine
  1 cup fresh or canned chicken broth
  1 tablespoon minced fresh ginger

2 tablespoons hoisin sauce
1 tablespoon cornstarch mixed with 3 tablespoons chicken broth
1 tablespoon chopped fresh coriander, optional
8 tablespoons chopped scallions

1. Heat the wine, broth, ginger, and hoisin sauce in a saucepan over medium heat, mixing well. Bring to a boil, reduce the heat, and simmer for 5 minutes.

2. Add the cornstarch-broth mixture and stir well. Strain the sauce through a fine sieve. Return to the pot, add the coriander and scallions, and keep warm until needed.

Yield: about 1½ cups.

Salmon and Shrimp Ravioli

³/₄ pound medium shrimp
½ pound salmon fillet, skin removed
1 tablespoon butter
8 scallions, minced, including some of the green part
Juice of ½ lemon
1 tablespoon chopped fresh dill
Salt and freshly ground pepper to taste
Cayenne pepper to taste
72 wonton skins
1 quart fresh fish or shrimp stock (or lightly salted water) for poaching
Dill Sauce (recipe follows)

1. Mince the shrimp and salmon with a large knife. Sauté the mixture in the butter with the scallions and lemon juice over medium heat for about 2 minutes, turning constantly with a spatula. You want to remove the raw look but not cook the fish thoroughly. Remove from the heat and add the dill, salt, pepper, and cayenne. Cool to room temperature before using with the wonton skins to make ravioli (see pages 273–74).

2. Poach the ravioli in the simmering stock, 5 or 6 at a time, for about 1 minute or until they rise to the surface. Drain well on paper towels and keep warm. Serve with the sauce.

Yield: about 36 ravioli.

Dill Sauce

> 1 stick plus 1 tablespoon butter, cut into pats
> 3 shallots, minced
> 2 tablespoons white-wine vinegar
> ½ cup fish stock or clam juice
> ¼ cup heavy cream
> 1½ tablespoons minced fresh dill
> Salt and freshly ground white pepper to taste

1. Melt 1 tablespoon butter in a saucepan over medium heat and in it sauté the shallots for 1 minute. Add the vinegar and fish stock. Reduce the liquid over high heat by half, leaving about ¼ cup.

2. Add the cream and reduce the liquid by half again. Place the sauce in a blender and drop in the remaining pats of butter while it is puréeing. Add the dill, purée briefly, and return the sauce to the pan to keep warm until serving. Add salt and white pepper to taste.

Yield: about 1 cup.

NOTE: Because of its richness, this sauce should be used sparingly.

Herbed Cheese Ravioli

    7 ounces Montrachet goat cheese at room temperature
    4 ounces St. André cheese at room temperature
    4 ounces cream cheese or any soft cheese at room temperature
    2 teaspoons chopped fresh rosemary or 1 teaspoon dry
    ¼ cup chopped parsley
    72 wonton skins
       Red Pepper Sauce (recipe follows)

1. Combine the cheeses, rosemary, and parsley in a mixing bowl. Use with the wonton skins to make ravioli (see pages 273–74).

2. Poach the ravioli in 1 quart simmering lightly salted water, 5 or 6 at a time, for about 1 minute or until they rise to the surface. Drain well on paper towels and keep warm. Serve with the sauce.

   Yield: about 36 ravioli.

Red Pepper Sauce

    ½ cup chopped onion
    2 tablespoons butter
    2 red sweet peppers, cored, seeded, and chopped coarsely (about
       2½ cups)
    ½ teaspoon loosely packed saffron threads
       Salt and freshly ground pepper to taste
    ½ cup fresh or canned chicken stock
    ½ cup heavy cream

1. Sauté the onion in the butter over medium-high heat until wilted. Add the red peppers, saffron, salt, and pepper. Stir well and add the stock.

2. Bring the liquid to a boil, cover, and simmer for 10 minutes. Add the cream, stir, and return to a boil. Pour the mixture into a blender and purée well. Keep warm until ready to serve.

   Yield: about 2½ cups.

Orzo with Fresh Tomato Sauce

Orzo is a Greek pasta shaped like rice that is widely available in supermarkets. It is an excellent accompaniment to all sorts of stews, sauces, and vegetables.

Salt to taste if desired
3/4 cup orzo (rice-shaped pasta)
2 tablespoons olive oil
1 teaspoon finely minced garlic
1/2 pound ripe tomatoes, peeled and cut into 1/2-inch cubes
Freshly ground pepper to taste
1/4 teaspoon red pepper flakes
2 tablespoons loosely packed shredded fresh basil or Italian parsley

1. Bring 4 cups water to a boil in a saucepan and add salt to taste. Add the orzo and cook, stirring briefly, about 10 minutes or until tender. Do not overcook. Drain.

2. Meanwhile, heat the oil in a saucepan and add the garlic. Cook briefly, stirring. Do not brown. Add the tomatoes and sprinkle with salt, pepper, and pepper flakes. Stir and bring to a boil.

3. Add the orzo and basil. Stir to blend and serve.

Yield: 4 servings.

Creole Rice with Tomatoes and Herbs

1 cup converted rice
2 tablespoons butter
1/2 cup finely chopped onion
1/2 cup diced tomatoes
Salt to taste if desired
Freshly ground pepper to taste
2 tablespoons finely chopped fresh basil
1 tablespoon fresh lemon juice

1. Rinse the rice and drain it well.

2. Bring 4 cups water to a boil in a saucepan. Add the rice. Cook at a full rolling boil exactly 17 minutes. Drain immediately and return the rice to the saucepan.

3. Meanwhile, heat the butter in a saucepan and add the onion. Cook, stirring, until wilted. Add the tomatoes, salt, and pepper and cook briefly, stirring. Add to the rice and stir. Stir in the basil and lemon juice.

Yield: 4 servings.

Rice Pilaf

2 tablespoons butter
2 tablespoons minced onion
1/2 teaspoon minced garlic
1 cup converted rice
1 1/2 cups fresh or canned chicken broth or water
3 sprigs parsley
1 sprig fresh thyme or 1/4 teaspoon dry
Salt and freshly ground pepper to taste
1 bay leaf

1. Melt 1 tablespoon butter in a saucepan and cook the onion and garlic in it, stirring with a wooden spoon, until the onion is translucent. Add the rice and stir briefly over low heat until the grains are coated with butter.

2. Stir in the broth, making sure there are no lumps in the rice. Add the parsley, thyme, salt, pepper, and bay leaf. Bring to a boil, cover with a close-fitting lid, and simmer for 17 minutes.

3. Remove the cover and discard the parsley, thyme, and bay leaf. Using a fork, stir in the remaining tablespoon butter. If the rice is not to be served immediately, keep covered in a warm place.

Yield: 4 servings.

Turmeric Rice

2 tablespoons butter
2 tablespoons finely chopped onion
½ teaspoon finely minced garlic
1 cup converted rice
1 tablespoon turmeric
1½ cups fresh or canned chicken broth
1 bay leaf
2 sprigs fresh thyme or ½ teaspoon dry
Salt and pepper to taste

1. Melt 1 tablespoon butter in a small saucepan and add the onion and garlic. Cook until wilted. Add the rice and turmeric. Stir to coat.

2. Add the broth, bay leaf, thyme, salt, and pepper. Cover and bring to a boil. Simmer and cook for 17 minutes. Uncover and stir in the remaining butter. Toss gently to blend well. Remove bay leaf.

Yield: 4 servings.

Rice with Raisins and Pine Nuts

2 tablespoons butter
3 tablespoons finely chopped onion
½ teaspoon minced garlic
1 cup converted rice
¼ cup raisins
1½ cups fresh or canned chicken broth
¼ cup pine nuts

1. Melt 1 tablespoon butter in a saucepan and add the onion and garlic. Cook, stirring, until wilted. Add the rice and stir. Add the raisins.

2. Add the broth and bring to a boil. Cover and simmer for exactly 17 minutes.

3. Add the pine nuts and remaining tablespoon butter. Stir to fluff the rice while blending in the nuts.

   Yield: 4 servings.

Rice with Mushrooms and Pistachios

>   2 tablespoons butter
> $1/2$ cup finely chopped onions
> $1/4$ pound mushrooms, diced (about $1^{1/3}$ cups)
> $1/3$ cup shelled pistachio nuts
>   1 cup rice
> $1^{1/2}$ cups fresh or canned chicken broth
>   Salt to taste if desired
>   Freshly ground pepper to taste

1. Heat 1 tablespoon butter in a saucepan and add the onions. Cook briefly, stirring, until wilted. Add the mushrooms and cook, stirring, about 2 minutes.

2. Add the nuts and rice and stir to blend. Add the broth, salt, and pepper and stir. Cover and simmer exactly 17 minutes.

3. Uncover and stir in the remaining butter.

   Yield: 4 to 6 servings.

◆ ◆ ◆

Risotto with Chicken and Veal

Different cultures prepare rice in different ways. The Chinese and Japanese prefer to serve rice that, when cooked, is just a bit sticky, so the grains hold together when picked up with chopsticks. For sushi, the Japanese also flavor their rice with a little vinegar. The French cook rice to a precise point of doneness so that the grains stand apart; usually they serve it buttered. The Italians like their rice in the form of risotto, where the rice is cooked in boiling or simmering broth added a little at a time until the rice is almost but not quite done. It should retain a slight bite in the center of each grain, but overall the rice should be quite creamy.

I recently planned to cook a chicken and rice dish for four people when a moment later four others showed up. There was a box of rice available (converted, not instant), as well as a pound of skinless, boneless chicken breasts, a few chicken livers, and a small amount of veal scaloppine.

With that in mind, I decided to experiment with a risotto that I have found to be stretchable and delectable as a main course, particularly if flavored with a good Parmesan cheese.

> $\frac{1}{4}$ pound thinly sliced veal scaloppine
> 1 pound skinless, boneless chicken breasts
> $\frac{1}{3}$ cup olive oil
> Salt and freshly ground pepper to taste
> 4 chicken livers, trimmed and cut into $\frac{1}{2}$-inch cubes
> $\frac{3}{4}$ cup finely chopped onion
> $\frac{1}{2}$ teaspoon finely minced garlic
> $\frac{1}{2}$ teaspoon loosely packed stem saffron
> 3 cups converted rice
> 2 cups dry white wine
> $7\frac{1}{2}$ cups fresh or canned chicken broth
> 4 tablespoons butter
> 1 cup freshly grated Parmesan or Romano cheese

1. Cut the veal into $\frac{1}{2}$-inch cubes. There should be about $\frac{1}{2}$ cup. Cut the chicken into $1\frac{1}{2}$-inch cubes. There should be about 2 cups.

2. Heat the oil in a deep skillet over medium-high heat. When it is hot and almost smoking, add the veal. Cook, stirring, about 30 seconds. Add the chicken, salt, and pepper. Cook, stirring, until the meat starts to brown lightly. Add the livers and cook, stirring, until they lose their raw look.

3. Add the onion, garlic, and saffron and stir about 1 minute.

4. Add the rice and stir to coat the grains. Add the wine and cook, stirring often, until the wine is absorbed.

5. Add 2 cups broth and cook about 6 minutes, stirring occasionally, or until the broth is absorbed.

6. Add 2 more cups broth and cook, stirring occasionally, about 6 minutes or until the broth is absorbed.

7. Add 2 more cups broth and cook, stirring occasionally, about 6 minutes or until the broth is absorbed.

8. Add the remaining 1½ cups broth and cook until it is almost absorbed and the rice is ready. The grains of rice must be whole and creamy. Just before serving stir in the butter and cheese.

Yield: 6 to 8 servings.

◆   ◆   ◆

Sauces, Condiments, & Bread

Fish Broth

    1 pound non-oily fish bones, cut into pieces
1½ cups water
    ½ cup dry white wine
    1 bay leaf
    1 cup coarsely chopped onion
    ½ teaspoon dry thyme
    6 black peppercorns, crushed
      Salt to taste if desired

1. Put all the ingredients in a saucepan and bring to a boil. Simmer 20 minutes. Strain and discard the solids.

   Yield: about 2 cups.

Mayonnaise

    1 large egg yolk
    2 tablespoons Dijon-style mustard
    1 tablespoon white-wine vinegar
      Salt and freshly ground pepper to taste
    1 cup vegetable oil
    1 tablespoon fresh lemon juice

1. Combine the egg yolk, mustard, vinegar, salt, and pepper in a mixing bowl. Stir with a wire whisk. Add the oil in a thin stream while beating briskly. When the oil is incorporated, add the lemon juice and blend well.

   Yield: 1 cup.

◆ ◆ ◆

Aïoli

(GARLIC MAYONNAISE)

½ teaspoon finely minced garlic
1 egg yolk
½ teaspoon white vinegar
  Salt to taste if desired
  Freshly ground pepper to taste
¾ cup olive oil

1. Ideally the garlic should be crushed using a mortar and pestle, but finely minced will suffice. Put the garlic in a mixing bowl.

2. Add the egg yolk, vinegar, salt, and pepper. Start beating with a wire whisk. Gradually add the oil, beating rapidly with the whisk until smooth and thickened.

   Yield: about ¾ cup.

Horseradish Sauce

½ cup sour cream
2 tablespoons horseradish, preferably freshly grated
1 teaspoon white-wine vinegar
  Salt to taste if desired
  Freshly ground pepper to taste
⅛ teaspoon Tabasco sauce

1. Put the sour cream in a mixing bowl. Add the horseradish, vinegar, salt, pepper, and Tabasco. Stir to blend the ingredients. If desired, add more horseradish to taste.

   Yield: about ½ cup.

Basic Vinaigrette

  1 tablespoon Dijon-style mustard
  $^1/_2$ teaspoon minced garlic
  1 tablespoon red-wine vinegar
  $^1/_3$ cup vegetable oil
  Salt and freshly ground pepper to taste

1. Put the mustard and garlic in a mixing bowl. Using a wire whisk, start beating the mixture.

2. Beat in the vinegar. Gradually add the oil, beating vigorously. Add salt and pepper to taste.

  Yield: about $^1/_2$ cup.

Fresh Tomato Sauce

  $1^1/_4$ pounds fresh tomatoes or 3 cups drained and
      chopped canned tomatoes
  2 tablespoons olive oil
  1 tablespoon finely minced garlic
  $1^1/_2$ teaspoons chopped fresh rosemary or 1 teaspoon dry
  $^1/_8$ teaspoon red pepper flakes
    Salt and freshly ground pepper to taste
  2 tablespoons butter

1. If fresh tomatoes are used, cut away and discard the cores. Cut the tomatoes into 1-inch cubes. There should be about 3 packed cups.

2. Heat the oil in a saucepan and add the garlic. Cook briefly, stirring, and add the tomatoes. Bring to a boil and add the rosemary, pepper flakes, salt, and pepper. Simmer about 10 minutes.

3. Pour the mixture into a food processor or blender and blend thoroughly. Or, preferably, line a saucepan with a sieve and pour the sauce into the sieve. Push the sauce through, discarding any solids that will not pass through. There should be about 2 cups. Return the sauce to the saucepan and bring to a simmer. Swirl in the butter.

Yield: about 2 cups.

Quick Tomato Sauce

$1\frac{1}{2}$ pounds fresh tomatoes or 4 cups imported canned
      tomatoes, drained
$\frac{1}{4}$ cup olive oil
2 tablespoons finely chopped garlic
1 dried red hot pepper
  Salt to taste if desired
  Freshly ground pepper to taste

1. Remove the core from each tomato. If using fresh tomatoes, cut them into 1-inch cubes. There should be about 3 cups. Put the tomatoes in a food processor and blend until coarsely chopped. There should be about $2\frac{1}{2}$ cups.

2. Heat the oil in a small skillet and add the garlic. Cook briefly, stirring, and add the tomatoes, hot pepper, salt, and ground pepper. Bring to a boil and simmer about 10 minutes.

Yield: about 2 cups.

Curry Sauce

1 Golden Delicious apple, about $\frac{3}{4}$ pound
1 tablespoon butter
2 tablespoons finely chopped shallots
2 teaspoons Curry Powder (recipe follows)

    $1/2$ cup fresh or canned chicken broth
    1 tablespoon tomato purée or crushed tomatoes
    $1/4$ cup heavy cream

1. Peel the apple and cut it into quarters. Cut away and discard the stem ends and the core. Cut each quarter into $1/4$-inch cubes.

2. Heat the butter in a saucepan and add the shallots and curry powder. Cook, stirring, about 1 minute. Add the apple and stir.

3. Add the broth and tomato purée. Cook over medium-high heat about 3 minutes or until reduced to about 1 cup. Add the cream and cook about 2 minutes.

    Yield: about 1 cup.

Curry Powder

Make a batch of this vibrant powder and store it in an airtight jar.

    $1/4$ cup turmeric
    3 tablespoons ground coriander
    2 tablespoons ground cumin
    1 tablespoon white peppercorns
    1 tablespoon whole cloves
    2 tablespoons ground ginger
    1 tablespoon ground cardamom
    2 teaspoons cayenne pepper
    1 tablespoon ground mace
    1 tablespoon dried fines herbes
    1 tablespoon fenugreek seeds

1. Put all the ingredients in a spice grinder or blender and grind them to a fine powder. Store in an airtight container.

    Yield: about 1 cup.

◆ ◆ ◆

Beurre Blanc aux Fines Herbes

(WHITE BUTTER SAUCE WITH HERBS)

- ¼ cup finely chopped shallots
- ¾ cup dry white wine
- ¼ cup heavy cream
- 8 tablespoons butter
- 2 tablespoons finely chopped parsley
- 2 tablespoons finely chopped fresh tarragon or 1 tablespoon dry
- 2 tablespoons finely chopped fresh chives
- 2 tablespoons finely chopped fresh chervil, optional
- Salt and freshly ground pepper to taste
- 1 tablespoon Pernod or Ricard, optional

1. Combine the shallots and wine in a heavy saucepan. Cook over medium-high heat until the wine has almost completely evaporated.

2. Add the cream and cook until reduced by half.

3. Add the butter quickly, 1 tablespoon at a time, stirring rapidly with a wire whisk. When totally blended, remove from the heat and add the herbs, salt, pepper, and Pernod.

   Yield: about ¾ cup.

◆ ◆ ◆

Quick French Bread

I make this bread several times a week. It is exceedingly easy, especially if you mix it in a food processor. I have found that using fast-rising packaged yeast, which is widely available in supermarkets, eliminates the need for a second proofing.

     2 envelopes fast-rising active dry yeast
 2¼ cups warm (90 degrees) water
     6 cups unbleached all-purpose flour
     1 tablespoon salt
     2 ice cubes

1. Preheat the oven to 400 degrees.

2. Place the chopping blade in the food processor bowl. Add the yeast and ¼ cup warm water. Mix by turning the chopping blade by hand. (Turn the stem without touching the sharp blade. Just to be extra cautious, unplug the machine.) Add all the flour. Turn on the machine and blend for 5 seconds. Add the salt and blend 5 seconds more. While the blade rotates, add the remaining 2 cups water. Blend until the batter begins to form a large ball, 20 to 25 seconds.

3. Flour a board and knead the dough on it, forming it into a ball. Flour a large mixing bowl and place the ball of dough in it. Sprinkle the top with flour. Cover it with a dish towel. Let the dough rise in a warm place until it doubles in size. The time required varies with environmental conditions, but at a room temperature of about 75 degrees it will take at least an hour.

4. Remove the dough from the bowl, punch it down, and shape it into loaves. This quantity is sufficient for 5 baguettes about 18 inches long, each stretched along the length of a tubular French loaf pan. Or make 2 thick French loaves about 14 inches long.

5. With a razor blade, diagonally score the surface of the loaves several times, making each incision about ½ inch deep.

6. Place the loaves in the oven and throw the ice cubes on the oven floor. The ice adds steam to help produce a thin crust. Bake for 30 minutes. Lower the oven temperature to 375 degrees and bake for 10 minutes. Transfer the bread to a rack and let it cool.

Yield: 5 baguettes or 2 thick French loaves.

Vegetables & Eggs

Asparagus with Shallot Butter

    1 pound medium asparagus
       Salt to taste if desired
    3 tablespoons finely chopped shallots
    4 tablespoons butter, cut into small pieces
       Freshly ground pepper to taste

1. Peel the asparagus, using a swivel-bladed peeler, starting about 2 inches from the top. Remove the tough ends.

2. Bring enough water to a boil to cover the asparagus. Add salt. Add the asparagus and cook until crisp-tender, 2 to 3 minutes. Drain well, reserving 3 tablespoons of the cooking liquid. Arrange on a warm platter.

3. Combine the shallots and the reserved liquid. Bring to a boil and cook over high heat until half the liquid evaporates. Add the butter gradually, stirring rapidly with a whisk. Add salt and pepper. Cook, stirring rapidly, 1 minute.

4. Spoon the mixture over the asparagus and serve hot.

    Yield: 4 servings.

Broccoli Purée

    1 bunch broccoli, about 1½ pounds
       Salt to taste if desired
    3 tablespoons butter
  ½ teaspoon finely minced garlic
       Freshly ground pepper to taste
    2 tablespoons freshly grated Parmesan cheese

1. Cut and trim the broccoli into florets. If the stems are large, trim them and cut them into large bite-size pieces. There should be about 6 cups.

2. Put the broccoli pieces in a saucepan and add cold water to cover and salt to taste. Bring to a boil and simmer about 10 minutes or until tender but not mushy. Drain.

3. Put the broccoli in a food processor and purée it. Or, preferably, put it in a conical food mill and press through into a saucepan.

4. Heat the purée gently while stirring in the butter, garlic, salt, pepper, and cheese. When piping hot, serve immediately.

Yield: 4 servings.

Broccoli di Rape

One of the finest vegetables I know of to acccompany an Italian meal is broccoli di rape or broccoli rabe. It is defined in certain books as a ''turnip green.'' The vegetable is widely available in supermarkets and greengrocers. Simple cooking is the best cooking for broccoli di rape—with a little olive oil, finely minced garlic, and a touch of red pepper flakes.

1½ **pounds broccoli di rape**
   Salt to taste
 3 **tablespoons olive oil**
 1 **teaspoon finely minced garlic**
 ½ **teaspoon red pepper flakes**
 1 **teaspoon anchovy paste**

1. Cut off and discard any tough stems from the broccoli di rape. The stems may be peeled and used if desired.

2. Bring enough salted water to a boil to cover the broccoli when added. Add the broccoli and cook about 1 minute. Drain, reserving ¼ cup of the cooking liquid.

3. Heat the oil in a large skillet and add the garlic. Cook briefly and add the broccoli, pepper flakes, anchovy paste, and reserved cooking liquid. Cook, stirring, about 2 minutes.

Yield: 4 servings.

Butternut Squash Purée

1 butternut squash, about 2½ pounds
Salt to taste
2 tablespoons butter
1 red sweet pepper (¼ pound), cut into ¼-inch pieces
¾ cup finely chopped onion
½ teaspoon minced garlic
⅛ teaspoon ground cumin
Freshly ground pepper to taste

1. Peel the squash and split it in half. Scoop out the seeds with a spoon and cut the squash into 1-inch cubes. There should be about 6 cups.

2. Drop the squash into boiling salted water. When the water returns to a boil, cook for about 5 minutes or until tender. Do not overcook.

3. Drain the squash thoroughly. Put it in a food processor or blender and purée it. Or, preferably, put it in a conical food mill and press it through into a bowl.

4. Heat the butter in a saucepan. Add the red pepper, onion, garlic, cumin, salt, and pepper. Cook, stirring, over medium heat for about 5 minutes. Add the squash, blend well, and reheat while stirring. When piping hot, remove from the heat and serve.

Yield: 4 servings.

Carrot Pudding

6 large carrots, about 1¼ pounds
¾ cup chopped scallions, green part included
2 large eggs, beaten
1 cup milk
Salt and freshly ground pepper to taste
⅛ teaspoon freshly grated nutmeg
2 teaspoons butter

1. Preheat the oven to 400 degrees.

2. Trim the carrots and scrape them all over. Cut the carrots crosswise into ¼-inch rounds. There should be about 4 cups.

3. Put the carrots in a saucepan and add water to cover. Bring to a boil and cook 5 minutes. Drain.

4. Put the carrots in a food processor or blender and blend thoroughly. Add the scallions and blend a second time. There should be about 3 cups. Put the mixture in a mixing bowl.

5. Beat the eggs with the milk, salt, pepper, and nutmeg. Add to the carrot mixture and beat to blend. Generously butter a 4-cup baking dish (a soufflé dish is recommended). Pour the carrot mixture into the baking dish. Dot the top with the butter. Bake 25 minutes.

Yield: 4 servings.

Carrots with Cumin Butter

18 baby carrots, about ¾ pound
    Salt to taste if desired
 1 tablespoon butter
¼ teaspoon ground cumin
 2 tablespoons finely chopped parsley

1. Peel the carrots and trim off the ends.

2. Put the carrots in a saucepan and add water to cover and salt. Bring to a boil and cook until tender, about 12 minutes.

3. Drain the carrots. Add the butter and cumin and toss to coat the carrots. Sprinkle with the parsley and serve.

Yield: 4 servings.

Chestnut Purée

  1 pound chestnuts
  Salt to taste
  1 stalk celery, diced
  1 cup fresh or canned chicken broth
  ½ cup heavy cream

1. Split the skins of the chestnuts and put them in a saucepan. Cover with water and add salt. Boil for 5 minutes or until they start to open. Drain. Cool slightly.

2. When cool enough to handle, remove the shells and thin skins. Put the chestnuts in a saucepan with the celery. Cover with water and bring to a boil. Cook for about 20 minutes or until the chestnuts are tender. Drain.

3. Purée the chestnuts and celery with a potato ricer, food mill, or food processor.

4. Add the broth and cream to the purée. Cook the mixture over medium-low heat for 5 minutes or until thick. If the purée seems too dry, add a bit more broth.

   Yield: 8 servings.

Corn with Red Peppers

  2 red sweet peppers, about ¾ pound
  1 or 2 ears corn or 1 cup frozen corn
  1 tablespoon olive oil
  1 tablespoon butter
  ⅓ cup finely chopped scallions
  ⅛ teaspoon ground cumin
  Salt to taste if desired
  Freshly ground pepper to taste
  ¼ teaspoon finely minced garlic

1. Core and seed the peppers. Cut the flesh into very thin strips about 1½ inches long. There should be about 2 cups.

2. Scrape the kernels from the corn. There should be about 1 cup.

3. Heat the oil and butter in a skillet and add the scallions, peppers, and corn. Sprinkle with the cumin, salt, pepper, and garlic. Cook, shaking the skillet and stirring, about 1½ minutes. Spoon the mixture into a warm serving dish.

   Yield: 4 servings.

Corn and Pepper Fritters

1¼ cups corn kernels, preferably fresh although frozen may be used
1 cup finely chopped sweet pepper, preferably red although green may be used
1 cup finely chopped scallions
1 teaspoon finely minced green hot pepper such as jalapeño, optional
1 teaspoon ground cumin
1¼ cups flour
2 teaspoons baking powder
Salt to taste if desired
Freshly ground pepper to taste
1 cup milk
¼ cup vegetable oil

1. Put the corn in a mixing bowl and add the sweet pepper, scallions, and hot pepper. Sprinkle with the cumin, flour, baking powder, salt, and pepper and stir to blend. Add the milk and stir to blend thoroughly.

2. Heat enough oil to barely cover the bottom of a skillet, preferably nonstick. Spoon the batter, about ¼ cup at a time, into the skillet and cook the fritters about 2 minutes or until golden brown on one side. Turn the fritters and cook about 2 minutes on the second side. As you prepare each batch of fritters add more oil as necessary.

   Yield: 12 fritters.

Cucumber and Chili Raita

    1 cucumber
    1 cup yogurt
      Salt to taste
    1 teaspoon or more finely chopped fresh green hot pepper
    $^1/_4$ teaspoon ground cumin
      White pepper to taste

1. Peel the cucumber and cut it in half lengthwise. Scrape out the seeds.

2. Cut the cucumber into $^1/_4$-inch slices. Stack the slices and cut them into $^1/_4$-inch strips. Cut the strips into $^1/_4$-inch cubes.

3. Combine the cucumber cubes with the remaining ingredients. Blend well.

    Yield: about 2$^1/_2$ cups.

Cucumbers and Carrots with Cumin

    2 large cucumbers, about 1$^1/_4$ pounds
    2 carrots, about $^1/_2$ pound
    2 tablespoons butter
    1 tablespoon finely chopped shallots
      Salt and freshly ground pepper to taste
    $^1/_4$ teaspoon ground cumin

1. Peel the cucumbers and cut them in half lengthwise. Scrape out the seeds.

2. Cut the cucumbers crosswise into thin slices. There should be about 4 cups.

3. Trim and scrape the carrots. Cut them crosswise into 1$^1/_2$-inch pieces. Cut the pieces lengthwise into thin julienne strips. There should be about 2 cups.

4. Bring enough water to a boil in a saucepan to cover the carrot strips when added. Add the carrots and cook about 4 minutes. Add the cucumbers and cook about 1 minute. Drain well.

5. Heat the butter in a skillet and add the shallots. Cook briefly, stirring. Add the carrots and cucumbers and sprinkle with the salt, pepper, and cumin. Cook, stirring occasionally, about 2 minutes.

   Yield: 4 servings.

Deep-Fried Eggplant

    2 medium eggplants, about ³/₄ pound each (see Note)
    1 egg, lightly beaten
    3 tablespoons cold water
    ¹/₂ teaspoon finely chopped fresh rosemary or ¹/₄ teaspoon dry
      Salt to taste if desired
      Freshly ground pepper to taste
    2 tablespoons freshly grated Parmesan cheese
    ¹/₂ cup flour
    2 cups fine fresh bread crumbs
    6 cups corn, peanut, or vegetable oil

1. Peel the eggplants and cut them crosswise into ³/₄-inch slices. Cut the slices into sticks about ³/₄ inch wide. There should be about 6 cups.

2. Put the egg in a large mixing bowl and add the water, rosemary, salt, pepper, and cheese. Beat well.

3. Dip the eggplant sticks in the flour to coat them. Put the sticks in the egg mixture and use your fingers to coat them well.

4. Put the bread crumbs in a flat dish and put the egg-coated eggplant sticks in. Toss to coat uniformly. Transfer the eggplant to a flat dish.

5. Heat the oil in a deep fryer or kettle to 375 degrees. Add half the eggplant sticks and cook 3 minutes or until crisp and golden brown. Drain thoroughly. Repeat with the remaining eggplant. Serve hot.

   Yield: 4 servings.

   NOTE: This technique also works well with zucchini.

Eggplant and Zucchini Casserole

   2 small eggplants, about ³/₄ pound
   2 small zucchini, about ³/₄ pound
   ¹/₄ cup olive oil
   1 tablespoon finely chopped garlic
   1 cup coarsely chopped onion
   1 bunch scallions, cut into 1-inch lengths
   4 plum tomatoes (about ³/₄ pound), cut into ¹/₄-inch cubes
   4 sprigs fresh thyme or 1 teaspoon dry
   1 bay leaf
   2 sprigs fresh rosemary or 1 teaspoon dry
   2 teaspoons grated orange rind
   ¹/₂ cup coarsely chopped fresh basil or parsley

1. Trim the eggplants but do not peel them. Cut them into ³/₈-inch cubes. There should be about 4 cups.

2. Trim the zucchini but do not peel them. Cut them into ³/₈-inch cubes. There should be about 4 cups.

3. Heat the oil in a heavy casserole. When it is very hot, add the eggplant and zucchini. Cook, stirring, for about 4 minutes. Add the garlic, onion, and scallions. Cook, stirring, about 5 minutes.

4. Add the tomatoes, thyme, bay leaf, rosemary, and orange rind. Stir well and cook over medium heat for 10 minutes. Stir often.

5. Remove the bay leaf and add the basil. Check the seasoning. Serve immediately.

   Yield: 4 servings.

Eggplant and Tomatoes au Gratin

> 1 slender eggplant about 3 inches in diameter, about 1 pound
> 4 plum tomatoes (about ¾ pound), cored
> Salt to taste if desired
> Freshly ground pepper to taste
> 3 tablespoons olive oil
> 2 tablespoons finely chopped parsley
> 2 teaspoons minced garlic
> ¼ cup finely chopped onion
> ¼ cup freshly grated Parmesan cheese

1. Preheat the broiler.

2. Trim the eggplant. Cut it into 16 slices of equal thickness.

3. Cut each tomato lengthwise into ¼-inch slices. There should be 16 slices. Sprinkle with salt and pepper.

4. Arrange the eggplant slices in one layer on a baking sheet. Brush the tops of the slices with 1 tablespoon oil. Sprinkle with salt and pepper.

5. Place the eggplant slices under the broiler about 4 inches from the heat. Broil about 3 minutes and turn the slices. Broil about 3 minutes more. Take care that the eggplant does not burn.

6. Arrange the eggplant and tomato slices in a baking dish, slightly overlapping.

7. Blend the parsley, garlic, and onion and sprinkle over the eggplant and tomatoes.

8. Dribble the remaining 2 tablespoons oil over the top and sprinkle evenly with the cheese.

9. Place the dish under the broiler about 6 to 7 inches from the heat and broil about 3 minutes.

10. Set the oven at 450 degrees. Put the vegetables in the oven and bake 3 minutes.

   Yield: 4 servings.

Escarole with Garlic and Olive Oil

   1½ **pounds escarole**
       Salt to taste
    3 **tablespoons olive oil**
    1 **tablespoon finely minced garlic**
       Freshly ground pepper to taste

1. Pull the leaves of the escarole apart. Trim the ends and cut out the core.

2. Drop the escarole into boiling water with salt to taste. Simmer until the escarole is tender, about 5 minutes.

3. Drain well. Squeeze to extract the excess liquid.

4. Heat the oil in a skillet and add the garlic. Cook until the garlic starts to brown. Do not let it brown or it will become bitter. Add the escarole, stirring so it heats evenly. Add salt and pepper to taste and serve.

   Yield: 4 servings.

Broiled Fennel with Parmesan Cheese

2 large unblemished fennel bulbs with stems, about 1 pound each
4 plum tomatoes, about ³/₄ pound
  Salt to taste if desired
  Freshly ground pepper to taste
¼ cup olive oil
¼ cup freshly grated Parmesan cheese
1 tablespoon finely chopped fresh herb such as basil or parsley

1. Preheat the broiler.

2. Trim the fennel, leaving the bulb intact. Each bulb should weigh about ³/₄ pound when trimmed. Cut each bulb lengthwise into ¹/₂-inch slices. Arrange the slices in one layer in a baking dish or pan.

3. Halve the plum tomatoes lengthwise.

4. Sprinkle the fennel with salt and pepper and brush the tops with 2 table-spoons oil. Place the fennel slices under the broiler about 6 inches from the heat, leaving the door partly open. Broil 5 minutes. Turn the fennel and brush with some of the remaining oil. Cook 5 minutes.

5. Arrange the tomatoes, cut side up, around the fennel. Brush with the remaining oil. Sprinkle the fennel and tomatoes with the Parmesan cheese and return to the broiler. Broil 1 minute and sprinkle with the herb.

Yield: 4 servings.

◆ ◆ ◆

Fennel Purée

 3 fennel bulbs
 2 potatoes, about ³/₄ pound
   Salt to taste if desired
 2 tablespoons butter
   Freshly ground pepper to taste
 2 tablespoons finely chopped parsley
 ¹/₈ teaspoon freshly grated nutmeg

1. Cut off and discard the upper stem portions of each bulb of fennel. Cut off and discard the bottom of each bulb. Cut each bulb in half and place the halves, cut side down, on a flat surface. Slice the halves into ¹/₂-inch lengths. There should be about 5 cups. Put the fennel in a large saucepan.

2. Peel the potatoes and cut them into ³/₄-inch cubes. There should be about 2 cups. Put the cubes in cold water to prevent discoloration. Drain the potatoes and add them to the fennel. Add water to cover and salt to taste.

3. Bring to a boil and cook about 15 minutes or until the fennel and potatoes are tender. Drain thoroughly. Purée, preferably in a food mill, or use a food processor. Return the mixture to the saucepan. Add the butter, salt, pepper, parsley, and nutmeg and heat briefly, stirring, until the butter is melted.

   Yield: 4 servings.

◆ ◆ ◆

Green Beans and Tomatoes Provençal

1 pound fresh green beans
Salt to taste if desired
3 tomatoes, about 1 pound
2 tablespoons butter
2 teaspoons finely minced garlic
1 bay leaf
Freshly ground pepper to taste

1. Cut the tips off the beans. If necessary, remove the strings. Cut the beans into 2-inch lengths. There should be 5 cups.

2. Bring enough water to a boil to cover beans when added. Add salt to taste. Add the beans and cook 5 to 10 minutes or until tender. Cooking time will depend on size and age. Drain thoroughly.

3. Peel the tomatoes. Remove the cores and cut the tomatoes in half crosswise. Gently squeeze out the seeds. Cut into ¹/₂-inch cubes. There should be about 2 cups.

4. Heat the butter in a skillet or casserole and add the garlic. When it is wilted and starting to brown, add the tomatoes, salt, and bay leaf. Cook, stirring, about 2 minutes and add the beans and pepper. Stir to blend well. Remove the bay leaf and serve.

    Yield: 4 servings.

Sautéed Lettuce with Garlic

3 or 4 heads bibb or Boston lettuce, about 1¹/₄ pounds
2 tablespoons olive oil
¹/₂ cup peeled and sliced white onion
2 teaspoons minced garlic

⅛ teaspoon red pepper flakes
Salt and freshly ground pepper to taste

1. Pick over the lettuce leaves and discard any tough stems.

2. Heat the oil in a large skillet. Add the onion and garlic. Cook over medium heat, stirring, until wilted. Add the lettuce, pepper flakes, salt, and pepper. Cook over high heat, stirring, about 2 minutes. Serve immediately.

   Yield: 4 servings.

Snap Peas with Mint

1 pound whole pod peas such as snap or sugar peas
Salt to taste if desired
2 tomatoes (about ¾ pound), cored
2 tablespoons butter
1 tablespoon shredded fresh mint
Freshly ground pepper to taste

1. Pluck off and discard the ends of each pea.

2. Bring enough water to a boil to cover the peas when they are added. Add salt.

3. Add the peas and, when the water returns to a boil, simmer 5 minutes. Drain.

4. Meanwhile, drop the tomatoes into boiling water and cook 9 seconds. Peel the tomatoes and cut them into ¼-inch cubes. There should be about 1½ cups.

5. Heat the butter in a saucepan and add the tomatoes. Cook over medium heat about 2 minutes and add the peas, mint, salt, and pepper. Stir to blend and bring to a boil. Serve.

   Yield: 4 servings.

Sautéed Potatoes with Garlic

14 red waxy new potatoes, about 1½ pounds
   Salt to taste if desired
2 tablespoons olive oil
   Freshly ground pepper to taste
2 tablespoons butter
2 tablespoons finely chopped shallots
1 teaspoon finely minced garlic
2 tablespoons finely chopped parsley

1. Put the potatoes in a saucepan. Add cold water to cover and salt.

2. Bring to a boil and cook until the potatoes are tender, about 20 minutes. Drain thoroughly. Cool.

3. Cut the potatoes into ¼-inch slices. There should be about 4½ to 5 cups.

4. Heat the oil in a nonstick skillet and, when it is quite hot, add the potatoes, salt, and pepper. Cook the potatoes until they start to brown on one side, about 4 minutes. Shake the skillet to toss and redistribute the potatoes. Add the butter. Shake and toss potatoes as they continue to cook.

5. When the potatoes have cooked for 4 minutes longer, sprinkle them with the shallots, garlic, and parsley. Toss and stir gently to blend. Serve immediately.

   Yield: 4 servings.

Buttered New Potatoes with Fennel

1 fennel bulb, about ½ pound
8 red waxy new potatoes
1½ cups water
   Salt to taste
1 tablespoon butter
2 tablespoons finely chopped fresh dill

1. Trim the stem and stalk ends of the fennel bulb. Cut the fennel into $1/2$-inch slices. Cut the slices into strips about $1/2$-inch wide. Cut the strips into $1/2$-inch cubes. There should be about 2 cups fennel cubes.

2. Trim the ends of the potatoes. Cut the potatoes into quarters and drop the pieces into cold water. Drain.

3. Combine the fennel and potatoes in a wide small skillet and add the water, salt, and butter. Bring to a boil. Do not cover. Cook about 15 minutes or until the water has evaporated and the vegetables are tender.

4. Put the vegetables in a serving dish. Sprinkle them with the dill and serve.

   Yield: 4 servings.

Purée de Pommes de Terre

(MASHED POTATOES)

> $2^{1}/_{2}$ **pounds russet potatoes**
> **Salt to taste**
> $1^{1}/_{2}$ **cups milk**
> 6 **tablespoons butter**

1. Peel the potatoes and cut them into 2-inch cubes.

2. Place the potatoes in a saucepan and cover with cold water. Add salt. Bring to a boil and simmer 20 minutes or until the potatoes are tender. Do not overcook them.

3. Meanwhile, heat the milk until it is hot.

4. Drain the potatoes and put them through a food mill or ricer or mash well with a potato masher. Return them to the saucepan. Using a wooden spatula, add the butter and blend well. Mix in the milk. Keep warm until ready to serve.

   Yield: 8 servings.

   NOTE: As a variation, add 1 cup sliced onion to the cooking water and purée it along with the potatoes.

Mashed Potatoes with Scallions

 7 Idaho potatoes, about 2¼ pounds
   Salt to taste if desired
 2 tablespoons butter
 ¾ cup milk
 ¼ cup heavy cream
 ½ cup finely chopped scallions or chives
   Freshly ground pepper, preferably white, to taste

1. Peel the potatoes and cut them into 1-inch cubes. There should be about 6 cups. Put the potatoes in a kettle and add salt.

2. Cover with water and bring to a boil. Cook 10 to 12 minutes or until the potatoes are tender. Remove from the heat. Drain the potatoes and put them through a ricer or food mill or mash well with a potato masher. Add the butter and beat to blend. Stir in the milk, cream, scallions, and pepper. Serve piping hot.

   Yield: 4 servings.

Puréed Garlic Potatoes

 4 russet potatoes, about 1½ pounds
 6 whole cloves garlic, peeled
   Salt to taste if desired
 3 tablespoons butter
 1⅓ cups milk
   Freshly ground white pepper to taste

1. Peel the potatoes and cut them crosswise into ¾-inch slices. Put the pieces in a saucepan and add water to cover. Add the garlic and salt.

2. Bring to a boil and cook 15 minutes or until the potatoes are tender. Drain and put the potatoes and garlic through a food mill and back in the saucepan.

3. Add the butter, milk, salt, and white pepper. Beat to blend.

   Yield: 4 servings.

Potato Pancakes

> 5 large russet potatoes, about 1½ pounds
> 1 onion, about ¼ pound
>   Salt to taste if desired
> ½ cup corn, peanut, or vegetable oil
>   Freshly ground pepper to taste

1. Grate the potatoes into a basin of cold water, using the grating surface with large holes. (Do not grate them, however, until you are ready to cook them.) Before cooking, drain the potatoes in a strainer.

2. Peel the onion and grate it on the same grating surface. There should be about ½ cup. Add the onion to the potatoes in the strainer and blend well. With a rubber spatula or your hands, push down on the potato-onion mixture to extract the liquid. Put the mixture in a mixing bowl and add salt.

3. To prepare the pancakes it is best to use 2 or more 6- or 7-inch nonstick frying pans.

4. Heat about 1 tablespoon oil in each skillet and add ¾ cup of the potato-onion mixture. Flatten the mixture and sprinkle it lightly with pepper. Cook about 3 minutes or until the "cake" is browned on the bottom. Flip the cake, trying not to break it. Flip the cake several times so that it cooks through, about 3 to 4 minutes longer. Slide the cake onto a flat surface.

5. Add 1 more tablespoon oil to each skillet and add another batch of potato mixture, cooking it as before. Continue cooking the cakes, adding more oil as necessary, until all the mixture is used.

   Yield: 8 potato pancakes.

◆ ◆ ◆

French-Fried Potatoes

Pommes frites, or French-fried potatoes, are a universal food. They come in all shapes and sizes, and each culture has its own term for what is essentially sliced potatoes fried (twice in the real French style) to achieve the ideal crispness. I prefer Idaho or Maine russet potatoes for French fries because they have a relatively low water content. You can make a big batch of sliced potatoes quickly using a mandoline or less elaborate (and less versatile) French-fry cutters available in kitchenware shops.

    5 medium-size potatoes (preferably Idaho or Maine russet)
  10 cups vegetable or corn oil for deep-frying
      Salt to taste

1. Peel potatoes and cut them into 1/4-inch slices. Cut each slice into 1/4-inch sticks. To prevent discoloration, drop the pieces into cold water until ready to cook. Drain extremely well and pat dry with paper towels.

2. Heat the oil to 365 degrees in a deep pan or fryer. You should have enough oil so that the potatoes do not fill more than half the volume. Drop the potatoes into the hot oil and cook about 5 to 7 minutes or until they are just losing their paleness (time varies with thickness of the potatoes). The potatoes should begin to blister but not brown. Drain and let cool. (They can sit in a cool place at this stage for an hour or more if needed, covered with paper towels.)

3. Return the potatoes to the hot oil and cook 4 to 5 minutes or until potatoes are nicely browned and crisp. Drain thoroughly. Sprinkle with salt and serve immediately.

    Yield: 4 servings.

◆ ◆ ◆

Ratatouille à la Minute

  1 yellow squash (about 1 pound), trimmed
  1 zucchini (about 1 pound), trimmed
  2 tomatoes (about 1 pound), cored
  2 tablespoons olive oil
  ³/4 cup finely chopped onion
  2 teaspoons finely minced garlic
  1 teaspoon finely chopped jalapeño pepper, optional
  4 sprigs fresh thyme, broken into ¹/2-inch lengths,
      or ¹/2 teaspoon dry
  1 bay leaf
    Salt to taste if desired
    Freshly ground pepper to taste
  2 tablespoons finely chopped fresh basil

1. Cut the yellow squash and zucchini crosswise into ¹/4-inch slices. There should be about 2 cups of each.

2. Cut the tomatoes into 1-inch cubes. There should be about 3 loosely packed cups.

3. Heat the oil in a heavy skillet and add the zucchini and yellow squash. Cook, stirring and tossing so the pieces cook evenly, about 3 minutes. Add the onion and garlic, and jalapeño if desired, and toss to blend.

4. Add the thyme, bay leaf, tomatoes, salt, and pepper. Stir to blend and cook, tossing and stirring, about 3 minutes. Add the basil and stir. Remove the bay leaf. Turn the mixture into a warm dish and serve hot.

    Yield: 4 servings.

◆ ◆ ◆

Purée de Rutabaga

(YELLOW TURNIP PURÉE)

1 rutabaga, about 2 pounds
Salt to taste if desired
Freshly ground pepper to taste
2 tablespoons butter
1/8 teaspoon freshly grated nutmeg
1/2 cup heavy cream

1. Peel the rutabaga. Cut it into 1-inch cubes. There should be about 8 cups. Put the cubes in a saucepan or kettle and add water to cover and salt to taste. Bring to a boil and cover. Cook 15 minutes or until tender.

2. Drain and put the cubes in a food processor. Add salt, pepper, butter, and nutmeg. Process while gradually adding the cream.

    Yield: 4 servings.

Spinach with Nutmeg

1 pound spinach leaves or a 10-ounce package spinach
2 tablespoons butter
Salt to taste if desired
Freshly ground pepper to taste
1/4 teaspoon freshly grated nutmeg

1. Cut away and discard any tough spinach stems and blemished leaves.

2. Heat the butter in a skillet and add the spinach, salt, pepper, and nutmeg. Stir as the spinach wilts. Cook over medium heat until the spinach is totally wilted. Remove from the heat and serve.

    Yield: 4 servings.

Broiled Tomatoes

>   2 large tomatoes, about 1 pound
>   Salt to taste if desired
>   Freshly ground pepper to taste
> ¹⁄₄ cup fine fresh bread crumbs
>   1 tablespoon finely chopped parsley
>   1 teaspoon finely minced garlic
>   2 teaspoons olive oil
>   2 tablespoons finely chopped shallots

1. Preheat a broiler.

2. Cut away and discard the core of each tomato. Cut the tomatoes crosswise through the center. Sprinkle with salt and pepper.

3. Combine the bread crumbs, parsley, garlic, olive oil, and shallots in a small mixing bowl. Blend well.

4. Top each tomato half with an equal portion of the crumb mixture, pressing down with your fingers to distribute the topping evenly. Arrange the tomato halves on a baking dish. Place them about 8 inches from the heat and cook about 5 minutes.

   Yield: 4 servings.

❖ ❖ ❖

White Beans Breton

White beans Breton, a classic accompaniment to lamb with garlic, are distinguished by their liberal seasoning. I cook them with onions, carrots, bay leaf, garlic, parsley, and tomatoes. Taste the mixture often to fine-tune the seasonings.

1 pound dried white navy or kidney beans, peas, or flageolets
8 cups water
Salt and freshly ground pepper to taste
1 carrot, scraped
1 onion, peeled and studded with 2 cloves
1 bay leaf
1 clove garlic, peeled
2 parsley sprigs
4 tablespoons butter
1 cup finely chopped onion
1 tablespoon finely chopped garlic
2 cups crushed imported tomatoes
2 sprigs fresh thyme, chopped, or ½ teaspoon dry
¼ cup chopped parsley

1. Put the beans in a mixing bowl and add water to a depth of about 2 inches above the top of the beans. Let soak for several hours or overnight.

2. Drain the beans and put them in a saucepan. Add the 8 cups water, salt, pepper, carrot, whole onion, bay leaf, garlic clove, and parsley sprigs. Bring to a boil and simmer 1 hour or until the beans are tender but not mushy.

3. While the beans cook, heat the butter. Add the chopped onion and chopped garlic. Cook and stir until the onions are translucent. Add the tomatoes, thyme, salt, and pepper. Simmer for 15 minutes.

4. When the beans are done, strain them. Reserve 1 cup cooking liquid. Add the beans and cooking liquid to the tomato sauce. Bring to a boil. Check the seasoning and simmer for 15 minutes. Sprinkle with the parsley before serving.

Yield: 6 to 8 servings.

French-Fried Yams

3 yams, about 1³/₄ pounds
8 cups vegetable oil

1. Peel the yams and cut them crosswise, slightly on the diagonal, into ¹/₈-inch slices. Stack a few slices at a time and cut them into matchstick strips about ¹/₈ inch wide. There should be about 6 cups.

2. Heat the oil in a deep-fat fryer or skillet to 360 degrees. Add half the potato sticks and cook about 5 minutes or until crisp. Drain on paper towels. Add the remaining potato sticks and cook and drain in the same manner.

   Yield: 4 servings.

Yam Purée

4 yams or sweet potatoes, about 2 pounds
  Salt to taste if desired
2 tablespoons butter
¹/₄ cup heavy cream
¹/₂ cup milk

1. Place the yams in a saucepan and add cold water to cover. Bring to a boil and cook 30 minutes. Drain.

2. When the yams are cool enough to handle, peel them. Cut the yams into 1-inch cubes and put them through a food mill or ricer.

3. Put the potatoes in a skillet and add the butter, cream, and milk. Heat thoroughly, stirring.

   Yield: about 3¹/₂ cups.

Yellow Squash au Gratin

  5 yellow squash, about 1 pound
  2 tomatoes, about 1 pound
  1 tablespoon olive oil
     Salt to taste if desired
     Freshly ground pepper to taste
 ¼ teaspoon dry thyme
  1 cup finely chopped onion
  1 cup grated Gruyère cheese

1. Trim the squash. Cut the squash diagonally into ovals about ¼-inch thick. There should be about 5 cups.

2. Core the tomatoes. Peel and cut them into ¼-inch cubes. There should be about 2 cups.

3. Heat the oil in a skillet over high heat. When it is almost smoking, add the squash. Add the salt, pepper, and thyme. Cook, shaking the skillet and stirring, about 2 minutes. Add the tomatoes and onion and cook, gently turning the ingredients with a spatula so they cook evenly. Cover and cook 5 minutes.

4. Meanwhile, preheat the broiler.

5. Spoon the mixture into a baking dish and sprinkle with the cheese.

6. Place the dish under the broiler about 6 inches from the heat. Leave the door open and broil about 5 minutes or until golden brown on top.

   Yield: 4 servings.

Deep-Fried Zucchini

Often when deep frying zucchini I dip them first in buttermilk, which gives fried food an extra crisp and flaky texture.

>   5 small zucchini, about 1¼ pounds
>   ½ cup buttermilk
>   1 cup flour
>   Salt to taste if desired
>   Freshly ground pepper to taste
>   Oil for deep frying

1. Trim the zucchini and cut it crosswise into thin slices. There should be about 4 cups.

2. Dip the zucchini slices in the buttermilk until well coated. Dip the slices in the flour seasoned with salt and pepper.

3. Heat 1½ inches oil to 325 degrees. Add the zucchini slices and cook, stirring often so that the pieces cook evenly, about 4 to 5 minutes or until the slices are crisp and golden brown. Drain on paper towels.

   Yield: 4 servings.

Summer Vegetables au Gratin

>   1 medium eggplant, about ¾ pound
>   1 yellow squash, about ¼ pound
>   1 small zucchini, about ¼ pound
>   7 tablespoons olive oil
>   1 cup finely chopped onion
>   1 teaspoon finely minced garlic
>   1 bay leaf
>   Salt to taste if desired
>   Freshly ground pepper to taste
>   ½ pound plum tomatoes
>   ¼ cup freshly grated Parmesan cheese

1. Preheat the broiler.

2. Trim the eggplant, squash, and zucchini. Cut the squash and zucchini into very thin rounds. There should be about 2 cups of each. Cut the eggplant lengthwise into quarters and cut each quarter into thin slices. There should be about 4 cups.

3. Heat 6 tablespoons oil in a skillet and add the eggplant, zucchini, and squash. Cook, shaking the skillet and stirring so slices cook evenly, about 8 minutes. Add the onion and garlic and stir to blend. Add the bay leaf, salt, and pepper. Cover and cook, stirring occasionally, about 3 minutes.

4. Meanwhile, core each tomato. Cut them crosswise into thin slices.

5. Remove and discard the bay leaf. Pour the cooked vegetables into a baking dish and arrange the tomato slices on top. Brush the tomatoes with the remaining tablespoon oil and sprinkle evenly with the cheese.

6. Place the dish under the broiler about 4 inches from the heat. Leave the door partly open and cook 5 minutes.

Yield: 4 or more servings.

Frittata with Potatoes

 6 small red waxy potatoes, about ³⁄₄ pound
 2 tablespoons vegetable oil
1¹⁄₂ cups chopped red sweet pepper
1¹⁄₂ cups chopped yellow sweet pepper
 ¹⁄₂ cup finely chopped red onion
 1 cup cubed lean ham
10 eggs
 1 tablespoon finely chopped fresh basil
   Salt to taste if desired
   Freshly ground pepper to taste
 ¹⁄₄ pound cheese, preferably Gruyère, cut into small dice
 2 tablespoons butter

1. Peel the potatoes and cut them into thin slices. Drop the slices into cold water to prevent discoloration. Drain.

2. Heat the oil and add the potatoes. Cook over medium heat, shaking the skillet and stirring, about 4 minutes. Add the peppers and onion. Cook, shaking the skillet and stirring, about 5 minutes.

3. Add the ham and cook, shaking the skillet and stirring, about 1 minute. Remove from the heat.

4. Beat the eggs with the basil. Add salt and pepper. Beat in the cheese.

5. Heat the butter in a 12-inch nonstick skillet and add the vegetable mixture. Add the egg and cheese mixture and cook over high heat, stirring gently but thoroughly with a fork or plastic spatula, about 45 seconds. Cover tightly and reduce the heat to medium. Cook about 2 minutes. Run a knife around the outside of the frittata. Invert a large round plate over the skillet and invert the skillet and plate quickly, letting the frittata fall into the plate.

6. Slide the frittata, browned side up, into the skillet and cook, covered, 1 to 2 minutes longer. Transfer it to a plate and cut it into wedges.

   Yield: 4 servings.

Ham and Cheese Frittata

> 1 red sweet pepper, about ¼ pound
> 1 green sweet pepper, about ¼ pound
> 1 red onion, about ¼ pound
> 10 eggs
>   Salt to taste if desired
>   Freshly ground pepper to taste
> 2 tablespoons olive oil
> ½ pound ham, cut into ½-inch cubes
> ¼ pound Gruyère or Swiss cheese, cut into ¼-inch cubes

1. Cut the peppers in half, remove the inner veins and seeds, and cut them into ½-inch cubes. There should be about 1½ cups of each.

2. Peel the onion and cut it into ¼-inch cubes. There should be about 1¼ cups.

3. Break the eggs into a mixing bowl. There should be about 2 cups. Add salt and pepper.

4. Heat 1 tablespoon oil in a large nonstick skillet and add the peppers. Cook, stirring often, about 3 minutes and add the onion, salt, and pepper. Cook about 2 minutes and cover. Continue cooking about 1 minute. Uncover and cook until the liquid from the vegetables evaporates. Sprinkle with the ham and cheese.

5. Add the remaining tablespoon oil. Beat the eggs thoroughly and add them. Cook, stirring from the bottom, until the eggs start to set, about 1 minute. Cover tightly and cook about 2 minutes.

6. Invert a large round dish over the skillet and invert the skillet and dish quickly, letting the frittata fall into the dish. It should be golden brown on top.

Yield: 4 servings.

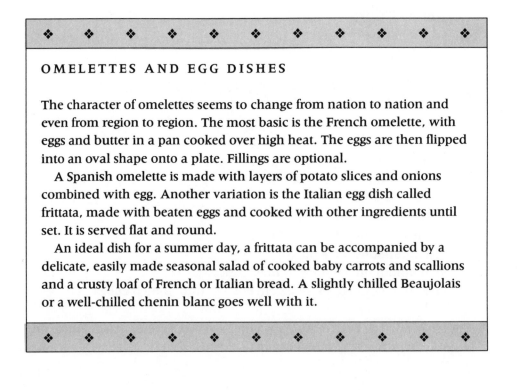

OMELETTES AND EGG DISHES

The character of omelettes seems to change from nation to nation and even from region to region. The most basic is the French omelette, with eggs and butter in a pan cooked over high heat. The eggs are then flipped into an oval shape onto a plate. Fillings are optional.

A Spanish omelette is made with layers of potato slices and onions combined with egg. Another variation is the Italian egg dish called frittata, made with beaten eggs and cooked with other ingredients until set. It is served flat and round.

An ideal dish for a summer day, a frittata can be accompanied by a delicate, easily made seasonal salad of cooked baby carrots and scallions and a crusty loaf of French or Italian bread. A slightly chilled Beaujolais or a well-chilled chenin blanc goes well with it.

Omelette Fines Herbes

> 12 eggs
> 8 teaspoons chopped parsley
> 4 teaspoons chopped fresh basil
> 4 teaspoons chopped fresh tarragon
> 4 teaspoons chopped fresh chervil
>   Salt and freshly ground pepper to taste
> 4 teaspoons butter

1. Use 3 eggs at a time to make individual omelettes. Put 3 eggs in a mixing bowl and add 2 teaspoons parsley and 1 teaspoon each basil, tarragon, and chervil. Add salt and pepper and beat well.

2. Melt 1 teaspoon butter for each omelette in an 8-inch omelette pan. Add the beaten egg mixture and cook over medium-high heat. As the eggs cook, stir them briskly with a fork, keeping the tines parallel to the bottom of the skillet. Stir almost constantly until the eggs are set, about 30 seconds. Increase the heat and cook about 30 seconds more or until the omelette is browned on the bottom. Turn the omelette onto a warm serving plate, cooked side up.

3. Repeat with the remaining ingredients.

   Yield: 4 servings.

◆ ◆ ◆

Desserts

Cantaloupe and Ginger Sorbet

2 ripe cantaloupes, about 4 pounds
2 tablespoons fresh lemon juice
1 cup sugar
2 cups water
2 tablespoons finely chopped bottled ginger in syrup
2 tablespoons ginger syrup from the bottled ginger
1 tablespoon finely chopped or grated fresh ginger
2 egg whites, lightly beaten

1. Cut the cantaloupes into eighths. Scrape away and discard the seeds and inner fibers. Cut away and discard the outer rind. There should be about 2 pounds flesh. Cut the flesh into small pieces and put them in a bowl. Add the lemon juice and toss.

2. Combine the sugar and water in a saucepan and bring to a boil. Simmer 5 minutes. Add the cantaloupe pieces and bring to a boil. Simmer 2 minutes. Drain, reserving both the cantaloupe and the cooking liquid. Cool.

SORBETS AND ICES

The idea of eating fruits and juices blended or frozen with ice is supposed to have been introduced to France by the chefs of the Medicis in the sixteenth century. French chefs expanded the notion of creating water ices by adding frozen creams to the mixture. It is said that the first advertisement for a machine to produce ices and cream desserts appeared in *The New York Gazette* on May 19, 1777, and that the first American patent for a hand-cranked freezer was issued in 1848.

There is a difference between ices (known in France as granités) and sorbets. Both are incredibly easy to make—as opposed to ice creams, which require a custard base. Ices are made with the juice of fruit or berries plus a simple syrup boiled for three or so minutes. A sorbet requires the addition of a ''stabilizer'' in the form of egg whites, cooked meringue, or gelatin.

One of the pleasures of preparing an ice or a sorbet is that both give you a chance to display inventiveness. You can play around with flavors.

3. Put the cantaloupe pieces in a food processor or blender. Add the chopped ginger, ginger syrup, and fresh ginger. Blend as thoroughly as possible. Put the mixture in a mixing bowl.

4. Add the reserved cooking liquid and blend. There should be about 7½ cups. Chill thoroughly.

5. Pour half the mixture into an ice cream machine and freeze according to the manufacturer's instructions. When the mixture starts to freeze, add 1 egg white and continue freezing to the desired consistency. Repeat with the remaining mixture and the remaining egg white.

   Yield: 12 to 14 servings.

Grapefruit and Campari Sorbet

> 3 large pink grapefruit (the redder the flesh the better),
>   about 1 pound each
> 2 cups water
> 1½ cups sugar
> ¼ cup Campari
> 1 egg white, lightly beaten

1. Peel the grapefruit, cutting away and discarding all the outer white membrane. Carefully section it, running the knife between each segment. There should be about 3 cups flesh and 1 cup juice. Discard any seeds.

2. Combine the grapefruit sections and juice in a food processor or blender and blend as thoroughly as possible. There should be about 3⅓ cups. Put the mixture in a mixing bowl.

3. Combine the water and sugar in a saucepan and bring to a boil. Cook about 5 minutes and cool. Add to the grapefruit mixture and blend. There should be about 5½ cups. Add the Campari and chill thoroughly.

4. Pour the mixture into an ice cream machine and freeze according to the manufacturer's instructions. When the mixture starts to freeze, add the egg white and continue freezing to the desired consistency.

Yield: 10 to 12 servings.

Pineapple and Mango Sorbet

> 1 ripe pineapple, about 2 pounds
> 2 ripe mangoes
> 3 tablespoons fruit liqueur, such as mango or
>   passion fruit, optional
> ½ cup sugar
> 2 tablespoons lemon juice

1. Trim the top and bottom of the pineapple. Slice down the sides to remove the skin and green flesh. Dig out any brown, fibrous spots.

2. Quarter the pineapple and remove the woody flesh in the center. Cut each quarter into ½-inch slices.

3. Peel the mangoes. Remove the ripe flesh with a knife. Do not use any of the fibrous sections close to the pit.

4. Place the pineapple and mango in a blender. Add the liqueur, sugar, and lemon juice. (You may need 2 batches, in which case add half the sugar and lemon juice to each batch.) Blend at high speed until very fine, about 1 minute or more.

5. Transfer the mixture to an ice cream maker and freeze according to the manufacturer's instructions. This sorbet is best if prepared about 1 hour before serving. If you want to use it later or the next day, partially thaw and reprocess it in the ice cream machine.

Yield: 6 servings.

Sorbet aux Pommes Vertes

(GREEN APPLE SORBET)

5 Granny Smith apples, about 3½ pounds
¼ cup lemon juice
2 cups confectioners' sugar
  Calvados if desired

1. Core and peel the apples. Cut them into eighths, then slice each section into thin strips. There should be about 4 cups. Place them in a food processor with the lemon juice. Add the sugar and blend until smooth.

2. Transfer the mixture to an ice cream freezer and freeze according to the manufacturer's instructions.

3. Serve in individual cups with a glass of Calvados on the side. Or pour the Calvados over the sorbet when serving.

    Yield: 8 to 10 servings.

Pear and Passion Fruit Sorbet

5 ripe pears, about 2¼ pounds
2 tablespoons fresh lemon juice
1 cup sugar
2 cups water
1 teaspoon vanilla extract
¼ cup passion fruit syrup or Grand Passion liqueur (see Note)

1. Cut the pears into quarters or eighths. Cut away and discard the cores, stems, and peel. The total weight of the trimmed pears should be about 1½ pounds. Toss with the lemon juice to prevent discoloration.

2. Put the sugar, water, and vanilla in a saucepan. Heat, stirring, until the sugar is dissolved. Add the pears and bring to a boil. Cook 5 minutes. Drain and save both the pears and the cooking liquid. Cool.

3. Put the pears in a food processor or blender and blend as thoroughly as possible. There should be about 3 cups. Put the mixture in a mixing bowl.

4. Add the reserved cooking liquid and passion fruit syrup and blend well. There should be about 4¹/₂ cups. Chill thoroughly.

5. Pour the mixture into an ice cream machine and freeze according to the manufacturer's instructions.

   Yield: 8 to 10 servings.

   NOTE: Grand Passion is a widely available commercially produced liqueur flavored with passion fruit.

Honeydew and Melon-Liqueur Ice

> 1 honeydew melon, about 3 pounds
> 2 tablespoons fresh lemon juice
> 2 cups water
> 1 cup sugar
> 5 tablespoons green melon liqueur such as Midori

1. Cut the honeydew into eighths. Scrape away and discard the inner seeds, fibers, and peel. The prepared melon should weigh about 1¹/₂ pounds.

2. Cut the melon into small pieces, place in a bowl, and add the lemon juice. Toss to coat the pieces.

3. Meanwhile, bring the water and sugar to a boil in a saucepan and simmer about 3 minutes. Add the melon pieces and cook 2 minutes. Drain, reserving both the melon pieces and cooking liquid. Cool.

4. Put the melon pieces in a food processor or blender and blend thoroughly. There should be about 3¹/₃ cups. Put the mixture in a mixing bowl. Add the reserved cooking liquid and blend. There should be about 5¹/₄ cups. Chill well. Add the liqueur.

5. Pour the mixture into an ice cream machine and freeze according to the manufacturer's instructions.

   Yield: 10 to 12 servings.

Rosemary and Mint Ice

3 cups water
1 cup sugar
2 tablespoons fresh or dry rosemary leaves
2 tablespoons lemon juice
1 tablespoon crème de menthe

1. Combine the water and sugar in a saucepan and simmer 3 minutes. Add the rosemary and stir. Cover tightly and let stand 15 minutes.

2. Line a bowl with a sieve and line the sieve with cheesecloth. Strain the liquid and discard the solids. Let the liquid stand until cool. Add the lemon juice and crème de menthe and chill thoroughly.

3. Pour the mixture into an ice cream machine and freeze according to the manufacturer's instructions.

Yield: 6 to 8 servings.

Basic French Vanilla Ice Cream

³/₄ cup sugar
5 egg yolks
2 cups milk
2 cups heavy cream
1 split vanilla bean (see Note)

1. Beat the sugar and yolks with a small whisk in a heavy 1-quart bowl, until bright yellow. Add 1 cup milk and stir.

2. Combine the egg mixture with the cream, the remaining cup milk, and the vanilla bean in a wide saucepan. Bring the mixture to 180 degrees (use a rapid-reading thermometer), stirring constantly. If the mixture boils it will take on an undesirable cooked flavor. Strain the mixture into a stainless steel bowl and cool. Remove the vanilla bean.

3. Place the mixture in an ice cream machine and freeze according to the manufacturer's instructions.

   Yield: 1 quart.

   NOTE: If you do not have vanilla beans, 2 teaspoons vanilla extract can be substituted. This ice cream is good topped with a sauce of $\frac{1}{2}$ cup cream of coconut beaten with 2 tablespoons dark rum.

French Apple Tart

    Basic Tart Pastry (recipe follows)
 6 or 7 **firm, unblemished apples, about** $2\frac{1}{2}$ **pounds**
 2 **tablespoons butter**
    Grated rind of 1 lemon
$\frac{1}{2}$ **cup sugar**
 1 **tablespoon Calvados, rum, or brandy, optional**
$\frac{1}{2}$ **cup apricot preserves**

1. Preheat the oven to 400 degrees.

2. Line a 10-inch pie tin (preferably a quiche pan with a removable bottom) with the pastry. Refrigerate or place in the freezer.

3. Core and peel 3 of the apples. Cut them into eighths. Cut these pieces into thin slices. There should be about 2 cups.

4. Heat 1 tablespoon butter in a small saucepan and add the apple slices. Sprinkle with the lemon rind and $\frac{1}{4}$ cup sugar. Cook, shaking the pan and stirring, for about 10 minutes. Add the Calvados. Mash the apples lightly with a fork. Chill.

5. Core, peel, and neatly slice the remaining apples.

6. Spoon the cooked apples over the bottom of the prepared shell. Arrange the raw apple slices in a circular pattern over the cooked pulp. Sprinkle with the remaining $\frac{1}{4}$ cup sugar and dot with the remaining tablespoon butter.

7. Bake for 40 or 45 minutes or until the apples are done and the pastry is browned.

8. Heat the preserves and put them through a sieve. Brush this over the tart.

Yield: 6 to 8 servings.

Basic Tart Pastry

2 cups all-purpose flour
¹/₄ teaspoon salt
2 tablespoons sugar
10 tablespoons very cold butter
2 egg yolks
2 tablespoons ice water

1. Place the flour, salt, and sugar in a food processor (see Note). Cut the butter into small pieces and add it. Add the yolks. Blend briefly and add the water. Blend just until the pastry pulls away from the sides of the container.

2. Gather the dough into a ball, wrap it in wax paper, and chill for at least 1 hour. The dough may also be frozen.

Yield: enough for a 10-inch tart.

NOTE: If a food processor is not used, place the flour, salt, and sugar in a mixing bowl. Cut the butter into small bits and add it. Using your fingers or a pastry blender, cut in the butter until it has the texture of coarse cornmeal. Beat the yolks and water together and add, stirring quickly with a fork.

French Cherry Tart

Basic Tart Pastry (see preceding recipe)
2 tablespoons all-purpose flour
3 tablespoons sugar
2 pounds fresh pitted cherries

1. Preheat the oven to 400 degrees.

2. Line a 10-inch pie tin (preferably a quiche pan with a removable bottom) with the pastry. Refrigerate or place in the freezer.

3. Blend the flour with 1 tablespoon sugar. Sprinkle the bottom of the shell evenly with the mixture. Place the cherries in the shell and sprinkle with the remaining 2 tablespoons sugar. Bake for 45 minutes.

   Yield: 8 servings.

   NOTE: This technique also works with pitted and sliced plums, apricots, peaches, and other fruit. Use the same quantities of ingredients.

Oeufs à la Neige

> 10 egg whites at room temperature
> ½ teaspoon cream of tartar
> 1½ cups sugar
> 1 cup strawberry jam
> 3 cups Crème Anglaise (recipe follows)
> 12 large strawberries

1. Preheat the oven to 350 degrees. Butter a 12-cup fluted tube pan.

2. Beat the egg whites with an electric beater in a large bowl until frothy. Add the cream of tartar. Gradually add the sugar, beating. Continue beating until the meringue is quite stiff and has a sheen.

3. Spoon the meringue into the mold, alternating it with spoonfuls of the jam. Smooth the top with a spoon or spatula. Tap the mold on the counter several times to pack the meringue down. Cover loosely with foil.

4. Place the mold in a baking dish and pour 2 inches boiling water around it. Place the dish on the bottom rack of the oven and bake for 15 minutes. The meringue will puff above the top of the mold.

5. Remove the mold from the oven and cool completely. If the meringue is being made a day ahead, refrigerate it in the mold at this point. To assemble, unmold the meringue onto a large round platter and spoon 1 cup crème anglaise around it and in the center. Place the strawberries around the meringue. Serve the remaining sauce on the side.

Yield: 10 to 12 servings.

Crème Anglaise

     6 large egg yolks
   2/3 cup sugar
       Pinch salt
     1 teaspoon vanilla extract
     2 cups milk
     2 tablespoons rum or Grand Marnier

1. Mix the yolks and sugar in a saucepan with a wire whisk until lemon colored. Add the salt and vanilla and blend well. Add the milk and blend.

2. Cook the mixture over medium heat, swirling it and constantly scraping the bottom and sides of the pan with a wooden spatula to ensure even cooking. It is important to keep the mixture moving during the entire process. The mixture is done when it coats the spatula evenly. This occurs at about 185 degrees. (To check, run your finger over the back of the spoon; the mixture should separate cleanly.)

3. Pour the mixture through a fine strainer into a small mixing bowl. Cool to room temperature, stirring occasionally to maintain smoothness.

4. Add the rum.

Yield: about 3 cups.

Caribbean Crêpes with Rum

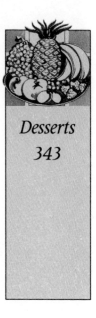

> 4 tablespoons butter
> 2 cups sliced bananas
> 2 tablespoons sugar
> 8 Basic Crêpes (recipe follows)
> ¼ cup heavy cream
> ¼ cup dark rum

1. Melt the butter in a shallow pan. Add the bananas and 1 tablespoon sugar. Sauté briefly until hot, turning the bananas.

2. Butter a large shallow gratin or presentation pan about 12 inches in diameter. With a serving spoon, place some of the banana mixture in each crêpe and roll it up. Arrange the crêpes in the pan.

3. Place over low heat, pour in the cream, and sprinkle with the remaining tablespoon sugar. Pour in the rum and tilt the pan slightly, then flambé. When the flame extinguishes, cook for about 1 minute and serve.

   Yield: 4 servings.

Basic Crêpes

> ½ cup all-purpose flour
> 1 large egg
> 1 teaspoon sugar
> ⅛ teaspoon salt
> ¾ cup milk
> 3 tablespoons butter
> ½ teaspoon vanilla extract

1. Blend the flour, egg, sugar, and salt in a mixing bowl. Gradually add the milk, stirring constantly.

2. Select a small crêpe pan (5 or 6 inches in diameter) and melt the butter. Pour the butter into the crêpe batter, stirring constantly. Strain through a fine sieve. Add the vanilla.

3. Add about 2 tablespoons or slightly less of the batter to the crêpe pan over medium heat. Cook for 45 seconds to 1 minute (the crêpe should be lightly browned) and turn the crêpe. Cook for about 30 seconds on the other side and transfer to a flat surface. Add more batter and repeat until finished.

Yield: 12 to 14 crêpes.

Crêpes Soufflé

12 Basic Crêpes (see preceding recipe)
 2 tablespoons butter
 2 tablespoons all-purpose flour
 1 tablespoon cornstarch
 2 cups milk
 ¼ teaspoon vanilla extract
 4 large eggs, separated
 1 tablespoon grated orange rind
 2 tablespoons melted butter
 2 tablespoons confectioners' sugar
   Crème Anglaise (see page 342) flavored with
     2 tablespoons dark rum

1. Preheat the oven to 425 degrees.

2. Melt the solid butter in a saucepan. Blend the flour and cornstarch and add them, stirring with a wire whisk. When blended, add the milk, stirring constantly with the whisk. When the mixture is thickened and smooth, lower the heat. Add the vanilla.

3. Beat the egg yolks and add them to the sauce, beating constantly and rapidly with the whisk. Do not boil or the sauce will curdle. When thickened, remove immediately from the heat and add the orange rind. Spoon the custard into a mixing bowl. Cool slightly.

4. Beat the egg whites until stiff and add about ⅓ of them to the custard mixture. Beat them in quickly with the whisk. Add the remaining whites and fold them in with a rubber spatula.

5. Butter a baking dish large enough to hold 12 filled crêpes.

6. Arrange the crêpes on a flat surface and fill them with the custard mixture. Roll them up.

7. Arrange the filled crêpes in the baking dish. Brush with the melted butter. Sprinkle 1 tablespoon confectioners' sugar over them.

8. Place in the oven and bake for 10 minutes or until puffed and slightly brown on top. Remove from the oven and sprinkle with the remaining tablespoon sugar. Serve with the Crème Anglaise on the side.

   Yield: 6 servings.

Chocolate Mousse

No dessert has more universal appeal than chocolate mousse. It seems to find favor with almost all cooks. To alter its flavor you may use bitter or semisweet chocolate instead of sweet chocolate. You may use any number of garnishes as decoration. Add sweetened whipped cream with candied violets or toasted nuts. All will be entirely fitting and irresistible.

> 4 ounces sweet chocolate, broken into pieces
> ¼ pound butter, cut into small pieces
> 3 eggs, separated
> ¼ cup dark rum or liqueur of your choice, optional
> ¼ cup sugar

1. Select a thin 2-quart stainless steel bowl and a saucepan large enough so that the bowl can fit snugly into it.

2. Add boiling water to the saucepan and set the bowl in the saucepan. Bring the water to a simmer. Add the chocolate to the bowl and stir. When it starts to melt, add the butter. Continue stirring until well blended and remove the bowl from the pan. Add the egg yolks, and liqueur if desired, and stir until thoroughly blended.

3. Place the bowl briefly in the refrigerator until the mixture is slightly cooler than lukewarm. If it becomes too chilled, it will harden; take care not to overchill it.

4. Beat the whites until they stand in soft peaks. Gradually add the sugar, beating briskly. Continue beating until the whites are stiff. Fold the whites into the chocolate mixture. Spoon the mousse into 4 serving dishes. Chill briefly until ready to serve.

   Yield: 4 servings.

Creole Pralines

It is not imperative that you use a candy thermometer to prepare these pralines, but a thermometer is an asset. It is also preferable that you cook the candy on a metal heat-control pad, the best-known brand of which is Flame-Tamer. This distributes the heat evenly and discourages burning.

   1½ **cups light brown sugar**
   1½ **cups granulated sugar**
     8 **tablespoons butter**
   ½ **cup heavy cream**
   ½ **cup milk**
     2 **tablespoons dark corn syrup**
     2 **cups coarsely broken pecan halves, toasted (see Note)**

1. Brush the insides of two baking sheets all over with melted butter.

2. Combine the sugars, butter, cream, milk, and syrup in a saucepan and bring to a boil, stirring. Cook about 20 minutes, stirring constantly and checking the temperature often if a thermometer is used. When the candy achieves the soft-ball stage, the syrup will form a soft ball when a small portion is dropped into a basin of cold water. It will register 235 degrees on a thermometer. Do not exceed that temperature at this point. Add the pecans and continue cooking, stirring constantly, until a temperature of 240 degrees—no more—is achieved. When ready, the syrup will have a non-glossy, matte look. Work quickly at this point.

3. Remove the saucepan from the heat while beating. Take care that the candy does not harden. Using 2 spoons, spoon about 4 teaspoons of the mixture at a time onto the buttered baking sheets, spacing the mounds about 3 inches apart to allow them to spread to about 2½ inches in diameter. Cool and transfer to a dessert plate with a wide metal spatula. The pralines should be crumbly and not chewy.

Yield: about 30 pralines.

NOTE: To toast pecans, preheat the oven to 425 degrees. Scatter the pecan pieces in one layer in a baking pan and place in the upper part of the oven. Bake 4 to 5 minutes or until the pecans are crisp. Check often as they bake to make certain they do not burn.

Prunes in Beaujolais

2 pounds large unpitted prunes
3 cups Beaujolais wine
1 teaspoon vanilla extract
2 cups sugar
Peel from 2 lemons

1. Place the prunes in a mixing bowl and add the wine. Let stand 24 hours at room temperature or until the prunes have softened well.

2. Place the prunes and wine in a saucepan. Add the vanilla, sugar, and lemon peel. Bring to a boil and simmer for 30 minutes. The mixture should be syrupy. Chill. Remove the peel. Serve alone or with vanilla ice cream.

Yield: 6 to 8 servings.

Poached Pears in Red Wine and Honey

8 Bartlett or Bosc pears, about 2 pounds
Juice of 1 lemon
¼ cup sugar
½ cup honey
1½ cups dry red wine
½ teaspoon vanilla extract
2 whole cloves
3 black peppercorns
¼ cup Cherry Marnier
1 sprig fresh thyme or ½ teaspoon dry

1. Peel and core the pears. Leave the stems attached. The pears can be whole, halved, or quartered.

2. Put the pears in a saucepan just large enough to hold them standing upright if whole. Add the lemon juice, sugar, honey, wine, vanilla, cloves, peppercorns, cherry liqueur, and thyme. Bring just to a boil and cover. Simmer 30 minutes.

3. Lift the pears out of the pan. Stand them upright in a serving bowl. Strain the sauce over the pears and allow them to cool before serving. Baste the pears periodically with the sauce as they cool.

Yield: 8 servings.

Strawberry Soufflé with Strawberry Sauce

1½ pints strawberries, sliced
1¼ cups sugar
8 eggs, separated
Strawberry Sauce (recipe follows)

1. Preheat the oven to 425 degrees. Butter well and chill eight 1¼-cup soufflé dishes.

2. Place the strawberries in a food processor or blender. Add ¾ cup sugar. Purée well. Taste for sweetness (amount of sugar varies with sweetness of fruit). Transfer to a bowl.

3. Add the yolks to the mixture and blend well with a wire whisk. In another bowl whisk the whites while gradually adding the remaining ½ cup sugar. Whisk until you have soft peaks. Fold ¼ of the whites into the strawberries, then the remainder. Do not overwork. Taste again for sweetness.

4. Place the soufflé dishes on a baking sheet and fill them to the rims. Before placing them in the oven run your thumb around the rim of each to remove any overflow which could cling and prevent the soufflé from rising fully. Bake for 10 minutes. The sauce should be served separately.

   Yield: 8 servings.

   NOTE: You can make a frozen soufflé by whipping 1 cup heavy cream and adding it to the strawberry mixture after folding in the whites. Make a collar of foil several inches high around the rim of the soufflé dishes before adding the strawberry mixture. Fill to the top of the collar and freeze for several hours. Remove the foil before serving.

Strawberry Sauce

   ½ **pint strawberries, sliced thinly**
   ¼ **cup sugar**
   2 **tablespoons Cherry Marnier or other fruit liqueur**

1. Place the strawberries and sugar in a saucepan over medium heat. Cook, stirring occasionally, for 5 minutes. Add the liqueur and keep warm until serving.

   Yield: about 1 cup.

Orange Soufflés

1 tablespoon butter
⅓ cup plus 3 tablespoons granulated sugar
6 eggs, separated
2 teaspoons finely grated orange rind
¼ cup orange juice with the pulp
1 tablespoon Grand Marnier
1 tablespoon confectioners' sugar
 Orange Sauce (recipe follows), optional

1. Preheat the oven to 450 degrees.

2. Use the butter to rub the bottom and sides of four 1¼-cup individual soufflé dishes. Use 1 tablespoon granulated sugar to sprinkle the insides of the dishes.

3. Put the egg yolks in a bowl and add ⅓ cup sugar, the orange rind, orange juice, and Grand Marnier. Beat briskly with a wire whisk.

4. Beat the egg whites until stiff. Toward the end, beat in the remaining 2 tablespoons granulated sugar.

5. Spoon and scrape the egg yolk mixture into the whites. Fold in the yolks rapidly and well. Spoon equal portions of the mixture into the prepared soufflé dishes.

6. Place the dishes on a baking sheet and put in the oven. Bake 12 minutes. Put the confectioners' sugar in a sieve and sprinkle an equal amount over each soufflé. If the sauce is used, spoon out a small portion in the center of each soufflé and serve the remainder on the side.

   Yield: 4 servings.

Orange Sauce

1 cup apricot preserves or jam
½ cup water
½ cup orange sections, cut into pieces
1 teaspoon grated orange rind
2 tablespoons Grand Marnier

1. Combine the preserves and water in a saucepan. Cook slowly over medium heat, stirring, until blended and smooth, about 5 minutes. Add the orange sections and orange rind. Remove from heat and stir in Grand Marnier. Serve.

    Yield: 1³/₄ cups.

Bittersweet Chocolate and Cherry Soufflé

> 4 ounces bittersweet chocolate
> ¹/₂ cup sugar
> 3 tablespoons cherry Grand Marnier or other cherry liqueur
> 8 eggs, separated
> 4 teaspoons confectioners' sugar

1. Preheat the oven to 450 degrees. Butter the bottoms and sides of 4 chilled individual 1¹/₂-cup soufflé dishes.

2. Shave or finely chop the chocolate and add it to a mixing bowl. Place the bowl over simmering water until the chocolate melts. Add ¹/₄ cup sugar and the liqueur and stir to blend. Cool briefly.

3. Add the yolks and heat until blended.

4. Beat the egg whites until they form soft peaks. Gradually add the remaining ¹/₄ cup sugar and continue beating until stiff.

5. Fold half the egg whites into the chocolate mixture. Fold in the remaining egg whites.

6. Pour the mixture into the soufflé dishes.

7. Place the dishes on a baking sheet and cook 10 to 12 minutes. Sprinkle with the confectioners' sugar and serve.

    Yield: 4 servings.

Grand Marnier Soufflé

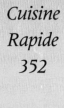

8 eggs, separated
²/₃ cup plus 2 tablespoons granulated sugar
¹/₃ cup Grand Marnier
2 tablespoons butter
Confectioners' sugar for garnish

1. Preheat the oven to 450 degrees. Place six 1¹/₄-cup individual soufflé dishes in the refrigerator to chill.

2. Beat the egg yolks and ¹/₃ cup granulated sugar in a double boiler over simmering water, whisking the mixture until it thickens to the consistency of heavy cream. Add the Grand Marnier.

3. Transfer the mixture to a mixing bowl set in a larger bowl of crushed ice. Continue beating over the ice until the mixture has cooled.

4. Butter the bottoms and sides of the soufflé dishes, paying special attention to the sides. Use 2 tablespoons granulated sugar to coat the insides of the dishes and return the dishes to the refrigerator.

5. Place the egg whites in a mixing bowl, preferably copper, and with a balloon whisk beat them to stiff peaks. Beat in the remaining ¹/₃ cup granulated sugar. With a large rubber spatula, fold the whites into the Grand Marnier mixture.

6. Spoon equal amounts of the mixture into the prepared dishes. The mixture should fill the dishes to a height of about ¹/₄ inch over the rims. With your thumb, create a channel around the periphery of the dish to allow for expansion. Place the dishes on a baking sheet and bake for 7 minutes. Lower the oven temperature to 425 degrees and bake for 5 minutes longer. Serve sprinkled with confectioners' sugar.

Yield: 6 servings.

Crème de Grand Marnier Ice Cream

    ¾ cup sugar
    5 egg yolks
    2 cups milk
    2 cups heavy cream
    1 vanilla bean, split
    ½ cup Crème de Grand Marnier

1. Beat the sugar and yolks with a small stiff whisk in a heavy 1-quart bowl until the yolks are bright yellow. Add 1 cup milk and stir.

2. Combine the egg mixture with the cream, the remaining cup milk, and the vanilla bean in a wide saucepan. Bring the mixture to 180 degrees (use a rapid-reading thermometer), stirring constantly. If the mixture boils, it will take on an undesirable cooked flavor. Strain the mixture into a stainless steel bowl and let it cool. Add the Crème de Grand Marnier. Remove the vanilla bean.

3. Place the mixture in an ice cream maker and freeze according to the manufacturer's instructions.

    Yield: 1 quart.

Grand Marnier Sauce

    2 egg yolks
    ¼ cup sugar
    2 tablespoons Grand Marnier
    ½ cup heavy cream, well chilled

1. Select a 1-quart mixing bowl that will fit snugly atop a slightly larger saucepan. Add about 2 inches of water to the saucepan and bring to a boil.

2. Put the yolks and sugar in the mixing bowl. Before placing the bowl over the heat, whisk vigorously until the mixture forms ribbons.

3. Place the mixing bowl over the saucepan. Whisk constantly and vigorously up to 10 minutes or until the mixture is thick and pale yellow.

4. Remove the bowl from the saucepan and stir in the Grand Marnier. Scrape the mixture into a cool bowl and refrigerate it.

5. Whip the cream until stiff and fold it into the cool custard mixture. Serve with fresh fruit or other desserts.

Yield: 4 servings.

Champagne Sabayon Sauce

6 egg yolks
¼ cup sugar
⅓ cup champagne
⅓ cup Grand Marnier

1. Place the yolks and sugar in a slant-sided saucepan. Whisk until the mixture is lemon-colored and forms ribbons.

2. Add the champagne and whisk well.

3. Whisk constantly over low heat or in a double boiler for 2 to 3 minutes. Add the Grand Marnier and cook, whisking, until the sauce forms a thickened cream. Remove from the heat immediately. Be careful not to overcook or it will curdle.

4. Serve with fresh fruit or other desserts, warm or cold, in a broad-mouthed wineglass.

Yield: 4 to 8 servings.

Index

aïoli (garlic mayonnaise), 290
anchovies:
   hamburgers with fried eggs and, 189
   sea trout with tomatoes and, 80
appetizers:
   artichokes vinaigrette, 19–20
   baked clams with garlic butter, 7
   cherrystone clam and corn fritters, 8–9
   chicken liver mousse, 18
   clam cocktail, 11
   cold lobster with basil vinaigrette, 11–12
   country pâté with pistachios, 3–4
   guacamole, 19
   smoked brook trout with horseradish
     sauce, 4–6
   smoked salmon mousse, 17
   tomatoes stuffed with curried shrimp,
     13–14
   tuna escabeche, 14–15
apple(s):
   caramelized, calf's liver with, 253
   green, sorbet (sorbet aux pommes vertes),
     336
   pork chops with sweet-and-sour sauce
     and, 205–6
   pork tenderloin with potatoes and, 203–4
   roast mallard duck with juniper berries
     and, 164–65
   sausage stuffing, roast breast of turkey
     with, 148–49
   tart, French, 339–40
artichoke bottoms:
   buttered, 116
   preparing, 117
artichokes:
   preparing for poaching, 20
   sautéed chicken breasts with (poulet
     noelle), 115–16
   vinaigrette, 19–20
arugula and red onion salad, 24
asparagus:
   fettuccine with, 262

and ham with cheese sauce (asperges et
   jambon mornay), 198–99
pasta with chicken and, 271
with shallot butter, 299
asperges et jambon mornay (asparagus and
   ham, with cheese sauce), 198–99
avocado(s):
   and broccoli salad, 21–22
   guacamole, 19

bacon, brochette of salmon with, 66–67
baked:
   clams with garlic butter, 7
   lobster with tarragon-cream sauce, 91–92
balsamic vinegar, chicken breasts with
   garlic and, 112–13
basic crêpes, 343–44
basic French vanilla ice cream, 338–39
basic tart pastry, 340
basic vinaigrette, 291
basil:
   fillets of sea bass with tomatoes and,
     54–55
   lemon marinade, grilled shrimp in, 102
   medallions of lamb with tomatoes and,
     231–32
   tomato-horseradish sauce with, 126
   veal rolls with, 243–44
   vinaigrette, cold lobster with, 11–12
bass, sea:
   fillets of, with basil and tomatoes, 54–55
   sautéed black, with red peppers, 53–54
bean(s), white:
   Breton, 322
   and lamb with vegetables, 228–29
   soup, Spanish, 30–31

Index
356

beans:
    braised lamb with (haricots d'agneau),
      227–28
    harira (Moroccan lamb and chickpea
      soup), 33–34
    lamb shanks with lentils, 230–31
    lentil salad with kielbasa, 22–23
    lentils with tomato sauce, 207–8
beans, green:
    spaghetti with clams and, 257–58
    and tomatoes Provençal, 312
    ziti with shrimp and, 266
Beaujolais:
    beef braised in (boeuf braisé au
      Beaujolais), 172
    prunes in, 347
    sauce, pheasant in, 153–54
beef:
    beer-braised, with onions, 173
    bitoks of veal and, 187–88
    boeuf bourguignon, 171
    braised in Beaujolais (boeuf braisé au
      Beaujolais), 172
    broiled skirt steak Cajun style, 179–80
    chateaubriand with chateau sauce,
      176–77
    filet mignon with mushrooms and
      Madeira sauce, 178
    fillet tied with string (filet de boeuf à la
      ficelle), 174–76
    German-style hamburgers with onions
      and vinegar, 191
    hamburger au poivre with red-wine
      sauce, 185–86
    hamburgers with fried eggs and ancho-
      vies, 189
    hamburgers with garlic and shallot butter,
      186–87
    hamburgers with goat cheese, 190
    moussaka with feta cheese, 237–39
    rib steak with marrow and red-wine
      sauce, 180–81
    rib steak with red-wine and shallot sauce,
      181–82
    roast fillet of, 174
    shell steaks with mustard butter, 182–83
    steak au poivre, 184
beer:
    batter, fish fillets in, 59.
    braised beef with onions, 173
beurre blanc aux fines herbes (white butter
    sauce with herbs), 294
Billi-Bi au safran (cream of mussel soup
    with saffron), 38–39

bitoks (Russian-style chicken burgers),
    133–34
bitoks of beef and veal, 187–88
bittersweet chocolate and cherry soufflé,
    351
blue cheese:
    dressing, mixed green salad with, 21
    sauce, chicken breasts with, 126–27
boeuf bourguignon, 171
boeuf braisé au Beaujolais (beef braised in
    Beaujolais), 172
boulettes of pork with cumin and coriander,
    214
braised:
    breast of veal (tendrons de veau braisés),
      247
    lamb with beans (haricots d'agneau),
      227–28
    quails with grapes, 157
bread:
    apple-sausage stuffing, 149
    crumbs, making fresh, 119
    garlic croutons, 28–29
    Parmesan cheese, 39–40
    quick French, 295
breaded chicken breasts with Parmesan
    cheese, 111–12
broccoli:
    and avocado salad, 21–22
    linguine with scallops and, 269–70
    purée, 299–300
broccoli di rape, 300
brochette(s):
    of honey-marinated pork, 199
    of salmon with bacon, 66–67
    scallop and zucchini, 100
broiled:
    fennel with Parmesan cheese, 310
    mustard-brushed chicken, 145
    quails with herb-sausage stuffing, 156–57
    shrimp with lemon-garlic butter, 101
    skirt steak Cajun style, 179–80
    tomatoes, 321
    tuna Provençal, 82
broth:
    fish, 289
    shrimp, 43
burgers:
    with fried eggs and anchovies, 189
    with garlic and shallot butter, 186–87
    German-style, with onions and vinegar,
      191
    with goat cheese, 190
    lamb, with feta cheese, 236–37

au poivre with red-wine sauce, 185–86
pork, with garlic and cumin, 218–19
butter:
    black, sauce, skate with, 75
    brown, sauce, salmon burgers with,
        70–71
    ginger sauce, grilled swordfish with, 77
    lemon sauce, poached cod with, 55–56
    maître d'hôtel, with mustard, 61
    parsley sauce, 89
    sauce, white, with herbs (beurre blanc
        aux fines herbes), 294
buttered:
    artichoke bottoms, 116
    new potatoes with fennel, 314–15
butternut squash purée, 301

cabbage:
    leaves stuffed with chicken and ginger,
        121–22
    packets stuffed with shrimp and salmon,
        105–7
    working with, 106
calf's liver:
    with caramelized apples, 253
    sautéed, with onions and capers (foie de
        veau Lyonnaise aux câpres), 251–52
Campari and grapefruit sorbet, 334–35
cantaloupe and ginger sorbet, 333–34
capers:
    breast of chicken with corn and, 123
    sautéed calf's liver with onions and (foie
        de veau Lyonnaise aux câpres), 251–52
    turkey breast with mushrooms and,
        146–47
capon, poached, with pistachio stuffing,
    151–52
Caribbean crêpes with rum, 343
carrot(s):
    and cucumbers with cumin, 305–6
    with cumin butter, 302
    egg noodles with lemon and, 272
    pudding, 301–2
cassoulet à la minute, 216–18
champagne sabayon sauce, 354
charcoal-grilled butterflied leg of lamb
    Provençal style, 225

chateaubriand with chateau sauce, 176–77
cheese:
    blue, dressing, mixed green salad with, 21
    blue, sauce, chicken breasts with, 126–27
    feta, lamb burgers with, 236–37
    feta, moussaka with, 237–39
    goat, hamburgers with, 190
    and ham frittata, 327–28
    macaroni and, 260
    Parmesan, bread, 39–40
    Parmesan, breaded chicken breasts with,
        111–12
    Parmesan, broiled fennel with, 310
    ravioli, herbed, 279
    sauce, asparagus and ham with (asperges
        et jambon mornay), 198–99
    turkey breast with prosciutto and, 147–48
    see also gratins
cherry:
    and bittersweet chocolate soufflé, 351
    tart, French, 340–41
cherry Marnier:
    bittersweet chocolate and cherry soufflé,
        351
    poached pears in red wine and honey,
        348
    strawberry sauce, 349
chestnut purée, 303
chicken:
    broiled mustard-brushed, 145
    burgers, Russian-style (bitoks), 133–34
    burgers with chive sauce, 119–20
    cabbage leaves stuffed with ginger and,
        121–22
    couscous, quick, 134–36
    cutting into ten serving pieces, 142–43
    fricassee with leeks, 140–41
    goujonettes, 124–25
    Mediterranean-style, 144
    nuggets with herb breading, 125–26
    pasta with asparagus and, 271
    pot-au-feu à la minute, 193–94
    in red wine (poulet au vin rouge), 137–38
    risotto with veal and, 284–85
    roast, with herbs, 138–40
    and winter-vegetable soup, 32–33
chicken breasts:
    with blue cheese sauce, 126–27
    bonne maman, 128
    breaded, with Parmesan cheese, 111–12
    with capers and corn, 123
    Chinese-style broiled, 130
    with fresh tomato and garlic, 129
    with garlic and balsamic vinegar, 112–13

chicken breasts *(continued)*
    lime-marinated grilled, 113–14
    with mustard-shallot sauce, 131
    saltimbocca, 132–33
    sautéed, with artichokes, 115–16
    sesame-coated (suprêmes de volaille aux
      sesames), 118
chicken liver(s):
    mousse, 18
    and mushroom ravioli, 273–74
chickpea and lamb soup, Moroccan
    (harira), 33–34
chili à la Franey, 192
chili and cucumber raita, 305
Chinese-style broiled chicken breasts, 130
chive sauce, chicken burgers with, 119–20
chocolate:
    bittersweet, and cherry soufflé, 351
    mousse, 345–46
choucroute garnie (garnished sauerkraut),
    215–16
cider, smoked pork shoulder with
    sauerkraut and, 213–14
clam(s):
    baked, with garlic butter, 7
    cherrystone, and corn fritters, 8–9
    chowder, Manhattan, 36
    cocktail, 11
    cornmeal-coated shrimp, scallops and,
      86–87
    green pasta with shrimp and, 263–64
    spaghetti with green beans and, 257–58
cod, poached, with lemon-butter sauce,
    55–56
cold:
cucumber and yogurt soup with fresh mint,
    27–28
    lobster with basil vinaigrette, 11–12
    lobster with hot-mustard sauce, 95–96
    pork with tuna sauce, 200
coriander:
    boulettes of pork with cumin and, 214
    orange vinaigrette, warm tuna and
      scallop salad with, 16
corn:
    breast of chicken with capers and, 123
    and cherrystone clam fritters, 8–9
    fresh, veal chops with, 241–42
    and pepper fritters, 304
    with red peppers, 303–4
Cornish game hen(s):
    bonne femme, 162–63
    with cranberry sauce, 158–59
    fricassee, 160–61

cornmeal-coated shrimp, scallops, and
    clams, 86–87
country pâté with pistachios, 3–4
country-style lamb loaf, 234
couscous:
    quick chicken, 134–36
    with raisins, 141–43
crab (meat):
    cakes with shrimp, Georges Perrier's,
      88–89
    gazpacho with, 29–30
    and shrimp gumbo, 41–43
    and spinach au gratin, 90–91
cranberry sauce:
    Cornish game hens with, 158–59
    fresh, pork chops with, 210–11
cream of leek soup, 27
cream of mussel soup with saffron (Billi-Bi
    au safran), 38–39
cream sauce:
    linguine in, 63
    tarragon, baked lobster with, 91–92
crème anglaise, 342
Crème de Grand Marnier ice cream, 353
creole pralines, 346–47
creole rice with tomatoes and herbs, 280–81
crêpes:
    basic, 343–44
    Caribbean, with rum, 343
    soufflé, 344–45
croutons, garlic, 28–29
cucumber(s):
    and carrots with cumin, 305–6
    and chili raita, 305
    salad, 6
    and yogurt soup with fresh mint, cold,
      27–28
cumin:
    boulettes of pork with coriander and, 214
    butter, carrots with, 302
    cucumbers and carrots with, 305–6
    pork burgers with garlic and, 218–19
curry(ied):
    lamb, 232–33
    lamb meatballs, 235–36
    powder, 293
    sauce, 292–93
    sauce, turkey patties with, 150
    shrimp, tomatoes stuffed with, 13–14

deep-fried:
 eggplant, 306–7
 zucchini, 325
desserts:
 basic crêpes, 343–44
 basic French vanilla ice cream, 338–39
 basic tart pastry, 340
 bittersweet chocolate and cherry soufflé,
  351
 cantaloupe and ginger sorbet, 333–34
 Caribbean crêpes with rum, 343
 chocolate mousse, 345–46
 crème de Grand Marnier ice cream, 353
 creole pralines, 346–47
 crêpes soufflé, 344–45
 French apple tart, 339–40
 French cherry tart, 340–41
 Grand Marnier soufflé, 352
 grapefruit and Campari sorbet, 334–35
 honeydew and melon-liqueur ice, 337
 ices, 333
 oeufs à la neige, 341–42
 orange soufflés, 350
 pear and passion fruit sorbet, 336–37
 pineapple and mango sorbet, 335
 poached pears in red wine and honey,
  348
 prunes in Beaujolais, 347
 rosemary and mint ice, 338
 sorbet aux pommes vertes (green apple
  sorbet), 336
 sorbets, 333
 strawberry soufflé with strawberry sauce,
  348–49
dessert sauces:
 champagne sabayon, 354
 crème anglaise, 342
 Grand Marnier, 353–54
 orange, 350–51
 strawberry, 349
dill sauce, 278
duck:
 braised in red wine and thyme, 163–64
 roast mallard, with juniper berries and
  apples, 164–65

egg noodles with carrots and lemon, 272
eggplant:
 deep-fried, 306–7
 and tomatoes au gratin, 308–9
 and zucchini casserole, 307–8
eggs, 328
 fried, hamburgers with anchovies and,
  189
 frittata with potatoes, 326–27
 ham and cheese frittata, 327–28
 oeufs à la neige, 341–42
 omelette fines herbes, 329
endive, scallops with, in saffron sauce, 98
escarole with garlic and olive oil, 309

faisan sauté aux herbes (sautéed pheasant
 with herbs), 152–53
farfalle and mussels with ginger-mustard
 vinaigrette, 268–69
fennel:
 broiled, with Parmesan cheese, 310
 buttered new potatoes with, 314–15
 purée, 311
feta cheese:
 lamb burgers with, 236–37
 moussaka with, 237–39
fettuccine:
 with asparagus, 262
 with pecans, 263
 with shrimp and vegetables, 260–61
filet de boeuf à la ficelle (beef fillet tied with
 string), 174–76
filet mignon with mushrooms and Madeira
 sauce, 178
fish:
 brochette of salmon with bacon, 66–67
 broiled tuna Provençal, 82
 broth, 289
 cabbage packets stuffed with shrimp and
  salmon, 105–7
 fillets, sesame-coated, 74
 fillets in beer batter, 59
 fillets of flounder with parsley-mustard
  sauce, 57

Index
360

fish *(continued)*
    fillets of sea bass with basil and tomatoes, 54–55
    flounder fillets à l'anglaise, 58
    grilled herbed salmon with shrimp, 71–72
    grilled swordfish with ginger-butter sauce, 77
    grilled tuna with fresh thyme, 85–86
    grilled tuna with Mediterranean salad, 83–84
    halibut fillets with leeks and linguine, 62–63
    lotte au poivre (monkfish coated with crushed pepper), 65
    matelote of salmon and shellfish, 72–73
    monkfish in red-wine sauce, 64
    paglia e fieno with salmon, 265
    peppered salmon with onion compote, 69–70
    poached cod with lemon-butter sauce, 55–56
    poached halibut with maitre d'hôtel butter, 60–61
    Provençal seafood stew, 44
    red snapper fillets with pine nut coating, 76
    salmon and shrimp ravioli, 277–78
    salmon baked in foil packages, 67–68
    salmon burgers with brown butter sauce, 70–71
    sautéed black sea bass with red peppers, 53–54
    sautéd trout with lime, 78–79
    sea trout with anchovies and tomatoes, 80
    and shellfish, soup, Japanese-style, 37–38
    skate with black butter sauce, 75
    smoked brook trout with horseradish sauce, 4–6
    smoked salmon mousse, 17
    soup, Marseilles-style, 45–46
    stew with vegetables, quick, 48–49
    stock, 38
    tuna escabeche, 14–15
    tuna Niçoise, 81
    tuna sauce, 200–201
    warm tuna and scallop salad with orange-coriander vinaigrette, 16
flounder:
    fillets à l'anglaise, 58
    fillets of, with parsley-mustard sauce, 57
foie de veau Lyonnaise aux câpres (sautéed calf's liver with onions and capers), 251–52
French apple tart, 339–40
French bread, quick, 295
French cherry tart, 340–41
French-fried:
    potatoes, 318
    yams, 323
fresh tomato sauce, 291–92
fricassee:
    chicken, with leeks, 140–41
    Cornish game hen, 160–61
frittatas, 328
    ham and cheese, 327–28
    with potatoes, 326–27
fritters:
    cherrystone clam and corn, 8–9
    corn and pepper, 304

game:
    birds, cooking, 154
    braised quails with grapes, 157
    broiled quails with herb-sausage stuffing, 156–57
    duck braised in red wine and thyme, 163–64
    faisan sauté aux herbes (sautéed pheasant with herbs), 152–53
    marinade for venison, 167
    pheasant in Beaujolais sauce, 153–54
    pheasant in onion sauce, 155
    roast mallard duck with juniper berries and apples, 164–65
    trussing, 138–39
    venison steaks in red-wine sauce, 168
    venison stew, 166
game hen(s), Cornish:
    bonne femme, 162–63
    with cranberry sauce, 158–59
    fricassee, 160–61
garlic:
    butter, baked clams with, 7
    chicken breasts with balsamic vinegar and, 112–13
    chicken breasts with fresh tomato and, 129
    croutons, 28–29

escarole with olive oil and, 309
lemon butter, broiled shrimp with, 101
mayonnaise (aïoli), 290
pork burgers with cumin and, 218–19
potatoes, puréed, 316
sautéed lettuce with, 312–13
sautéed potatoes with, 314
and shallot butter, hamburgers with,
186–87
garnished sauerkraut (choucroute garnie),
215–16
gazpacho with crab meat, 29–30
Georges Perrier's crab cakes with shrimp,
88–89
German-style hamburgers with onions and
vinegar, 191
ginger:
butter sauce, grilled swordfish with, 77
cabbage leaves stuffed with chicken and,
121–22
and cantaloupe sorbet, 333–34
flavored veal loaf, 250–51
hoisin sauce, 276–77
mustard vinaigrette, farfalle and mussels
with, 268–69
and pork ravioli, 276
goat cheese, hamburgers with, 190
goujonettes, chicken, 124–25
Grand Marnier:
champagne sabayon sauce, 354
crème anglaise, 342
orange sauce, 350–51
orange soufflés, 350
sauce, 353–54
soufflé, 351
Grand Marnier, cherry:
bittersweet chocolate and cherry soufflé,
351
poached pears in red wine and honey,
348
strawberry sauce, 349
Grand Marnier, Crème de, ice cream, 353
grapefruit and Campari sorbet, 334–35
grapes, braised quails with, 157
gratins:
crab meat and spinach, 90–91
eggplant and tomatoes, 308–9
summer vegetables, 325–26
yellow squash, 324
green apple sorbet (sorbet aux pommes
vertes), 336
green beans:
spaghetti with clams and, 257–58
and tomatoes Provençal, 312

ziti with shrimp and, 266
green pasta with shrimp and clams, 263–64
grilled:
herbed salmon with shrimp, 71–72
shrimp in lemon-basil marinade, 102
swordfish with ginger-butter sauce, 77
tuna with fresh thyme, 85–86
tuna with Mediterranean salad, 83–84
guacamole, 19
gumbo, crab and shrimp, 41–43

halibut:
fillets with leeks and linguine, 62–63
poached, with maître d'hôtel butter,
60–61
ham:
and asparagus with cheese sauce
(asperges et jambon mornay), 198–99
and cheese frittata, 327–28
Spanish white bean soup, 30–31
steaks with Madeira and mustard sauce,
197
turkey breast with prosciutto and cheese,
147–48
ziti with prosciutto and tomato sauce, 267
hamburgers, see burgers
haricots d'agneau (braised lamb with
beans), 227–28
harira (Moroccan lamb and chickpea soup),
33–34
harissa, 136
herb(s):
breading, chicken nuggets with, 125–26
creole rice with tomatoes and, 280–81
omelette fines herbes, 329
pork cutlets with vinegar and, 201–2
roast chicken with, 138–40
sausage stuffing, broiled quails with,
156–57
sautéed pheasant with (faisan sauté aux
herbes), 152–53
white butter sauce with (beurre blanc aux
fine herbes), 294
herbed:
cheese ravioli, 279
grilled salmon with shrimp, 71–72
hoisin-ginger sauce, 276–77

hominy and pork stew, Mexican (pozole),
    34–35
honey:
    marinated pork, brochettes of, 199
    poached pears in red wine and, 348
honeydew and melon-liqueur ice, 337
horseradish:
    sauce, 290
    sauce, smoked brook trout with, 4–6
    and tomato sauce, 194
    tomato sauce with basil, 126

ice cream:
    basic French vanilla, 338–39
    Crème de Grand Marnier, 353
ices, 333
    honeydew and melon-liqueur, 337
    rosemary and mint, 338
individual meat loaves, 239–40

Japanese-style fish and shellfish soup,
    37–38
julienne of veal with mustard sauce, 245
julienne of veal with paprika and sour
    cream, 246
juniper berries, roast mallard duck with
    apples and, 164–65

kielbasa, lentil salad with, 22–23

lamb:
    braised, with beans (haricots d'agneau),
        227–28
    burgers with feta cheese, 236–37
    charcoal-grilled butterflied leg of,
        Provençal style, 225
    and chickpea soup, Moroccan (harira),
        33–34
    curry, 232–33
    loaf, country-style, 234
    meatballs, curried, 235–36
    medallions of, with tomatoes and basil,
        231–32
    moussaka with feta cheese, 237–39
    parsleyed rack of, 223
    preparing a leg of, for grilling, 226–27
    roast leg of, with rosemary, 224
    shanks with lentils, 230–31
    and white beans with vegetables, 228–29
leek(s):
    chicken fricassee with, 140–41
    cream of, soup, 27
    halibut fillets with linguine and, 62–63
    sauce, 275
lemon:
    basil marinade, grilled shrimp in, 102
    butter sauce, poached cod with, 55–56
    egg noodles with carrots and, 272
    garlic butter, broiled shrimp with, 101
lentil(s):
    lamb shanks with, 230–31
    salad with kielbasa, 22–23
    with tomato sauce, pork chops with,
        206–8
lettuce:
    sautéed, with garlic, 312–13
    three-, chiffonade, 12–13
lime:
    marinated grilled chicken breasts, 113–14
    sautéed trout with, 78–79
linguine:
    in cream sauce, halibut fillets with leeks
        and, 62–63
    with scallops and broccoli, 269–70
liver, calf's:
    with caramelized apples, 253
    sautéed, with onions and capers (foie de
        veau Lyonnaise aux câpres), 251–52
liver(s), chicken:
    mousse, 18

and mushroom ravioli, 273–74
livers, rice pilaf with, 161
lobster:
    américaine, 93–95
    baked, with tarragon-cream sauce, 91–92
    cold, with basil vinaigrette, 11–12
    cold, with hot-mustard sauce, 95–96
    cutting up, 94
lotte au poivre (monkfish coated with
    crushed pepper), 65
Lyonnaise oyster stew, 46–47

macaroni:
    and cheese, 260
    and veal soup, 31–32
Madeira:
    and mushrooms sauce, filet mignon with,
      178
    and mustard sauce, ham steaks with, 197
maître d'hôtel butter with mustard, 61
mango and pineapple sorbet, 325
Manhattan clam chowder, 36
marinade for venison, 167
Marseilles-style fish soup, 45–46
mashed potatoes (purée de pommes de
    terre), 315
mashed potatoes with scallions, 316
matelote of salmon and shellfish, 72–73
mayonnaise, 289
    garlic (aïoli), 290
    with scallions, 87
    sweet red pepper, 60
meatballs:
    boulettes of pork with cumin and
      coriander, 214
    curried lamb, 235–36
    veal, avgolemono, 249–50
meat loaves, individual, 239–40
meats:
    asperges et jambon mornay (asparagus
      and ham with cheese sauce), 198–99
    beer-braised beef with onions, 173
    bitoks of beef and veal, 187–88
    boeuf bourguignon, 171
    boeuf braisé au Beaujolais (beef braised in
      Beaujolais), 172
    boulettes of pork with cumin and
      coriander, 214

brochettes of honey-marinated pork, 199
broiled skirt steak Cajun style, 179–80
calf's liver with caramelized apples, 253
cassoulet à la minute, 216–18
charcoal-grilled butterflied leg of lamb
    Provençal style, 225
chateaubriand with chateau sauce,
    176–77
chili à la Franey, 192
choucroute garnie, 215–16
cold pork with tuna sauce, 200
country pâté with pistachios, 3–4
country-style lamb loaf, 234
curried lamb meatballs, 235–36
filet de boeuf à la ficelle (beef fillet tied
    with string), 174–76
filet mignon with mushrooms and
    Madeira sauce, 178
foie de veau Lyonnaise aux câpres
    (sautéed calf's liver with onions and
    capers), 251–52
German-style hamburgers with onions
    and vinegar, 191
ginger-flavored veal loaf, 250–51
ham and cheese frittata, 327–28
hamburger au poivre with red-wine
    sauce, 185–86
hamburgers with fried eggs and
    anchovies, 189
hamburgers with garlic and shallot butter,
    186–97
hamburgers with goat cheese, 190
ham steaks with Madeira and mustard
    sauce, 197
haricots d'agneau (braised lamb with
    beans), 227–28
harira (Moroccan lamb and chickpea
    soup), 33–34
individual meat loaves, 239–40
julienne of veal with mustard sauce, 245
julienne of veal with paprika and sour
    cream, 246
lamb, leg of, preparing for grilling, 226–27
lamb and white beans with vegetables,
    228–29
lamb burgers with feta cheese, 236–37
lamb curry, 232–33
lamb shanks with lentils, 230–31
lentil salad with kielbasa, 22–23
marinade for venison, 167
medallions of lamb with tomatoes and
    basil, 231–32
moussaka with feta cheese, 237–39
parsleyed rack of lamb, 223

**Index
364**

meats *(continued)*
 pork and ginger ravioli, 276
 pork burgers with garlic and cumin, 218–19
 pork chops and sausage with sauerkraut, 209–10
 pork chops Basque style, 208–9
 pork chops Milanese, 211–12
 pork chops with apples and sweet-and-sour sauce, 205–6
 pork chops with fresh cranberry sauce, 210–11
 pork chops with lentils, 206–8
 pork cutlets with vinegar and herbs, 201–2
 pork tenderloin with potatoes and apples, 203–4
 pot-au-feu à la minute, 193–94
 pozole (Mexican pork and hominy stew), 34–35
 rib steak with marrow and red-wine sauce, 180–81
 rib steak with red-wine and shallot sauce, 181–82
 risotto with chicken and veal, 284–85
 roast fillet of beef, 174
 roast leg of lamb with rosemary, 224
 roast pork tenderloin with sweet peppers and paprika sauce, 204–5
 sautéed medallions of pork with port, 202–3
 shell steaks with mustard butter, 182–83
 smoked pork shoulder with cider and sauerkraut, 213–14
 Spanish white bean soup, 30–31
 steak au poivre, 184
 tendrons de veau braisés (braised breast of veal), 247
 veal and macaroni soup, 31–32
 veal chops with fresh corn, 241–42
 veal meatballs avgolemono, 249–50
 veal rolls with basil, 243–44
 veal scaloppine Milanese, 242–43
 veal shanks with Oriental vegetables, 248
 venison steaks in red-wine sauce, 168
 venison stew, 166
medallions of lamb with tomatoes and basil, 231–32
Mediterranean salad with tomato dressing, 84–85
Mediterranean-style chicken, 144
melon-liqueur and honeydew ice, 337
Mexican pork and hominy stew (pozole), 34–35
mint:
 fresh, cold cucumber and yogurt soup with, 27–28

and rosemary ice, 338
 snap peas with, 313
mixed green salad with blue cheese dressing, 21
monkfish:
 coated with crushed pepper (lotte au poivre), 65
 in red-wine sauce, 64
Moroccan lamb and chickpea soup (harira), 33–34
moussaka with feta cheese, 237–39
mousse:
 chicken liver, 18
 chocolate, 345–46
 smoked salmon, 17
mushroom(s):
 and chicken livers ravioli, 273–74
 and Madeira sauce, filet mignon with, 178
 and paprika sauce, shrimp with, 103
 rice with pistachios and, 283
 tomato sauce with, 240–41
 turkey breast with capers and, 146–47
mussel(s):
 cleaning, 40
 cream of, soup with saffron (Billi-Bi au safran), 38–39
 and farfalle with ginger-mustard vinaigrette, 268–69
 soup, Vietnamese-style, 41
mustard:
 brushed chicken, broiled, 145
 butter, shell steaks with, 182–83
 ginger vinaigrette, farfalle and mussels with, 268–69
 hot-, sauce, cold lobster with, 95–96
 and Madeira sauce, ham steaks with, 197
 maître d'hôtel butter with, 61
 parsley sauce, fillets of flounder with, 57
 sauce, julienne of veal with, 245
 shallot sauce, chicken breasts with, 131

noodles:
 egg, with carrots and lemon, 272
 see also pasta
nutmeg, spinach with, 320
nuts:
 chestnut purée, 303

country pâté with pistachios, 3–4
fettuccine with pecans, 263
poached capon with pistachio stuffing, 151–52
red snapper fillets with pine nut coating, 76
rice with mushrooms and pistachios, 283
rice with raisins and pine nuts, 282–83

oeufs à la neige, 341–42
omelettes, 328
fines herbes, 329
see also frittatas
onion(s):
beer-braised beef with, 173
compote, peppered salmon with, 69–70
German-style hamburgers with vinegar and, 191
mincing, 120
red, and arugula salad, 24
sauce, pheasant in, 155
sautéed calf's liver with capers and (foie de veau Lyonnaise aux câpres), 251–52
orange:
coriander vinaigrette, warm tuna and scallop salad with, 16
sauce, 350–51
soufflés, 350
see also Grand Marnier
orzo with fresh tomato sauce, 280
oyster stew, Lyonnaise, 46–47

paglia e fieno with salmon, 265
paprika:
julienne of veal with sour cream and, 246
and mushrooms sauce, shrimp with, 103
and sweet peppers sauce, roast pork tenderloin with, 204–5
Parmesan cheese:
bread, 39–40
breaded chicken breasts with, 111–12

broiled fennel with, 310
parsley(ed):
butter sauce, 89
mustard sauce, fillets of flounder with, 57
rack of lamb, 223
passion fruit and pear sorbet, 336–37
pasta:
with chicken and asparagus, 271
chicken livers and mushroom ravioli, 273–74
egg noodles with carrots and lemon, 272
farfalle and mussels with ginger-mustard vinaigrette, 268–69
fettuccine with asparagus, 262
fettucine with pecans, 263
fettuccine with shrimp and vegetables, 260–61
green, with shrimp and clams, 263–64
herbed cheese ravioli, 279
linguine in cream sauce, 63
linguine with scallops and broccoli, 269–70
macaroni and cheese, 260
orzo with fresh tomato sauce, 280
paglia e fieno with salmon, 265
pork and ginger ravioli, 276
salmon and shrimp ravioli, 277–78
spaghettini with vegetables and pepper-vodka sauce, 258–59
spaghetti with clams and green beans, 257–58
wonton skins, filling, to make ravioli, 273–74
ziti with prosciutto and tomato sauce, 267
ziti with shrimp and green beans, 266
pastry, basic tart, 340
pâté, country, with pistachios, 3–4
pea(s):
snap, with mint, 313
snow, and roasted pepper salad, 23–24
pear(s):
and passion fruit sorbet, 336–37
poached, in red wine and honey, 348
pecans, fettuccini with, 263
pepper(s):
and corn fritters, 304
roasting, 10
tomato sauce with, 212
pepper, sweet red:
corn with, 303–4
mayonnaise, 60
and paprika sauce, roast pork tenderloin with, 204–5
purée, 9

pepper, sweet red *(continued)*
  roasted, and snow pea salad, 23–24
  sauce, 279
  sautéed black sea bass with, 53–54
peppercorns:
  crushed, monkfish coated with (lotte au poivre), 65
  peppered salmon with onion compote, 69–70
  Szechuan-style shrimp with, 104–5
  pepper-vodka sauce, spaghettini with vegetables and, 258–59
pheasant:
  in Beaujolais sauce, 153–54
  in onion sauce, 155
  sautéed, with herbs (faisan sauté aux herbes), 152–53
pilaf, rice, 281
  with livers, 161
pineapple and mango sorbet, 335
pine nut(s):
  coating, red snapper fillets with, 76
  rice with raisins and, 282–83
pistachio(s):
  country pâté with, 3–4
  rice with mushrooms and, 283
  stuffing, poached capon with, 151–52
poached:
  capon with pistachio stuffing, 151–52
  cod with lemon-butter sauce, 55–56
  halibut with maître d'hôtel butter, 60–61
  pears in red wine and honey, 348
pork:
  boulettes of, with cumin and coriander, 214
  burgers with garlic and cumin, 218–19
  choucroute garnie, 215–16
  cold, with tuna sauce, 200
  cutlets with vinegar and herbs, 201–2
  and ginger ravioli, 276
  and hominy stew, Mexican (pozole), 34–35
  honey-marinated, brochettes of, 199
  sautéed medallions of, with port, 202–3
  shoulder, smoked, with cider and sauerkraut, 213–14
  tenderloin, roast, with sweet peppers and paprika sauce, 204–5
  tenderloin with potatoes and apples, 203–4
pork chops:
  with apples and sweet-and-sour sauce, 205–6
  Basque style, 208–9

with fresh cranberry sauce, 210–11
with lentils, 206–8
Milanese, 211–12
and sausage with sauerkraut, 209–10
port, sautéed medallions of pork with, 202–3
potato(es):
  buttered new, with fennel, 314–15
  French-fried, 318
  frittata with, 326–27
  mashed (purée de pommes de terre), 315
  mashed, with scallions, 316
  pancakes, 317
  pork tenderloin with apples and, 203–4
  puréed garlic, 316
  sautéed, with garlic, 314
pot-au-feu à la minute, 193–94
poulet au vin rouge (chicken in red wine), 137–38
poulet noelle (sautéed chicken breasts with artichokes), 115–16
poultry:
  bitoks (Russian-style chicken burgers), 133–34
  braised quails with grapes, 157
  breaded chicken breasts with Parmesan cheese, 111–12
  breast of chicken with capers and corn, 123
  breasts of chicken bonne maman, 128
  broiled mustard-brushed chicken, 145
  broiled quails with herb-sausage stuffing, 156–57
  cabbage leaves stuffed with chicken and ginger, 121–22
  chicken, cutting into ten serving pieces, 142–43
  chicken and winter-vegetable soup, 32–33
  chicken breasts saltimbocca, 132–33
  chicken breasts with blue cheese sauce, 126–27
  chicken breasts with fresh tomato and garlic, 129
  chicken breasts with garlic and balsamic vinegar, 112–13
  chicken breasts with mustard-shallot sauce, 131
  chicken burgers with chive sauce, 119–20
  chicken fricassee with leeks, 140–41
  chicken goujonettes, 124–25
  chicken liver mousse, 18
  chicken livers and mushroom ravioli, 273–74

chicken nuggets with herb breading,
125–26
Chinese-style broiled chicken breasts, 130
Cornish game hen fricassee, 160–61
Cornish game hens with cranberry sauce,
158–59
duck braised in red wine and thyme,
163–64
faisan sauté aux herbes (sautéed pheasant
with herbs), 152–53
game birds, cooking, 154
game hens bonne femme, 162–63
lime-marinated grilled chicken breasts,
113–14
Mediterranean-style chicken, 144
pasta with chicken and asparagus, 271
pheasant in Beaujolais sauce, 153–54
pheasant in onion sauce, 155
poached capon with pistachio stuffing,
151–52
poulet au vin rouge (chicken in red wine),
137
poulet noelle (sautéed chicken breasts
with artichokes), 115–16
quick chicken couscous, 134–36
risotto with chicken and veal, 284–85
roast breast of turkey with apple-sausage
stuffing, 148–49
roast chicken with herbs, 138–40
roast mallard duck with juniper berries
and apples, 164–65
suprêmes de volaille aux sesames
(sesame-coated chicken breasts), 118
trussing, 138–39
turkey breast with capers and
mushrooms, 146–47
turkey breast with prosciutto and cheese,
147–48
turkey patties with curry sauce, 150
pozole (Mexican pork and hominy stew),
34–35
pralines, creole, 346–47
prosciutto:
and tomato sauce, ziti with, 267
turkey breast with cheese and, 147–48
Provençal sauce, 82–83
Provençal seafood stew, 44
prunes in Beaujolais, 347
purée(d):
broccoli, 299–300
butternut squash, 301
chestnut, 303
fennel, 311
garlic potatoes, 316
de pommes de terre (mashed potatoes),
315
red pepper, 9
de rutabaga (yellow turnip purée), 320
yam, 323

quails:
braised, with grapes, 157
broiled, with herb-sausage stuffing,
156–57
quick chicken couscous, 134–36
quick fish stew with vegetables, 48–49
quick French bread, 295
quick tomato sauce, 292

raisins:
couscous with, 141–43
rice with pine nuts and, 282–83
raita, cucumber and chili, 305
ratatouille à la minute, 319
ravioli:
chicken livers and mushroom, 273–74
herbed cheese, 279
pork and ginger, 276
salmon and shrimp, 277–78
wonton skins, filling to make, 273–74
red snapper fillets with pine nut coating, 76
rib steak:
with marrow and red-wine sauce, 180–81
with red-wine and shallot sauce, 181–82
rice:
creole, with tomatoes and herbs, 280–81
with mushrooms and pistachios, 283
pilaf, 281
pilaf with livers, 161
with raisins and pine nuts, 282–83
risotto with chicken and veal, 284–85
turmeric, 282
roast:
breast of turkey with apple-sausage
stuffing, 148–49

Index
368

roast *(continued)*
    chicken with herbs, 138–40
    fillet of beef, 174
    leg of lamb with rosemary, 224
    mallard duck with juniper berries and
        apples, 164–65
    pork tenderloin with sweet peppers and
        paprika sauce, 204–5
roasted pepper and snow pea salad, 23–24
rosemary:
    and mint ice, 338
    roast leg of lamb with, 224
roses, tomato, 5
rum:
    Caribbean crêpes with, 343
    chocolate mousse, 345–46
    crème anglaise, 342
Russian-style chicken burgers (bitoks),
    133–34
rutabaga, purée de (yellow turnip purée),
    320

sabayon sauce, champagne, 354
saffron:
    cream of mussel soup with (Billi-Bi au
        safran), 38–39
    sauce, scallops with endive in, 98
salads:
    arugula and red onion, 24
    broccoli and avocado, 21–22
    cucumber, 6
    lentil, with kielbasa, 22–23
    Mediterranean, with tomato dressing,
        84–85
    mixed green, with blue cheese dressing,
        21
    roasted pepper and snow pea, 23–24
    three-lettuce chiffonade, 12–13
    warm shrimp, 108
    warm tuna and scallop, with orange-
        coriander vinaigrette, 16
salmon:
    baked in foil packages, 67–68
    brochette of, with bacon, 66–67
    burgers with brown butter sauce, 70–71
    cabbage packets stuffed with shrimp and,
        105–7
    grilled herbed, with shrimp, 71–72

    matelote of shellfish and, 72–73
    paglia e fieno with, 265
    peppered, with onion compote, 69–70
    and shrimp ravioli, 277–78
    smoked, mousse, 17
saltimbocca, chicken breasts, 132–33
sauces:
    aïoli (garlic mayonnaise), 290
    basic vinaigrette, 291
    champagne sabayon, 354
    crème anglaise, 342
    cucumber and chili raita, 305
    curry, 292–93
    dill, 278
    fresh tomato, 291–92
    ginger-butter, 78
    Grand Marnier, 353–54
    harissa, 136
    hoisin-ginger, 276–77
    horseradish, 176, 290
    leek, 275
    maître d'hôtel butter with mustard, 61
    mayonnaise, 289
    mayonnaise with scallions, 87
    orange, 350–51
    parsley butter, 89
    Provençal, 82–83
    quick tomato, 292
    red pepper, 279
    red pepper purée, 9
    strawberry, 349
    sweet-and-sour, 122
    sweet red pepper mayonnaise, 60
    tomato, with mushrooms, 240–41
    tomato, with peppers, 212
    tomato and horseradish, 194
    tomato-horseradish, with basil, 126
    tuna, 200–201
    white butter, with herbs (beurre blanc
        aux fines herbes), 294
sauerkraut:
    garnished (choucroute garnie), 215–16
    pork chops and sausage with, 209–10
    smoked pork shoulder with cider and,
        213–14
sausage:
    apple stuffing, roast breast of turkey with,
        148–49
    herb stuffing, broiled quails with, 156–57
    lentil salad with kielbasa, 22–23
    and pork chops with sauerkraut, 209–10
sautéed:
    black sea bass with red peppers, 53–54
    calf's liver with onions and capers (foie de
        veau Lyonnaise aux câpres), 251–52

chicken breasts with artichokes, 115–16
lettuce with garlic, 312–13
medallions of pork with port, 202–3
pheasant with herbs (faisan sauté aux
    herbes), 152–53
potatoes with garlic, 314
trout with lime, 78–79
scallions:
    mashed potatoes with, 316
    mayonnaise with, 87
scallop(s):
    américaine, 99
    cornmeal-coated shrimp, clams and,
        86–87
    with endive in saffron sauce, 98
    linguine with broccoli and, 269–70
    sea, with watercress sauce, 96–97
    and tuna salad, warm, with orange-
        coriander vinaigrette, 16
    and zucchini brochettes, 100
scaloppine, veal, Milanese, 242–43
sea bass:
    fillets of, with basil and tomatoes, 54–55
    sautéed black, with red peppers, 53–54
seafood, *see* fish; shellfish; *specific fish and*
        shellfish
sesame-coated:
    chicken breasts (suprêmes de volaille aux
        sesames), 118
    fish fillets, 74
shallot:
    butter, asparagus with, 299
    and garlic butter, hamburgers with,
        186–87
    mustard sauce, chicken breasts with, 131
    and red-wine sauce, rib steak with,
        181–82
shellfish:
    baked clams with garlic butter, 7
    baked lobster with tarragon-cream sauce,
        91–92
    Billi-Bi au safran (cream of mussel soup
        with saffron), 38–39
    broiled shrimp with lemon-garlic butter,
        101
    cabbage packets stuffed with shrimp and
        salmon, 105–7
    cherrystone clam and corn fritters, 8–9
    clam cocktail, 11
    cold lobster with basil vinaigrette, 11–12
    cold lobster with hot-mustard sauce,
        95–96
    cornmeal-coated shrimp, scallops, and
        clams, 86–87
    crab and shrimp gumbo, 41–43
    crab meat and spinach au gratin, 90–91
    farfalle and mussels with ginger-mustard
        vinaigrette, 268–69
    fettuccini with shrimp and vegetables,
        260–61
    and fish soup, Japanese-style, 37–38
    gazpacho with crab meat, 29–30
    Georges Perrier's crab cakes with shrimp,
        88–89
    green pasta with shrimp and clams,
        263–64
    grilled herbed salmon with shrimp,
        71–72
    grilled shrimp in lemon-basil marinade,
        102
    linguine with scallops and broccoli,
        269–70
    lobster, cutting up, 94
    lobster américaine, 93–95
    Lyonnaise oyster stew, 46–47
    Manhattan clam chowder, 36
    matelote of salmon and, 72–73
    mussels, cleaning, 40
    salmon and shrimp ravioli, 277–78
    scallop and zucchini brochettes, 100
    scallops américaine, 99
    scallops with endive in saffron sauce, 98
    sea scallops with watercress sauce, 96–97
    shrimp broth, 43
    shrimp with mushrooms and paprika
        sauce, 103
    spaghetti with clams and green beans,
        257–58
    Szechuan-style shrimp with peppercorns,
        104–5
    tomatoes stuffed with curried shrimp,
        13–14
    Vietnamese-style mussel soup, 41
    warm shrimp salad, 108
    warm tuna and scallop salad with orange-
        coriander vinaigrette, 16
    ziti with shrimp and green beans, 266
shell steaks with mustard butter, 182–83
shrimp:
    broiled, with lemon-garlic butter, 101
    broth, 43
    cabbage packets stuffed with salmon and,
        105–7
    cornmeal-coated scallops, clams and,
        86–87
    and crab gumbo, 41–43
    curried, tomatoes stuffed with, 13–14
    fettuccine with vegetables and, 260–61
    Georges Perrier's crab cakes with, 88–89
    green pasta with clams and, 263–64

shrimp *(continued)*
  grilled, in lemon-basil marinade, 102
  grilled herbed salmon with, 71–72
  with mushrooms and paprika sauce, 103
  with peppercorns, Szechuan-style, 104–5
  salad, warm, 108
  and salmon ravioli, 277–78
  ziti with green beans and, 266
skate with black butter sauce, 75
smoked:
  brook trout with horseradish sauce, 4–6
  pork shoulder with cider and sauerkraut, 213–14
  salmon mousse, 17
snap peas with mint, 313
snapper, red, fillets with pine nut coating, 76
snow pea and roasted pepper salad, 23–24
sorbets, 33
  cantaloupe and ginger, 333–34
  grapefruit and Campari, 334–35
  pear and passion fruit, 336–37
  pineapple and mango, 335
  aux pommes vertes (green apple sorbet), 336
soufflés:
  bittersweet chocolate and cherry, 351
  crêpes, 344–45
  Grand Marnier, 352
  orange, 350
  strawberry, with strawberry sauce, 348–49
soups:
  chicken and winter-vegetable, 32–33
  cold cucumber and yogurt, with fresh mint, 27–28
  cream of leek, 27
  cream of mussel, with saffron (Billi-Bi au safran), 38–39
  gazpacho with crab meat, 29–30
  Japanese-style fish and shellfish, 37–38
  Manhattan clam chowder, 36
  Marseilles-style fish, 45–46
  Moroccan lamb and chickpea (harira), 33–34
  Spanish white bean, 30–31
  veal and macaroni, 31–32
  Vietnamese-style mussel, 41
  see also stews
sour cream, julienne of veal with paprika and, 246
spaghettini with vegetables and pepper-vodka sauce, 258–59
spaghetti with clams and green beans, 257–58

Spanish white bean soup, 30–31
spinach:
  and crab meat au gratin, 90–91
  with nutmeg, 320
squash:
  butternut, purée, 301
  yellow, au gratin, 324
steak(s):
  au poivre, 184
  broiled skirt, Cajun style, 179–80
  rib, with marrow and red-wine sauce, 180–81
  rib, with red-wine and shallot sauce, 181–82
  shell, with mustard butter, 182–83
stews:
  crab and shrimp gumbo, 41–43
  Lyonnaise oyster, 46–47
  Mexican pork and hominy (pozole), 34–35
  Provençal seafood, 44
  quick fish, with vegetables, 48–49
  venison, 166
stock, fish, 38
strawberry(ies):
  oeufs à la neige, 341–42
  soufflé with strawberry sauce, 348–49
stuffing, apple-sausage, 149
summer vegetables au gratin, 325–26
suprêmes de volaille aux sesames (sesame-coated chicken breasts), 118
sweet-and-sour sauce, 122
sweet-and-sour sauce, pork chops with apples and, 205–6
swordfish, grilled, with ginger-butter sauce, 77
Szechuan-style shrimp with peppercorns, 104–5

tarragon-cream sauce, baked lobster with, 91–92
tart:
  French apple, 339–40
  French cherry, 340–41
  pastry, basic, 340
tendrons de veau braisés (braised breast of veal), 247
three-lettuce chiffonade, 12–13

thyme:
    duck braised in red wine and, 163–64
    fresh, grilled tuna with, 85–86
tomato(es):
    broiled, 321
    creole rice with herbs and, 280–81
    dressing, Mediterranean salad with,
        84–85
    and eggplant au gratin, 308–9
    fillets of sea bass with basil and, 54–55
    fresh, chicken breasts with garlic and, 129
    gazpacho with crab meat, 29–30
    and green beans Provençal, 312
    medallions of lamb with basil and,
        231–32
    roses, making, 5
    sea trout with anchovies and, 80
    stuffed with curried shrimp, 13–14
tomato sauce:
    fresh, 291–92
    fresh, orzo with, 280
    horseradish, with basil, 126
    horseradish and, 194
    lentils with, 207–8
    prosciutto and, ziti with, 267
    quick, 292
    with mushrooms, 240–41
    with peppers, 212
trout:
    sautéed, with lime, 78–79
    sea, with anchovies and tomatoes, 80
    smoked brook, with horseradish sauce,
        4–6
tuna:
    broiled, Provençal, 82
    escabeche, 14–15
    grilled, with fresh thyme, 85–86
    grilled, with Mediterranean salad, 83–84
    Niçoise, 81
    sauce, cold pork with, 200
    and scallop salad, warm, with orange-
        coriander vinaigrette, 16
turkey breast:
    with capers and mushrooms, 146–47
    with prosciutto and cheese, 147–48
    roast, with apple-sausage stuffing,
        148–49
    turkey patties with curry sauce, 150
    turmeric rice, 282
    turnip, yellow, purée (purée de rutabaga),
        320

vanilla ice cream, basic French, 338–39
veal:
    bitoks of beef and, 187–88
    braised breast of (tendrons de veau
        braisés), 247
    chops with fresh corn, 241–42
    julienne of, with mustard sauce, 245
    julienne of, with paprika and sour cream,
        246
    loaf, ginger-flavored, 250–51
    and macaroni soup, 31–32
    meatballs, avgolemono, 249–50
    risotto with chicken and, 284–85
    rolls with basil, 243–44
    scaloppine Milanese, 242–43
    shanks with Oriental vegetables, 248
vegetable(s):
    quick fish stew with, 48–49
    fettuccine with shrimp and, 260–61
    lamb and white beans with, 228–29
    Oriental, veal shanks with, 248
    ratatouille á la minute, 319
    spaghettini with pepper-vodka sauce
        and, 258–59
    summer, au gratin, 325–26
    winter, and chicken soup, 32–33
    see also specific vegetables
venison:
    marinade for, 167
    steaks in red-wine sauce, 168
    stew, 166
Vietnamese-style mussel soup, 41
vinaigrette:
    artichokes, 19–20
    basic, 291
vinegar:
    balsamic, chicken breasts with garlic and,
        112–13
    German-style hamburgers with onions
        and, 191
    pork cutlets with herbs and, 201–2
vodka:
    pepper-, sauce, spaghettini with
        vegetables and, 258–59
    spaghetti with clams and green beans,
        257–58